WordPress 2.8 Themes Cookbook

Over 100 simple but incredibly effective recipes for creating powerful, custom WordPress themes

Lee Jordan

Nick Ohrn

[PACKT] open source
PUBLISHING   community experience distilled

BIRMINGHAM - MUMBAI

WordPress 2.8 Themes Cookbook

First published: June 2010

Production Reference: 1220610

Published by Packt Publishing Ltd.
32 Lincoln Road
Olton
Birmingham, B27 6PA, UK.

ISBN 978-1-847198-44-0

www.packtpub.com

Cover Image by Vinayak Chittar (vinayak.chittar@gmail.com)

Credits

Authors
Lee Jordan
Nick Ohrn

Reviewers
Jose Argudo Blanco
Taeke Reijenga

Acquisition Editor
Sarah Cullington

Development Editor
Ved Prakash Jha

Technical Editor
Dayan Hyames

Copy Editors
Janki Mathuria
Lakshmi Menon

Editorial Team Leader
Akshara Aware

Project Team Leader
Lata Basantani

Project Coordinator
Srimoyee Ghoshal

Indexers
Tejal Daruwale
Monica Ajmera Mehta

Proofreader
Dirk Manuel

Production Coordinator
Shantanu Zagade

Cover Work
Shantanu Zagade

About the Authors

Lee Jordan is a web designer and new media developer who designs and maintains websites, web-based applications, templates, and social media for a privately-held technical services company. She brings a strong design background and concern for the visual and emotional impact of media to web-based projects. Experienced in multiple CMS platforms including Expression Engine, Plone, WordPress, PostNuke, and Google's Blogger, she has maintained, explored, and used most of them on a day-to-day basis. She spends her spare time as the leader of a local scout troop, taking long hikes with her family in the beautiful North Georgia woods, trying to taste every variety of chocolate that exists, and playing with code and pixels. Design topics, or whatever she can think of at the time, are posted on her blog at `http://leejordan.net`.

Lee has previously written two books with Packt Publishing: *Project Management with dotProject*, and *Blogger: Beyond the Basics*.

A big thank you to my family: Brian, Celeste, Jason and Mom for looking over my shoulder and giving hugs when I needed encouragement, knowing when to give me space, and learning way more than they ever wanted to about this "WordPress theme stuff". They are responsible for helping me keep my reader's point of view in mind. I love you all.

Nick Ohrn holds a bachelors degree in Computer Science from the Rose-Hulman Institute of Technology. He graduated in 2008 and has been running his own independent software development company ever since.

As an independent business owner, Nick has had the pleasure of working on a variety of high profile projects. He enjoys creating applications that are both usable and have a high-quality codebase. Nick specializes in custom WordPress development and web applications.

Nick balances his time between programming, managing others, reading, writing on a variety of technical platforms, and contributing to open source software. When he isn't working, he enjoys weight training, bodybuilding, and other athletic endeavors.

Find Nick's custom WordPress development business at http://plugin-developer.com. You can find his personal site at http://nickohrn.com.

I'd like to first thank my wonderful fiancee and soon to be wife, Angela Tokarz. Without her gentle prompting along the way, this book may never have been finished. Thanks also to Peter Chester and Shane Pearlman for introducing me to the Packt Publishing team.

Finally, a big thank you to my entire family who showed interest throughout the process and were constantly asking when the book would be done. It is because of them that I have the skills to be able to write this book in the first place.

About the Reviewers

Jose Argudo is a web developer from Valencia, Spain. After finishing his studies, he started working for a web design company. Then, six years later, he decided to start working as a freelancer.

Now that some years have passed as a freelancer, he thinks it's the best decision he has ever taken—a decision that lets him work with the tools he likes, such as Joomla!, Codeigniter, Cakephp, Jquery and other known open source technologies.

His desire to learn and share his knowledge has led him to be a regular reviewer of books from Packt, including *Drupal E-commerce*, *Joomla! with Flash*, *Joomla! 1.5 SEO*, *Magento 1.3 Theme Design* or *Symfony 1.3 WebApplication Development*.

Recently he has even published his own book, *Codeigniter 1.7*, which you can also find at Packt's site. If you work with PHP, take a look at it!

Jose is currently working on a new book for Packt, this time Joomla! related; check for it soon!

If you want to know more about Jose, you can check his site at www.joseargudo.com.

To my Brother.

Taeke Reijenga is the co-founder of Level Level, a young and versatile graphic and web design agency from Rotterdam, The Netherlands.

Level Level is well known for their WordPress expertise. From a small-scale personal blog to a multilingual corporate website or e-commerce website, Level Level does it all.

In his spare time Taeke loves to travel, cook a nice meal, and enjoy a good glass of wine with friends.

You can contact Taeke via http://level-level.com.

Table of Contents

Preface

In the last few years, WordPress has exploded in popularity. What started as simple blogging software has become an amazingly-capable content management system. As the capabilities of the software have grown, so have the unique and novel ways in which WordPress data is displayed.

Nowadays, developers and designers utilize the WordPress theme system to build everything from simple blogs to fully-fledged news sites. You can display different content in unique ways, highlight your most important posts and pages, and engage your users by allowing them to comment on and share your content, quickly and easily.

In short, WordPress makes it easy for people to show the world what they have to offer. Theming WordPress is easy, and template files are readily-modifiable by users of any skill level. However, if you're willing to put in the time, you will find a powerful system hidden by this simplicity that allows you to build almost anything you want. This book will teach you how to use that power to build robust and high-quality themes that take full advantage of WordPress and the WordPress ecosystem.

What this book covers

Chapter 1, WordPress Theme Basics gets you started with developing WordPress themes teaching you about the documentation and finding, creating and installing themes.

Chapter 2, Creating Navigation shows you how to implement a variety of techniques that allow your users to navigate around your site.

Chapter 3, The Loop teaches you about The Loop, the main building block of WordPress. It shows you how to display your content in unique and interesting ways, and shows you how to change the data that is fetched and presented.

Chapter 4, Template Tags shows you how to display the content that the user enters in the administrative back-end. It teaches you to use unique WordPress functions to show titles, content, and other post data.

Chapter 5, Comments shows you how to start the conversation on your blog by allowing users to view and post comments. It teaches you to modify how the comments are shown and the information shown for each comment.

Chapter 6, Sidebars covers how to display secondary content on your blog by using WordPress' fabulous widget and sidebar system.

Chapter 7, Custom Page Templates shows you unique content and unique needs for displaying it. It teaches you how to use the powerful template system to make WordPress display the content that you want and the way you want it.

Chapter 8, Integrating Media discusses multimedia types, such as audio and video, which are now commonplace on blogs. It teaches you to take control of how images and media are displayed and create custom media templates for images, audio, video, or any other file type.

Chapter 9, Showing Author Information introduces why your site's authors are important. It teaches you how to display author bios, latest posts, and custom data.

Chapter 10, Adding JavaScript Effects shows you how to make your theme interactive and easy to use, by adding small pieces of JavaScript functionality.

Chapter 11, Advanced WordPress Themes covers how to take your theme to the next level, by adding theme options, creating multiple color schemes, and packaging and uploading your theme to the WordPress.org theme repository.

Chapter 12, Layout shows you how to extend your theme layout options through global toolbar navigation, centered theme design, tabbed navigation, drag-and-droppable components, and added accessibility through the use of skip navigation links.

What you need for this book

You need to have the following:

- PHP, Apache and MySQL (MAMP or WAMP for local development)
- WordPress (latest release)

Who this book is for

This book is intended for people interested in working with WordPress themes. Some experience with PHP and HTML is assumed, but no prior knowledge of the way in which WordPress works is needed. Users with a background in WordPress themes will still be able to learn from the more advanced recipes in this book.

Conventions

In this book, you will find a number of styles of text that distinguish between different kinds of information. Here are some examples of these styles, and an explanation of their meaning.

Code words in text are shown as follows: "Locate the `title` tag and remove whatever value is contained within it".

A block of code is set as follows:

```
<div class="notice-snippet">
Thanks for visiting my site!
</div>
```

When we wish to draw your attention to a particular part of a code block, the relevant lines or items are set in bold:

```
<?php get_sidebar(); ?>
<?php get_footer(); ?>
```

New terms and **important words** are shown in bold. Words that you see on the screen, in menus, or dialog boxes for example, appear in the text like this: "If you don't wish to preview your new theme, you can click on the **Activate** link directly".

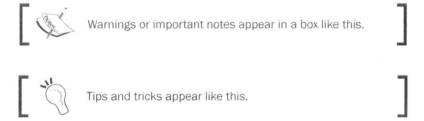

Warnings or important notes appear in a box like this.

Tips and tricks appear like this.

Reader feedback

Feedback from our readers is always welcome. Let us know what you think about this book—what you liked or may have disliked. Reader feedback is important for us to develop titles that you really get the most out of.

To send us general feedback, simply send an e-mail to feedback@packtpub.com, and mention the book title in the subject of your message.

If there is a book that you need and would like to see us publish, please send us a note via the **SUGGEST A TITLE** form on www.packtpub.com or e-mail suggest@packtpub.com.

If there is a topic that you have expertise in and you are interested in either writing or contributing to a book on, see our author guide on www.packtpub.com/authors.

Customer support

Now that you are the proud owner of a Packt book, we have a number of things to help you to get the most from your purchase.

Downloading the example code for this book

You can download the example code files for all Packt books you have purchased from your account at http://www.PacktPub.com. If you purchased this book elsewhere, you can visit http://www.PacktPub.com/support and register to have the files emailed directly to you.

Errata

Although we have taken every care to ensure the accuracy of our content, mistakes do happen. If you find a mistake in one of our books—maybe a mistake in the text or the code—we would be grateful if you would report this to us. By doing so, you can save other readers from frustration, and help us to improve the subsequent versions of this book. If you find any errata, please report them by visiting http://www.packtpub.com/support, selecting your book, clicking on the **let us know** link, and entering the details of your errata. Once your errata are verified, your submission will be accepted and the errata will be uploaded on our website, or added to any list of existing errata, under the Errata section of that title. Any existing errata can be viewed by selecting your title from http://www.packtpub.com/support.

Piracy

Piracy of copyright material on the Internet is an ongoing problem across all media. At Packt, we take the protection of our copyright and licenses very seriously. If you come across any illegal copies of our works, in any form, on the Internet, please provide us with the location address or website name immediately, so that we can pursue a remedy.

Please contact us at copyright@packtpub.com with a link to the suspected pirated material.

We appreciate your help in protecting our authors, and our ability to bring you valuable content.

Questions

You can contact us at questions@packtpub.com if you are having a problem with any aspect of the book, and we will do our best to address it.

1
WordPress Theme Basics

In this chapter, we will cover:

- ▶ Finding documentation on WordPress.org
- ▶ Downloading themes from the WordPress theme repository
- ▶ Downloading themes from third-party websites
- ▶ Installing and activating a theme
- ▶ Displaying the blog name
- ▶ Getting the absolute directory path of the active theme
- ▶ Creating a theme from scratch
- ▶ Creating a child theme
- ▶ Creating a theme by using a theme framework
- ▶ Adding expected WordPress hooks
- ▶ Including PHP files from your theme

Introduction

If you're going to be creating or modifying a WordPress theme, it pays to start with the basics. That's what this chapter is all about. By reviewing the recipes contained within, you'll learn how to find useful documentation, how to download and install themes from various places, and what is required if you want to create your own theme from scratch.

As you progress through the recipes in this book, you'll need a theme to work with. If you're an experienced WordPress developer, you'll probably want to create your own theme by using the recipe *Creating a theme from scratch* contained later in this chapter. If you're just starting out, I recommend using either of the two themes distributed with the base install of WordPress. Both "WordPress Default" and "WordPress Classic" offer solid bases on which you can build your custom theme.

Finding documentation on WordPress.org

This book will help you through the most common tasks you may encounter when developing a WordPress theme. However, you'll certainly have questions along the way that need further investigation. When these questions arise, you should consult the official WordPress documentation.

Getting ready

A web browser with Internet access is required to access the documentation.

How to do it...

First fire up your browser and go to http://codex.wordpress.org. This is the home page for the codex, where you'll spend a lot of time as a WordPress developer. The page looks like the following screenshot:

From the home page, you can browse to a topic that you are interested in. In the following screenshot, you can see the topic page for the WordPress **Database Description**:

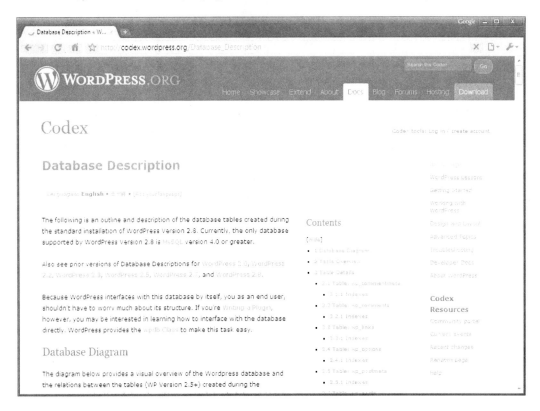

How it works...

The WordPress Codex is a user-generated set of documentation for the WordPress system. Most functions and functionality are well-documented, and most theme-related questions can be answered through careful browsing and reading.

For questions related to specific topics, it may be useful to consult that topic's page. Here is a short guide:

- ► Theme development—http://codex.wordpress.org/Theme_Development
- ► Template tags—http://codex.wordpress.org/Template_Tags
- ► Conditional tags—http://codex.wordpress.org/Conditional_Tags
- ► Function reference—http://codex.wordpress.org/Function_Reference

Downloading themes from the WordPress theme repository

The best place to find reputable WordPress themes free for use is the official WordPress theme repository. Every theme in the official repository is licensed under the GPL, which means that you can download it, modify it, and distribute your changes as you please.

You'll find themes for almost every use in the repository. There are themes for business sites, blogs, and even team communication. If you look hard, you'll probably find a theme you can use, or at least one you can modify to look the way that you want.

Getting ready

A web browser with Internet access is required to download themes from the official theme repository.

How to do it...

First fire up your browser and visit `http://wordpress.org/extend/themes/`. This is the theme repository home page, and looks like the following screenshot:

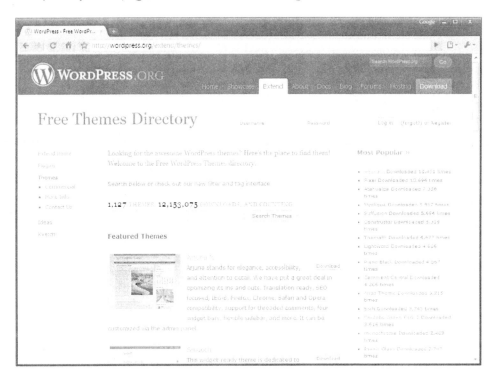

From the home page, you can browse themes by several different sorting criteria. Of note are the most popular, the newest, and the most recently-updated themes. If a theme appeals to you and you want to try it out, click on the name of the theme and then click on the download button on the resulting page. Be sure to read the theme's description to determine the type and placement of the dynamic sidebars, default widgets, and the different options that you can configure for the theme. As an example, you can see Arjuna X's theme page in the following image:

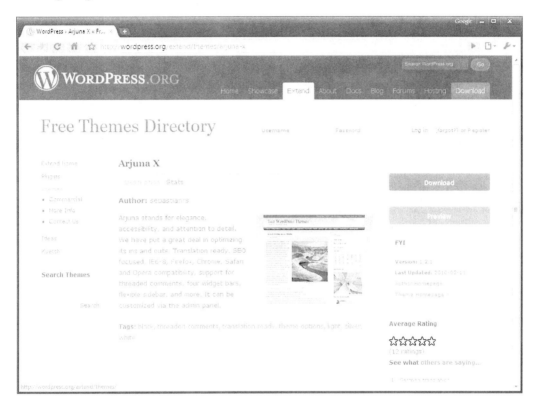

How it works...

The WordPress Theme Repository hosts WordPress themes submitted by individual theme developers and that conform to the GPL—the same license that ships with WordPress. This means that all themes contained within the theme repository are free to use, modify, and redistribute as you wish.

When downloading items from the theme repository, you are almost guaranteed a stable well-developed theme that will work when you first install it. In addition, the themes that you download from there will not contain affiliate links or other malicious or obfuscated code that could negatively affect your WordPress blog.

There's more...

Although browsing the repository by theme type or one of the special categories (like featured, new, or popular) is great in some instances, there are other ways to find a theme that will fit your exact needs. The following techniques will help you in your search for the perfect WordPress theme.

Try search

The Theme Repository includes a basic search function. Simply type in the search terms that you're looking for and the system will return the best-matched results. This is great if you're looking for a theme built for a particular purpose, such as photoblogging, podcasting, content aggregation, or business. The following image shows the search results page when searching for **"2 column"**:

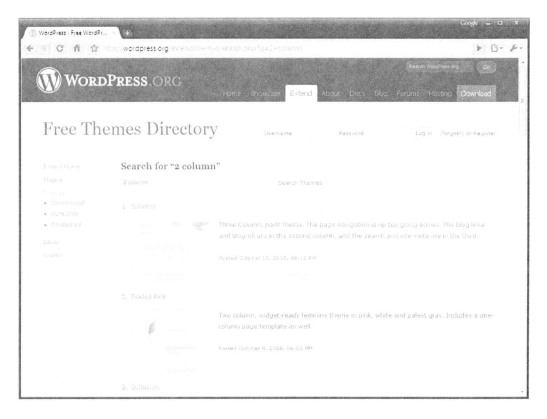

Tag filter

Another great way to find a theme that fits your particular needs is to use the WordPress theme repository's tag filter functionality. You can find this at `http://wordpress.org/extend/themes/tag-filter/`. After checking your desired filtering criteria, click on the **Find Themes** button. You'll be presented with a screen like the one shown in the following screenshot:

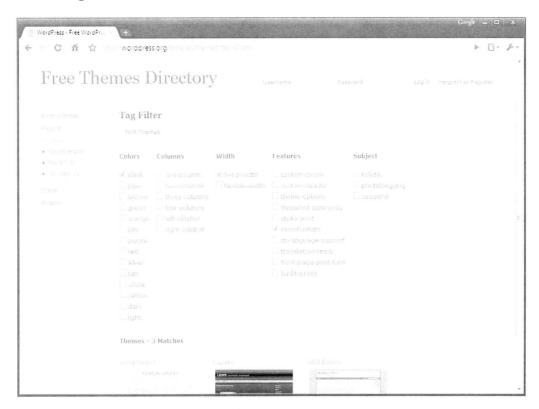

Downloading themes from third-party websites

Another place to find good, sometimes great, WordPress themes is on third-party websites. You have to be careful, though. Although most themes released to the public are done with the best intentions, there have been some instances where people have released themes full of backdoors into your site and spam links.

As such, care needs to be taken to make sure that the theme you are downloading doesn't give hackers and crackers a backdoor into your website, or populate your blog with hidden spam links.

How to do it...

The first thing that you need to do is find a theme you'd like to download. A search on Google or Bing for **best free WordPress themes** will return a list of results that should get you started. You can try more specific searches, such as **best one column WordPress themes** or **best business WordPress themes**, if you already have a good idea of what you want.

After you find a theme that you'd like to download, you have some due diligence to perform. You need to check the reputation of the theme developer to ensure that the theme is safe to download. Some things to look for are:

  ▶ Does the theme developer have support forums for their themes?

  ▶ Does the developer have a blog that is updated somewhat frequently?

  ▶ Have other users commented on the theme, either on the theme's website or their own?

If you're comfortable with the reputation of the theme developer, it is usually safe to download the theme and try it out. Just remember that you're taking a risk every time you download software from the web. You should test the theme in a non-critical environment before deploying it to a site that you actually care about.

How it works...

Developers release WordPress themes on their site instead of on the official theme repository for a variety of reasons. The theme may use a different license than the GPL, the author may be trying to garner publicity, or market themselves, and so on. Be sure to read any materials distributed with the theme to make sure that you know your rights in regards to it.

Be cautious with themes that you download from third-party sites. Again, most themes are safe, but it never hurts to have a friend or colleague familiar with WordPress check it out to make sure. If that is not an option, you can always try contacting the developer before using his theme and ask him if there is anything that you should watch out for. No matter what, make sure that you test the theme in a non-critical environment before deploying it somewhere important.

There's more...

There are several trusted developers who release high-quality themes on a regular basis. You can find them at the following places:

  ▶ Justin Tadlock—http://justintadlock.com/

  ▶ Ian Stewart—http://themeshaper.com/

  ▶ Ptah Dunbar—http://ptahdunbar.com/

In addition, there are several sites available where you can purchase high-quality WordPress themes at very reasonable prices. Some of the best sites to visit are:

- ▶ ThemeForest Marketplace—`http://themeforest.net`
- ▶ Thesis Theme—`http://diythemes.com`
- ▶ WooThemes—`http://woothemes.com`

It is important to point out that paying $30-$100 for a theme (the average price range across these and similar sites) is much less costly than taking an entire week to build a theme from scratch. Although you may lose some of the individual flavor that you might have had if you had developed a theme from scratch, the cost and time savings may be worth it to you.

Installing and activating a theme

Once you find or create a theme that is right for you, there is a need to install and activate it so that it can start providing the output for your WordPress install. Installation is easy once you know where WordPress expects theme files to be located, and activation is done through the administration panel with a few clicks. In this recipe, you'll learn exactly how to do both.

Getting ready

Download or create a theme that you wish to install. The theme's files should be contained in a single directory, exactly like the default WordPress themes are packaged.

How to do it...

First, you need to get your theme into the proper location in your WordPress install. Unless you've configured your installation in an unusual way, the correct directory to install your theme is `wp-content/themes/`. If you're working with a fresh install of WordPress, the directory should contain two subdirectories: `default` and `classic`. This is shown in the following screenshot:

Once you get to the correct place, you need to create a new subdirectory for your theme. Here we create a directory called `wordpress-themes-cookbook` that will hold all of the files for the new theme:

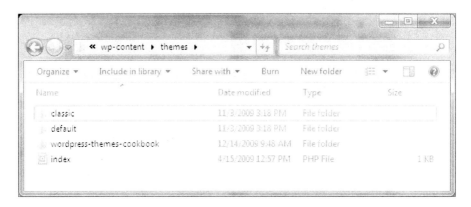

After you've created the directory, place all of your theme's files into the new directory. At this point, if your theme has been constructed properly and contains the necessary files, you can activate the theme for use on your site. Open up your WordPress administrative area and click on the **Appearance** menu item. You'll see the **Manage Themes** page, as shown in the screenshot below:

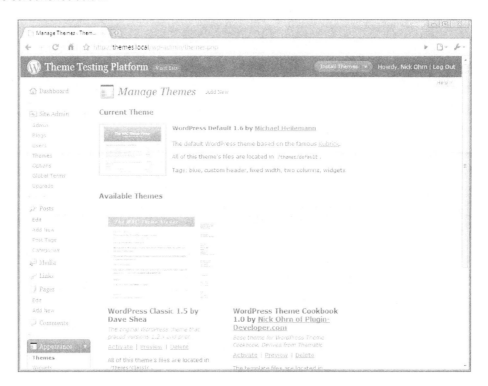

If you need to preview your theme before activating it, click on the **Preview** link under the theme that you're interested in. After confirming that the view is correct, click on the **Activate** link in the upper-right corner of the preview box, as shown in the next screenshot:

If you don't wish to preview your new theme, you can click on the **Activate** link directly. After activation, the page will refresh and you'll be greeted with a message regarding the switch:

How it works...

When you activate a new theme, WordPress stores two values in the database, indicating which theme is active, and what template files should be used. Whenever a page is viewed on the website, WordPress looks up the active theme and uses the correct template files to display the appropriate output.

The two values are located in the WordPress options table for your install and have keys of `stylesheet` and `template`. In most circumstances, these two values will be the same. However, if you are using a child theme, the template option will be the name of the folder in which the parent theme is located.

Displaying the blog name

A variety of information about a blog can be entered in the WordPress administration panel. Displaying that information publicly is the responsibility of the active theme. One piece of information that you may want to display is the name of the blog.

How to do it...

First, you must locate the position at which the blog name should be displayed in your theme. Open the appropriate theme file (`header.php` is a good place to start) and place your cursor at the desired location. For the purposes of this recipe, you'll be inserting the blog's name as the value of the `title` tag.

Locate the `title` tag and remove whatever value is contained within it. Now, insert the `bloginfo` function and make the markup look like the following:

```
<title><?php bloginfo('name'); ?></title>
```

How it works...

When the blog name is set in the administrative panel, the value that the user enters is stored in the options table within the WordPress database. When you call `bloginfo` with `name` as the argument, the name of the blog is retrieved from the options table and displayed.

Benefits of open source

WordPress is open source software. As such, you can examine the code base directly when you want to see how things are implemented. To get the most out of WordPress, you should look up functions that you use frequently, and `bloginfo` is a great place to start. It gives you a good idea of the way WordPress stores and retrieves miscellaneous information, and can be found in `wp-includes/general-template.php`.

There's more...

Template tags, of which `bloginfo` is one, often take one or more parameters that modify the output produced. With `bloginfo`, the single parameter you can pass determines which piece of information about the blog should be displayed.

Blog info available

The sole parameter accepted by the `bloginfo` function is a simple string. The following strings are supported, and must be passed in place of `name` in the above code sample:

String	Data Displayed
name	The blog's title
description	The blog's tag line
url	The URL to the blog's home page
wpurl	The URL to the WordPress installation
rdf_url	The URL for the blog's RDF/RSS 1.0 feed
rss_url	The URL for the blog's RSS 0.92 feed
atom_url	The URL for the blog's ATOM feed
comments_rss2_url	The URL for the blog's comments RSS 2.0 feed
pingback_url	The URL for the pingback XML-RPC file
stylesheet_url	The URL for the primary CSS file of the active theme
stylesheet_directory	The URL of the style sheet directory of the active theme
template_directory	The URL of the active theme's directory
template_url	
admin_email	The e-mail address of the blog administrator
charset	The blog's encoding for pages and feeds
version	The blog's version of WordPress
html_type	The content type of WordPress HTML pages

Retrieving information without displaying it

To retrieve a piece of information for storage in a variable or for further manipulation, use the `get_bloginfo` function instead of `bloginfo`. `get_bloginfo` returns information instead of printing it, and supports the same parameters as `bloginfo`.

As an example, perhaps you want to capitalize the blog name for some reason. The following would allow you to do so:

```
<?php echo strtoupper(get_bloginfo('name')); ?>
```

Getting the absolute directory path of the active theme

It sometimes becomes necessary to directly access files within the active theme's directory. Binary file loading, PHP or HTML includes, and iteration over custom file structures (as used in some theme frameworks) are some of the reasons for using direct access.

How to do it...

You can access the STYLESHEETPATH constant from any PHP file in your theme. The STYLESHEETPATH constant is defined when WordPress first loads.

To give you an idea of how the constant works, consider the case where you want to load a file containing some variable declarations for your theme. Create a new file in your theme's directory called config-variables.php, and add the following code to it:

```php
<?php
$blue = 1;
$red = 2;
$green = 3;
```

Next, open up your theme's header file—header.php—and add the following code at the very beginning of the file:

```php
<?php include (STYLESHEETPATH . '/config-variables.php '); ?>
```

Now, anywhere inside of your theme, you'll be able to access the variables defined within config-variables.php.

How it works...

The STYLESHEETPATH constant contains the absolute directory path to the file system location that contains the active theme. This is true for both regular themes and child themes. The STYLESHEETPATH constant does not contain a trailing slash, so one will need to be appended when accessing individual files within the directory.

Creating a theme from scratch

Creating a great theme from scratch is a challenging task. You have to define markup and behaviour, and add all of the necessary styles yourself. That being said, building from the ground up is sometimes the only thing that makes sense if you're building something really special.

Although making sure everything works correctly when you're finished will be difficult, getting started with your theme is not. There are only a few files required to get you going. After that, though, you'll be on your own as far as making sure that all of the appropriate information gets displayed.

How to do it...

First, create a new directory to contain your theme, and name it whatever you want. If you need help figuring out where to place your theme, see the recipe *Installing and activating a theme.*

Next, create the following files inside your newly-created directory:

- style.css
- index.php

The theme's main stylesheet (style.css) is required to contain information about the theme in a particular format. This is very important. Without this information, WordPress will not be able to correctly recognize your theme. Open style.css and insert the following:

```
/*
Theme Name: Your Theme Name
Theme URI: http://example.com
Description: Write a short description.
Author: Your Name
Author URI: http://example.com
*/
```

After inserting the base structure, you are free to change it to whatever you see fit. For my purposes, I've changed the code to read as follows:

```
/*
Theme Name: WordPress Themes Cookbook
Theme URI: http://plugin-developer.com/wordpress-themes-cookbook-
theme/
Description: A demonstration theme for the WordPress Themes Cookbook.
Author: Nick Ohrn
Author URI: http://plugin-developer.com
*/
```

Now, to test that you correctly entered all the information, you need to visit the *Manage Themes* section of the WordPress administration panel. Open up the WordPress administration interface and click on **Appearance**. Scroll down, and you should see a box that contains all of the information for your newly-created theme. Given the information that I entered, my box looks like the following:

WordPress Themes Cookbook by Nick Ohrn

A demonstration theme for the WordPress Themes Cookbook.

Activate | Preview | Delete

All of this theme's files are located in /themes/wordpress-themes-cookbook .

Your **Manage Themes** page should display the information that you entered. For more information on the different items that your `style.css` file can contain, see the official WordPress documentation at `http://codex.wordpress.org/Theme_Development#Theme_Style_Sheet`.

There's more...

WordPress themes generally contain a variety of different files to display data of different types and organizations. In addition to the required `style.css` and `index.php` files, you can create specially-named files that will handle certain situations.

Recognized WordPress files

WordPress recognizes and uses a variety of files for different situations. A full list of files and their use can be found at `http://codex.wordpress.org/Theme_Development#Theme_Template_Files_List`. The following list describes the most common files and the purposes for which they are used:

- `home.php`—used to display the home page
- `single.php`—used to display a single post
- `page.php`—used to display a single page

- `category.php`—used to display a category archive
- `author.php`—used to display an author archive
- `date.php`—used to display a date- or time-based archive
- `archive.php`—used to display a generic archive if `category.php`, `author.php`, or `date.php` are not present
- `search.php`—used to display search results
- `404.php`—used when no results match a query

Organizing a theme

WordPress recognizes that a good theme will be well-organized and often has a consistent header, sidebar, footer, and comments section. As such, the following files are supported for separating those elements out, and are included with special WordPress functions:

- `header.php`—`get_header()`
- `footer.php`—`get_footer()`
- `sidebar.php`—`get_sidebar()`
- `comments.php`—`comment_form()`

For more information on these functions, see `http://codex.wordpress.org/Theme_Development#Basic_Templates`.

See also

- *Installing and activating a theme*

Creating a child theme

One of the features that is really gaining traction in the WordPress theme development community is the concept of child themes. A child theme is a theme that has a unique stylesheet but inherits the template files from a parent theme. That is, the parent theme is largely responsible for producing the template output, and the child theme is responsible for styling that output.

In addition, a child theme can selectively override certain template files. So, if a child theme wishes to have a special home page or wants to list a specific archive type in a unique way, it can override only those pages and everything else will still display as defined by the parent theme.

Getting ready

Before creating a child theme, you must choose a parent to base it on. You can use any existing WordPress theme as your parent when creating a child theme. When deciding on a parent theme, remember that the child theme can both style the output of the parent and use its own template files to override the parent theme's display of information.

How to do it...

First, you need to determine which theme you want to use as the parent. Pick a theme that generates markup that you're happy with and feel that you can style appropriately. For the purposes of this recipe, we'll use the WordPress Default theme.

When you choose your parent theme, you need to make a note of the name of the directory containing the parent theme. The directory for the WordPress Default theme is named `default`.

Now create a new a directory to contain your child theme. You can name the new directory whatever you want. Create a new file—`style.css`—inside your newly-created directory. Then insert the following code:

```
/*
Theme Name: Your Child Theme Name
Theme URI: http://example.com
Description: Write a short description.
Template: Parent Theme Directory Name
Author: Your Name
Author URI: http://example.com
*/
```

Replace the information in the above code snippet with your desired theme information. For example purposes, we've modified this code snippet to read as follows:

```
/*
Theme Name: WordPress Themes Cookbook Child
Theme URI: http://plugin-developer.com/wordpress-themes-cookbook-
theme/
Description: A demonstration child theme for the WordPress Themes
Cookbook.
Template: default
Author: Nick Ohrn
Author URI: http://plugin-developer.com
*/
```

After creating the child theme's `style.css` file, visit the **Manage Themes** page in your WordPress administration panel. If you've done everything correctly and put the correct string next to the `Template:` item, you'll see something like the following:

WordPress Themes Cookbook Child by Nick Ohrn

A demonstration child theme for the WordPress Themes Cookbook.

Activate | Preview | Delete

The template files are located in `/themes/default`. The stylesheet files are located in `/themes/wordpress-themes-cookbook`. **WordPress Themes Cookbook Child** uses templates from **WordPress Default**. Changes made to the templates will affect both themes.

However, if you put a nonexistent or incorrect folder name next to the `Template:` item, you'll see an error message like the following:

Broken Themes

The following themes are installed but incomplete. Themes must have a stylesheet and a template.

Name	Description
WordPress Themes Cookbook Child	Template is missing.

How it works...

When you activate a child theme, WordPress reads the `style.css` file for that theme and recognizes that it has a parent. It then stores the values as discussed in the recipe *Installing and activating a theme*. The parent theme's folder name is stored in the `template` option, whereas the child theme's folder name is stored in the `stylesheet` option.

When WordPress starts to render a page, it looks for appropriate templates first in the directory defined by the `stylesheet` option, and then falls back to the directory specified by the `template` option. Other than that, there isn't that much difference between a child theme and a regular theme.

There's more...

The concept of child themes is a really powerful one. As a theme developer, you can create a base theme with good markup and a layout that you're happy with, and then make small style tweaks by using a child theme. If you're doing this, then there is one trick in particular that you'll want to use.

Maintaining default styling

If you've got a carefully-styled base theme, you can choose to selectively override styling while maintaining the basic look of the parent theme. To do so, you include an `import` statement in the `style.css` file. Insert the following statement after the theme definition header that you copied earlier in the recipe:

```
@import url('../folder-name/style.css');
```

Replace `folder-name` with the directory name of your parent theme. At this point, refresh your browser and you'll notice that the child theme looks exactly the same as the parent theme. Individual styles can then be selectively overridden in the child theme's style sheet by placing style declarations after the `import` statement.

See also

▶ *Installing and activating a theme*

Creating a theme by using a theme framework

Creating a theme by using a theme framework allows for the ultimate in customization. Theme frameworks tend to allow easy modification of template output in addition to customization of element styles. This puts more power into the hands of the derivative theme developer.

Getting ready

Download and install the theme framework of your choice. For more information on this, please see the recipe *Installing and activating a theme*.

How to do it...

First, you need to pick a theme framework to build on. There are several theme frameworks listed in the *There's more...* section of this recipe, and all of them consist of quality markup and carefully chosen styles, making them a snap to build on top of.

After you've chosen a theme framework, it is time to create a theme based on that framework. To do so, you'll use the technique described in *Creating a child theme*. After you've created the base child theme, you can start to customize it.

In most cases, you override the markup of a parent theme by supplying template files directly in your child theme. With a theme framework, things generally work a little differently. You supply your custom markup by attaching callbacks to custom action and filter hooks, as defined by the theme framework. To find out what the custom hooks are, you need to read the theme framework's documentation.

To add appropriate functionality via the custom hooks, you create a `functions.php` file inside your child theme, and use the Plugin API to add callbacks to the theme framework's custom hooks.

How it works...

A theme framework is a theme created for the sole purpose of being extended by child themes. They are built to be modified by users for use on their own websites. Although most theme frameworks can be used out of the box, it is the personalization and customization that end users and developers perform that really allow their particular use of the framework to shine.

There's more...

There are several quality theme frameworks in existence at the time of writing this book. The best are as follows:

- ▶ Thematic—`http://themeshaper.com/thematic/`
- ▶ Hybrid—`http://themehybrid.com/archives/2008/11/hybrid-wordpress-theme-framework`
- ▶ Carrington—`http://carringtontheme.com/`
- ▶ Vanilla—`http://code.google.com/p/vanilla-theme/`
- ▶ Whiteboard—`http://plainbeta.com/2008/05/20/whiteboard-a-free-wordpress-theme-framework/`
- ▶ WPFramework—`http://wpframework.com/`

See also

- ▶ *Installing and activating a theme*
- ▶ *Creating a child theme*

Adding expected WordPress hooks

WordPress themes should possess a number of different hooks by default, allowing active plugins to alter or add output when pages are rendered. WordPress development guidelines specify the names and locations of the expected WordPress hooks in themes.

How to do it...

There are three WordPress hooks that you need to add to almost every custom theme. They are:

- `wp_head`
- `wp_footer`
- `comment_form`

First, add the `wp_head` hook. Find the end tag of the HTML `head` element (`</head>`, often in `header.php`) and place your cursor on the line before it. Insert the following:

```php
<?php do_action( 'wp_head' ); ?>
```

Next, add the `wp_footer` hook. Find the end tag of the HTML `body` element (`</body>`, often in `footer.php`) and place your cursor on the line before it. Insert the following:

```php
<?php do_action( 'wp_footer' ); ?>
```

Finally, insert the `comment_form` hook. Locate the end tag of the HTML `form` element for the comment form (`</form>`, often in `comments.php` and `comments-popup.php`) and place your cursor on the line before it. Insert the following:

```php
<?php do_action( 'comment_form', $post->ID ); ?>
```

If you are using the default comments form layout, you won't have to explicitly add the `comment_form` hook because it is provided in the default theme's `comments.php` file.

How it works...

Plugins use these hooks to add to or modify the rendered output of a theme's template files. Often the modification includes linking to or outputting JavaScript, CSS, or HTML code. Many popular plugins use the above hooks, and making sure that they are present is essential to the plugin's proper operation.

Although `wp_head`, `wp_footer`, and `comment_form` are the only hooks necessary for a complete theme, it is possible to add many more custom hooks that allow individuals to customize a theme after it has been fully developed by its author.

Including PHP files from your theme

For organizational or reuse purposes, you will often separate components of your theme into separate files to be used in several different places.

Getting ready

Before getting started, you need to identify the pieces of output that will be reused throughout your theme, and separate them into different PHP files. You may wish to separate common post listing structures or advertisement blocks.

How to do it...

First, you should identify the piece of output that you wish to reuse and separate it into a new file. For this recipe, we'll say that you have a notice snippet that you may wish to include in several places. Place the following code in a new file called `notice-snippet.php`:

```
<div class="notice-snippet">
Thanks for visiting my site!
</div>
```

After you've separated it, you need to decide where you want to display the snippet. Wherever you want to display the snippet, insert the following:

```
<?php include TEMPLATEPATH . '/notice-snippet.php'; ?>
```

You'll notice that your snippet is now shown in the template wherever you inserted the above statement.

How it works...

The `include` function does exactly what you would think it does: it includes the contents of the separate file wherever you use it. The important thing to remember about this example is the `TEMPLATEPATH` constant used in the `include` statement.

`TEMPLATEPATH` is a constant defined by WordPress that holds the directory path to the directory that contains the template used to render output for the theme. You should use the `TEMPLATEPATH` constant whenever you need to have PHP access files from your theme.

There's more...

In addition to the TEMPLATEPATH constant, WordPress provides a STYLESHEETPATH constant. Generally, these two constants hold the same variable. However, if a child theme is active, then the STYLESHEETPATH constant will contain the file system path to the style sheet in use, whereas the TEMPLATEPATH constant will contain the file system path to the parent theme directory.

2
Creating Navigation

In this chapter, we will cover:

- ▶ Listing all of the pages that exist on a blog
- ▶ Listing all of the categories defined for a blog
- ▶ Listing all of the tags in use on a blog
- ▶ Highlighting the current page in the navigation
- ▶ Adding a search function to a theme
- ▶ Getting the category page link from a category name
- ▶ Displaying page links only if the destination page exists
- ▶ Creating a category drop-down menu
- ▶ Creating drop-downs using child pages

Introduction

One of the most important aspects of any website is navigation. Making sure that a visitor can get around is paramount to increasing traffic, user engagement, and visit length. By offering a variety of navigation methods, you give the user multiple ways to find the content that interests them. There are several techniques built into WordPress that you can use to build the navigation that lets your users find what they need on your site.

When thinking about the topic of navigation in the context of this chapter, it is important to also consider the subject as a whole. Don't limit yourself to the concept of a top or side main navigation item. Those types of navigation are very important, but for the purposes of this chapter, you'll consider navigation as a whole—meaning any way that helps the user to get around your site.

Listing all of the pages that exist on a blog

WordPress pages often contain static content that should be reachable at any time. Common uses for WordPress pages are website and author descriptions, contact forms, affiliate information, and more. Making sure that these pages can be found and navigated to quickly is paramount.

How to do it...

First, decide where you want to generate a linked list of all your pages. If you're comfortable using pages for navigation, then you probably want to put the pages listing directly below your main site identification elements, in `header.php`. Open your chosen template file and insert the following:

```
<ul>
  <?php wp_list_pages(); ?>
</ul>
```

Next, open your theme in your browser and take a look at the spot where you inserted the appropriate code. Depending on your site's styles and the pages that you've created, the output for this function call should look like the main content area in the following screenshot:

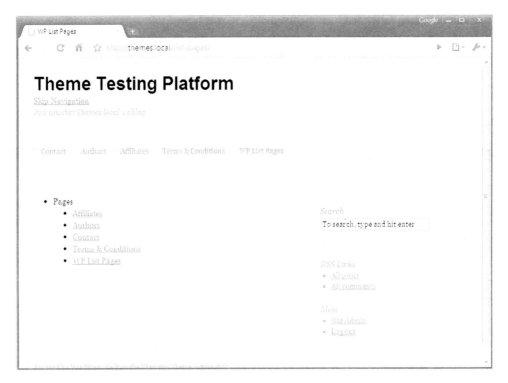

How it works...

When you call `wp_list_pages`, WordPress performs a database query, fetching the appropriate pages based on the parameters that you pass to the function. After fetching the pages, WordPress builds the markup for the list. The markup consists of an `<li>` tag containing a link to the page for each page that was fetched. If the `title_li` parameter is not empty, then the entire list is wrapped in a containing `<li>`. By default, the previous code will produce markup that is similar to the following:

```
<li class="pagenav">Pages<ul>
    <li class="page_item page-item-271">
      <a title="Affiliates"
      href="http://themes.local/affiliates/">Affiliates</a>
    </li>
    <li class="page_item page-item-269">
      <a title="Authors"
      href="http://themes.local/authors/">Authors</a>
    </li>
    <li class="page_item page-item-267">
      <a title="Contact"
      href="http://themes.local/contact/">Contact</a>
    </li>
    <li class="page_item page-item-273">
      <a title="Terms &amp; Conditions"
      href="http://themes.local/terms-conditions/">Terms &amp;
      Conditions</a>
    </li>
    <li class="page_item page-item-256 current_page_item">
      <a title="WP List Pages"
      href="http://themes.local/list-pages/">WP List Pages</a>
    </li>
  </ul>
</li>
```

There's more...

The default output for `wp_list_pages` might not fit your specific use cases. Luckily, modifying the output from `wp_list_pages` is easy.

Passing parameters

The `wp_list_pages` output can be changed by passing different values for a wide array of parameters, as follows:

```php
<?php
wp_list_pages(array('parameter_name' => 'parameter_value'));
?>
```

Some of the more important parameters are as follows:

Parameter Name	Effect
echo	Set to false to cause wp_list_pages to return a string containing HTML markup instead of printing the markup
child_of	Pass a numeric ID to only retrieve child pages of the page with that ID
exclude	Pass a comma-delimited list of page IDs (for example: '#,#,#') to exclude them from the pages displayed

Taking this into account, consider the case where you only want to display pages that are a child of the affiliate information page. If the affiliate information page has an ID of 4, then you would use wp_list_pages as follows:

```php
<?php wp_list_pages(array('child_of'=>4)); ?>
```

For more information on the available parameters, visit http://codex.wordpress.org/Template_Tags/wp_list_pages.

Listing all of the categories defined for a blog

Proper categorization of posts is a great way to help visitors find what they are looking for. To make it even easier, a theme could include a list of all of the categories in which there are posts. This technique works best on blogs with a small number of categories.

Alternatively, you can use category drill-downs that change based on the category level that you're at. If you're writing a site about music, you might have Rock, Hip Hop, and Country as top-level categories, each containing second-level categories such as Reviews, Recommendations, and News. In this way, your users can navigate directly to the information that they're looking for, quickly and easily.

How to do it...

First, decide where you want to generate a linked list of all of your categories. If you're taking a drill-down approach as talked about in the introduction to this recipe, then you may wish to put the list of links in the header of your site. Otherwise, category links would be best served in a sidebar or footer. Open the appropriate template file and insert the following:

```html
<ul>
  <?php wp_list_categories(); ?>
</ul>
```

Next, open your theme in your browser and take a look at the spot where you inserted the appropriate code. Depending on your site's styles, and the categories that you've created, the output for this function call should look like the following:

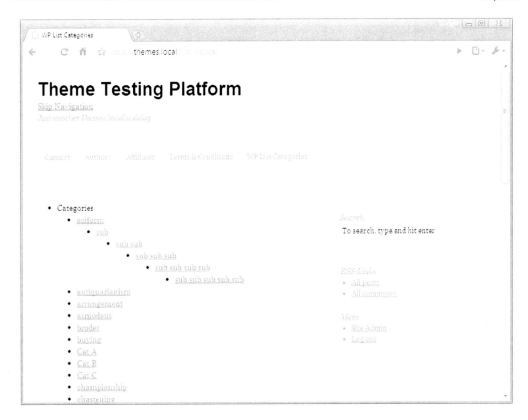

How it works...

When you call `wp_list_categories`, WordPress performs a database query, fetching all of the categories that match the parameters that you pass to the function. After fetching the categories, WordPress builds the markup for the list. The markup consists of an `<li>` tag containing a link to the categories archive page for each category that was fetched. If the `title_li` parameter is not empty, then the entire list is wrapped in a containing `<li>`. By default, the previous code will produce markup that is similar to the following:

```
<li class="categories">Categories<ul>
    <li class="cat-item cat-item-3">
        <a title="View all posts filed under aciform"
        href="http://themes.local/category/aciform/">aciform</a>
        <ul class="children">
          <li class="cat-item cat-item-41">
            <a title="View all posts filed under sub"
            href="http://themes.local/category/aciform/sub/">sub</a>
            <ul class="children">
              <li class="cat-item cat-item-102">
```

```
        <a title="View all posts filed under sub sub"
        href="http://themes.local/category/aciform/sub/sub-sub/"
        >sub sub</a>
      </li>
    </ul>
  </li>
</ul>
</li>
<li class="cat-item cat-item-4">
  <a title="View all posts filed under antiquarianism"
  href="http://themes.local/category/antiquarianism/"
  >antiquarianism</a>
</li>
<li class="cat-item cat-item-5">
  <a title="View all posts filed under arrangement"
  href="http://themes.local/category/arrangement/">arrangement</a>
</li>
<li class="cat-item cat-item-6">
  <a title="View all posts filed under asmodeus"
  href="http://themes.local/category/asmodeus/">asmodeus</a>
</li>
<li class="cat-item cat-item-7">
  <a title="View all posts filed under broder"
  href="http://themes.local/category/broder/">broder</a>
</li>
<li class="cat-item cat-item-8">
  <a title="View all posts filed under buying"
  href="http://themes.local/category/buying/">buying</a>
</li>
</ul>
</li>
```

There's more...

The default output for `wp_list_categories` might not fit your specific use cases. Luckily, modifying the output is easy.

Passing parameters

Similar to `wp_list_pages`, the categories retrieved by `wp_list_categories` can be modified by passing parameters to the function. Parameters are passed as follows:

```php
<?php
wp_list_categories(array('parameter_name' => 'parameter_value'));
?>
```

Some of the more important ones are as follows:

Parameter Name	Effect
Number	Pass a numeric value to limit the number of categories retrieved. This is especially helpful for blogs with a large number of categories.
Feed	Pass true to cause a link to each category's feed to be printed
current_category	Pass the ID of a category to force the output to contain the current-cat class on a particular category.

For example, say you wanted to limit your category list to the first five categories. To do so, you would use the following code:

```php
<?php
wp_list_categories(array('number' => 5));
?>
```

For more information on the available parameters, visit http://codex.wordpress.org/Template_Tags/wp_list_categories.

Listing all of the tags in use on a blog

Generally, tags are used liberally to indicate the subject matter of a post. For this reason, a list of tags is a great way to help visitors to get around a blog and view a wide array of posts that they're interested in. By default, WordPress lists tags in a cloud, varying the size of each tag according to the number of times it was used. However, this default output can be modified to produce a list that might make more sense to your users.

How to do it...

First, decide where you want to generate a linked list of all of your tags. Open the appropriate template file, and insert the following:

```php
<?php
wp_tag_cloud(array(
    'format' => 'list',
    'unit' => ''
));
?>
```

Next, open your theme in your browser and take a look at the spot where you inserted the appropriate code. Depending on your site's styles, the output for this function call should look like the example shown in following screenshot:

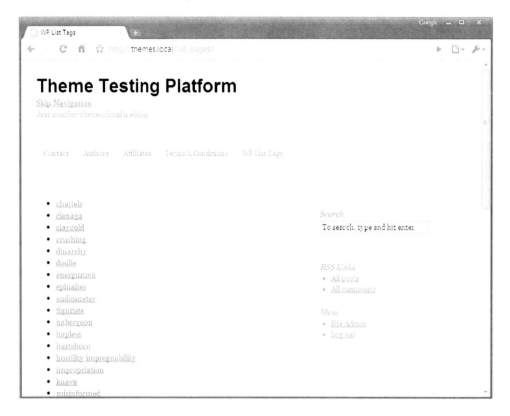

How it works...

When you call wp_tag_cloud, WordPress performs a database query, fetching all of the tags that match the parameters you pass to the function. After fetching the tags, WordPress builds the markup for the list. Using the parameters in the previous code, the markup consists of an <li> tag containing a link to the categories archive page for each category that was fetched. The entire list is then wrapped in a containing <ul> tag, producing output similar to the following:

```
<ul class="wp-tag-cloud">
  <li>
    <a style="" title="1 topic" class="tag-link-53"
    href="http://themes.local/tag/chattels/">chattels</a>
  </li>
  <li>
    <a style="" title="1 topic" class="tag-link-54"
```

```
      href="http://themes.local/tag/cienaga/">cienaga</a>
    </li>
    <li>
      <a style="" title="1 topic" class="tag-link-55"
      href="http://themes.local/tag/claycold/">claycold</a>
    </li>
    <li>
      <a style="" title="1 topic" class="tag-link-56"
      href="http://themes.local/tag/crushing/">crushing</a>
    </li>
    <li>
      <a style="" title="1 topic" class="tag-link-58"
      href="http://themes.local/tag/dinarchy/">dinarchy</a>
    </li>
    <li>
      <a style="" title="1 topic" class="tag-link-59"
      href="http://themes.local/tag/doolie/">doolie</a>
    </li>
  </ul>
```

You'll notice that each of the `<a>` tags that link to the tag archive page has an empty in-line style attribute. This is a consequence of the processing that `wp_tag_cloud` does internally. You'll also notice that unlike `wp_list_pages` and `wp_list_categories`, this function produces a surrounding `<ul>` element for its items.

There's more...

In most cases, the default display of `wp_tag_cloud` will not be the one that is most beneficial to your users. This is especially true for business blogs and professional sites. Luckily, there is an easy way to change how `wp_tag_cloud` displays.

Passing parameters

As seen earlier, the output from `wp_tag_cloud` can be modified by using parameters with the function call. Parameters are passed in the same way as with many other WordPress functions, which is in the following format:

```php
<?php
wp_tag_cloud(array('parameter_name' => 'parameter_value'));
?>
```

You've already seen a couple of the parameters that `wp_tag_cloud` supports. Another important one is the `number` parameter, which limits the number of tags placed in the cloud. If you wanted to limit the number of tags to 5, then you'd call the function as follows:

```php
<?php
wp_tag_cloud(array('number' => 5));
?>
```

For more information on the available parameters,
visit `http://codex.wordpress.org/Template_Tags/wp_tag_cloud`.

Highlighting the current page in the navigation

One easy way to provide a great user experience is to make sure that the user's current location on a website is plainly visible to them. The best way to accomplish this is to visibly highlight the navigation item for the page that the user is on.

How to do it...

First, ensure that you have used `wp_list_pages` to generate a list of links for use in navigation. Most likely, you'll do this in the site header where your main navigation is located. After you've done this, open your theme's stylesheet (`style.css`) and add the following CSS:

```
.current_page_item a {
  color: #fff;
  background: #000;
}
```

If you've done everything correctly, depending on your theme's styles, you'll see something like the following on your home page:

After you navigate to the page with the title **Lorem Ipsum**, you'll see the following on your home page:

How it works...

When `wp_list_pages` creates output, it adds the `current_page_item` class to the list item for the page that is currently being viewed. You style this class to ensure that the current page appears differently from other pages.

The previous CSS code simply changes the background color of the list item to black, while changing the text color to white. However, you can use any CSS declarations to customize the style of the highlighted item to your heart's content.

If your blog has a small number of top-level categories and you are using `wp_list_categories` for your main navigation items, you might want to take advantage of the highlighting capabilities demonstrated for pages. Doing so is easy, because you can use the earlier-featured code in full. You just have to change the targeted class from `current_page_item` to `current-cat`, as follows:

```
.current-cat a {
  color: #fff;
  background: #000;
}
```

Adding a search function to a theme

In spite of your best efforts, static navigation for a website will always be left wanting when a user wants to quickly and easily find content matching a specific term or phrase. That is where search comes in, and with WordPress, it is easy to implement.

How to do it...

Open your theme and decide where you want to place the search form. The best place for a search form is either in the header or at the top of a sidebar in the site. When you figure out where you want to place the search form, insert the following code at the appropriate place:

```
<form method="get" id="searchform" action="<?php echo site_url('/');
?>">
<label class="hidden" for="s"><?php _e('Search for:'); ?></label>
  <div>
    <input type="text"
    value="<?php echo attribute_escape(get_search_query()); ?>"
    name="s" id="s" />
    <input type="submit" id="searchsubmit"
    value="<?php _e('Search'); ?>" />
  </div>
</form>
```

After you've inserted the search form markup, style the form elements as desired. By default, you'll end up with output that looks like the following:

Search for:

Search

How it works...

In this recipe, you've created the standard markup for a WordPress search form. In the markup, there is a label describing the search input, the search text input itself, and the submit button for the form. When a user types text into the form and submits it, WordPress detects the parameters contained in the query and responds accordingly.

Of particular note in this recipe is the use of two WordPress functions. The first is `get_search_query`. This function retrieves the search query text that a user submitted, so that the user can see what they searched for. In addition, the `site_url` function is used to output the home page for the blog. This function is a handy utility that lets you easily construct URLs to your site.

There's more...

Searching is a complicated thing, and many developers feel that the default search functionality in WordPress is inadequate. Luckily, because of WordPress' extensive plugin system, there is a solution. That solution is the Search Everything plugin by Dan Cameron of Sprout Venture.

The Search Everything plugin, found at `http://wordpress.org/extend/plugins/search-everything/`, allows for searching tags, categories, pages, comments, and more. It might be a great addition to your WordPress installation, so check it out.

Getting the category page link from a category name

There are several situations where a particular category should be linked to directly. If the name of the category is known, but the ID of the category could differ (for instance, between production and development environments), then it is useful to be able to retrieve the category page link directly from the category name. In addition, it is helpful to not display the link at all if the category doesn't exist.

How to do it...

For this recipe, consider the situation where you need to link to three different categories: Testimonials, Portfolio, and Thoughts. You've established each of these categories in your local development environment and in your staging environment, but you haven't yet created them on the blog where you'll be launching your theme. This is a good situation to use conditional linking.

Given this situation, you need code similar to the following:

```php
<?php
$nav_categories = array('Testimonials','Portfolio','Thoughts');
?>
<ul id="site-nav">
  <?php
  foreach($nav_categories as $cat_name) {
    $cat_id = get_cat_ID($cat_name);
    if($cat_id) {
    ?>
    <li>
      <a href="<?php echo get_category_link($cat_id); ?>">
      <?php echo $cat_name; ?>
      </a>
    </li>
    <?php
    }
  }
  ?>
</ul>
```

This code produces a nice list of links for the categories that exist. You remove the chance of fatal errors from using non-existent categories, and you provide your users with a better experience.

How it works...

The get_cat_ID function returns the ID for a specific category name. If a category with that name does not exist, the function returns the value 0. Therefore, the condition that checks the $cat_id variable will prevent the system from trying to retrieve a link for categories that do not exist. If the category does exist, the category link will be displayed appropriately.

Displaying page links only if the destination page exists

In themes intended for distribution, you may want to provide a link to an **About** or **Contact** page somewhere in the theme template. However, you won't want to display the link if the page doesn't actually exist. To get around this, you can use some WordPress functions to see if the destination page exists.

How to do it...

Identify all of the pages that you wish to link to individually in your theme. For each of them, insert the following code, replacing Page Name with the name of the page you're referencing:

```php
<?php
$page = get_page_by_title('Page Name');
if( null !== $page ) {
  echo '<a href="' . get_page_link($page->ID) . '">Page Name</a>';
}
?>
```

How it works...

The get_page_by_title function returns an object containing all of the information about the page with the specified title if the page exists. If the page does not exist, the function returns null. In this recipe, you check the value of the $page variable to make sure that the page exists. If it does, a link to the page is printed, utilizing get_page_link to retrieve the correct URL for the page.

get_page_link respects the front page options of WordPress and bypasses a lot of checks that get_permalink has for non-page links. If you know that you are linking to a page and not a post, you should use get_page_link.

Creating a category drop-down menu

For highly-categorized and deeply-hierarchical sites, showing a full list of categories and subcategories can take up a lot of space in your design. To get around this, you can change your categories list from static to dynamic by using a simple JavaScript technique.

How to do it...

First, download the Superfish package from http://users.tpg.com.au/j_birch/ plugins/superfish/ and place all of the JavaScript files contained within it in your theme directory. Next, insert the following code in your theme's <head> section, above the wp_head function call:

```php
<?php
wp_enqueue_script('superfish',
get_bloginfo( 'stylesheet_directory' ) . '/superfish.js',
array('jquery'));
?>
```

Place the following code after the `wp_head` call:

```
<script type="text/javascript">
// <![CDATA[
jQuery(document).ready(function() { jQuery('ul.superfish').
superfish(); });
// ]]>
</script>
```

Now, open the template file in which you wish to display your **Category** drop-down.
Insert the following:

```
<ul class="nav superfish">
  <?php wp_list_categories(array('title_li'=>'','hide_empty'=>false));
?>
</ul>
```

Finally, load your page. Unstyled, you'll see something like the following:

When you hover over a category name that has a child, you'll see the following:

How it works...

The Superfish script is a JavaScript solution to realize true cross-browser drop-downs. It takes advantage of the semantic markup generated by the `wp_list_categories` function to create drop-downs with fully-realized submenus for subcategories. The internals of Superfish are beyond the scope of this recipe.

The empty `title_li` parameter in this recipe prevents a separate list item containing a title string from being generated and displayed. This extra list item could prove confusing to users and should generally be removed with this parameter, when using categories for navigation.

Creating drop-downs using child pages

Complex sites can be created with WordPress by using only the system of pages and subpages. In order to allow the user to easily drill down through a topic, it can be beneficial to create drop-downs from the parent-child page relationship.

Getting started

For this recipe to be useful, you must first create a series of pages and subpages that you'll be using for your site's content. An example of a desirable hierarchical content organization that would be useful to structure in this way would be a top-level "Teams" page with subpages for each team in the league that you're writing about.

How to do it...

Follow the steps for the recipe *Creating a category drop-down menu* until you get to the point where you use the function `wp_list_categories`. Then insert the following code:

```
<ul class="nav superfish">
  <?php wp_list_pages(array('title_li'=>'')); ?>
</ul>
```

Depending on your theme's styles, you should see something similar to the following, before hovering over a parent page:

- About
- Level 1 »
- Lorem Ipsum
- Parent page »

And you should see the following after hovering over a parent page:

- About
- Level 1 »
    - Level 2
- Lorem Ipsum
- Parent page »

How it works...

Again, the semantic markup output by the `wp_list_pages` function is the real star here. The Superfish JavaScript takes the nested lists generated by WordPress and transforms them into easy-to-use and efficient drop-down menus. The internals of the Superfish JavaScript is beyond the scope of this recipe, but the basic idea is that it uses hover events on the hierarchical list items to make the drop-downs work appropriately.

See also

▶ *Creating a category drop-down menu*

3
The Loop

In this chapter, we will cover:

- ▶ Creating a basic Loop
- ▶ Displaying ads after every third post
- ▶ Removing posts in a particular category
- ▶ Removing posts with a particular tag
- ▶ Highlighting sticky posts
- ▶ Creating multiple loops in a single template
- ▶ Displaying only posts in a particular category
- ▶ Styling every other post differently
- ▶ Styling posts in a particular category differently
- ▶ Showing every post in a category on a category archive page

Introduction

The Loop is the basic building block of WordPress template files. You'll use The Loop when displaying posts and pages, both when you're showing multiple items or a single one. Inside of The Loop you use WordPress' template tags to render information in whatever manner your design requires.

WordPress provides the data required for a default Loop on every single page load. In addition, you're able to create your own custom Loops that display post and page information that you need. This power allows you to create advanced designs that require a variety of information to be displayed. This chapter will cover both basic and advanced Loop usage and you'll see exactly how to use this most basic WordPress structure.

Creating a basic Loop

The Loop nearly always takes the same basic structure. In this recipe, you'll become acquainted with this structure, find out how The Loop works, and get up and running in no time.

How to do it...

First, open the file in which you wish to iterate through the available posts. In general, you use The Loop in every single template file that is designed to show posts. Some examples include `index.php`, `category.php`, `single.php`, and `page.php`. Place your cursor where you want The Loop to appear, and then insert the following code:

```php
<?php
if( have_posts() ) {
  while( have_posts() ) {
    the_post();
    ?>
    <h2><?php the_title(); ?></h2>
    <?php
  }
}
?>
```

Using the WordPress theme test data with the above Loop construct, you end up with something that looks similar to the example shown in following screenshot:

Depending on your theme's styles, this output could obviously look very different. However, the important thing to note is that you've used The Loop to iterate over available data from the system and then display pieces of that data to the user in the way that you want to. From here, you can use a wide variety of template tags in order to display different information depending on the specific requirements of your theme.

How it works...

A deep understanding of The Loop is paramount to becoming a great WordPress designer and developer, so you should understand each of the items in the above code snippet fairly well.

First, you should recognize that this is just a standard `while` loop with a surrounding `if` conditional. There are some special WordPress functions that are used in these two items, but if you've done any PHP programming at all, you should be intimately familiar with the syntax here. If you haven't experienced programming in PHP, then you might want to check out the syntax rules for `if` and `while` constructs at `http://php.net/if` and `http://php.net/while`, respectively.

The next thing to understand about this generic loop is that it depends directly on the global `$wp_query` object. `$wp_query` is created when the request is parsed, request variables are found, and WordPress figures out the posts that should be displayed for the URL that a visitor has arrived from. `$wp_query` is an instance of the `WP_Query` object, and the `have_posts` and `the_post` functions delegate to methods on that object.

The `$wp_query` object holds information about the posts to be displayed and the type of page being displayed (normal listing, category archive, date archive, and so on). When `have_posts` is called in the `if` conditional above, the `$wp_query` object determines whether any posts matched the request that was made, and if so, whether there are any posts that haven't been iterated over.

If there are posts to display, a `while` construct is used that again checks the value of `have_posts`. During each iteration of the `while` loop, the `the_post` function is called. `the_post` sets an index on `$wp_query` that indicates which posts have been iterated over. It also sets up several global variables, most notably `$post`.

Inside of The Loop, the `the_title` function uses the global `$post` variable that was set up in `the_post` to produce the appropriate output based on the currently-active post item. This is basically the way that all template tags work.

If you're interested in further information on how the `WP_Query` class works, you should read the documentation about it in the WordPress Codex at http://codex.wordpress.org/Function_Reference/WP_Query. You can find more information about *The Loop* at `http://codex.wordpress.org/The_Loop`.

Displaying ads after every third post

If you're looking to display ads on your site, one of the best places to do it is mixed up with your main content. This will cause visitors to view your ads, as they're engaged with your work, often resulting in higher click-through rates and better paydays for you.

How to do it...

First, open the template in which you wish to display advertisements while iterating over the available posts. This will most likely be a listing template file like `index.php` or `category.php`. Decide on the number of posts that you wish to display between advertisements. Place your cursor where you want your loop to appear, and then insert the following code:

```php
<?php
if( have_posts() ) {
  $ad_counter = 0;
  $after_every = 3;
  while( have_posts() ) {
    $ad_counter++;
    the_post();
    ?>
    <h2><?php the_title(); ?></h2>
    <?php

    // Display ads
    $ad_counter = $ad_counter % $after_every;
    if( 0 == $ad_counter ) {
      echo '<h2 style="color:red;">Advertisement</h2>';
    }
  }
}
?>
```

If you've done everything correctly, and are using the WordPress theme test data, you should see something similar to the example shown in the following screenshot:

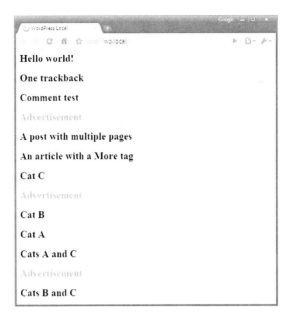

Obviously, the power here comes when you mix in paying ads or images that link to products that you're promoting. Instead of a simple heading element for the **Advertisement** text, you could dynamically insert JavaScript or Flash elements that pull in advertisements for you.

How it works...

As with the basic Loop, this code snippet iterates over all available posts. In this recipe, however, a counter variable is declared that counts the number of posts that have been iterated over. Every time that a post is about to be displayed, the counter is incremented to track that another post has been rendered. After every third post, the advertisement code is displayed because the value of the $ad_counter variable is equal to 0.

It is very important to put the conditional check and display code after the post has been displayed. Also, notice that the $ad_counter variable will never be greater than 3 because the modulus operator (%) is being used every time through The Loop.

Finally, if you wish to change the frequency of the ad display, simply modify the $after_every variable from 3 to whatever number of posts you want to display between ads.

Removing posts in a particular category

Sometimes you'll want to make sure that posts from a certain category never implicitly show up in the Loops that you're displaying in your template. The category could be a special one that you use to denote portfolio pieces, photo posts, or whatever else you wish to remove from regular Loops.

How to do it...

First, you have to decide which category you want to exclude from your Loops. Note the name of the category, and then open or create your theme's `functions.php` file. Your `functions.php` file resides inside of your theme's directory and may contain some other code. Inside of `functions.php`, insert the following code:

```php
add_action('pre_get_posts', 'remove_cat_from_loops');

function remove_cat_from_loops( $query ) {
  if(!$query->get('suppress_filters')) {
    $cat_id = get_cat_ID('Category Name');
    $excluded_cats = $query->get('category__not_in');
    if(is_array($excluded_cats)) {
      $excluded_cats[] = $cat_id;
    } else {
      $excluded_cats = array($cat_id);
    }
    $query->set('category__not_in', $excluded_cats);
  }
  return $query;
}
```

How it works...

In the above code snippet, you are excluding the category with the name `Category Name`. To exclude a different category, change the `Category Name` string to the name of the category you wish to remove from loops.

You are filtering the `WP_Query` object that drives every Loop. Before any posts are fetched from the database, you dynamically change the value of the `category__not_in` variable in the `WP_Query` object. You append an additional category ID to the existing array of excluded category IDs to ensure that you're not undoing work of some other developer. Alternatively, if the `category__not_in` variable is not an array, you assign it an array with a single item. Every category ID in the `category__not_in` array will be excluded from The Loop, because when the `WP_Query` object eventually makes a request to the database, it structures the query such that no posts contained in any of the categories identified in the `category__not_in` variable are fetched.

Please note that the denoted category will be excluded by default from all Loops that you create in your theme. If you want to display posts from the category that you've marked to exclude, then you need to set the `suppress_filters` parameter to true when querying for posts, as follows:

```
query_posts(
  array(
    'cat'=>get_cat_ID('Category Name'),
    'suppress_filters'=>true
  )
);
```

Removing posts with a particular tag

Similar to categories, it could be desirable to remove posts with a certain tag from The Loop. You may wish to do this if you are tagging certain posts as asides, or if you are saving posts that contain some text that needs to be displayed in a special context elsewhere on your site.

How to do it...

First, you have to decide which tag you want to exclude from your Loops. Note the name of the tag, and then open or create your theme's `functions.php` file. Inside of `functions.php`, insert the following code:

```
add_action('pre_get_posts', 'remove_tag_from_loops');
function remove_tag_from_loops( $query ) {
  if(!$query->get('suppress_filters')) {
    $tag_id = get_term_by('name','tag1','post_tag')->term_id;
    $excluded_tags = $query->get('tag__not_in');
    if(is_array( $excluded_tags )) {
      $excluded_tags[] = $tag_id;
    } else {
      $excluded_tags = array($tag_id);
    }
```

```
    $query->set('tag__not_in', $excluded_tags);
  }
  return $query;
}
```

How it works...

In the above code snippet, you are excluding the tag with the slug `tag1`. To exclude a different tag, change the string `tag1` to the name of the tag that you wish to remove from all Loops.

When deciding what tags to exclude, the WordPress system looks at a query parameter named `tag__not_in`, which is an array. In the above code snippet, the function appends the ID of the tag that should be excluded directly to the `tag__not_in` array. Alternatively, if `tag__not_in` isn't already initialized as an array, it is assigned an array with a single item, consisting of the ID for the tag that you wish to exclude. After that, all posts with that tag will be excluded from WordPress Loops.

Please note that the chosen tag will be excluded, by default, from all Loops that you create in your theme. If you want to display posts from the tag that you've marked to exclude, then you need to set the `suppress_filters` parameter to `true` when querying for posts, as follows:

```
query_posts(
  array(
    'tag'=>get_term_by('name','tag1','post_tag')->term_id,
    'suppress_filters'=>true
  )
);
```

Highlighting sticky posts

Sticky posts are a feature added in version 2.7 of WordPress and can be used for a variety of purposes. The most frequent use is to mark posts that should be "featured" for an extended period of time. These posts often contain important information or highlight things (like a product announcement) that the blog author wants to display in a prominent position for a long period of time.

How to do it...

First, place your cursor inside of a Loop where you're displaying posts and want to single out your sticky content. Inside The Loop, after a call to `the_post`, insert the following code:

```
<?php
if(is_sticky()) {
  ?>
```

```
<div class="sticky-announcer">
  <p>This post is sticky.</p>
</div>
<?php
}
?>
```

Create a sticky post on your test blog and take a look at your site's front page. You should see text appended to the sticky post, and the post should be moved to the top of The Loop. You can see this in the following screenshot:

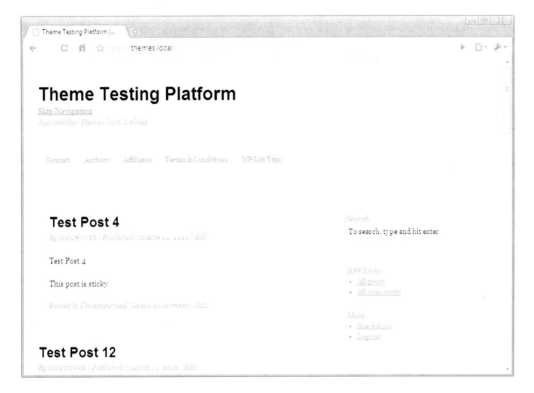

The `is_sticky` function checks the currently-active post to see if it is a sticky post. It does this by examining the value retrieved by calling `get_option('sticky_posts')`, which is an array, and trying to find the active post's ID in that array.

In this case, if the post is sticky then the `sticky-announcer` div is output with a message. However, there is no limit to what you can do once you've determined if a post is sticky. Some ideas include:

- ▶ Displaying a special icon for sticky posts
- ▶ Changing the background color of sticky posts
- ▶ Adding content dynamically to sticky posts
- ▶ Displaying post content differently for sticky posts

Creating multiple loops in a single template

In advanced themes, there are often situations where you would want to display multiple Loops consisting of posts with different criteria. When doing so, you should make sure not to alter the normal default Loop or else some template tags will not work appropriately.

How to do it...

First, decide what kind of Loops you want to create. Perhaps you want to create two Loops, based on different categories. Perhaps one Loop should have featured posts while the other has the default posts based on the page URL. For this example, we're going to create two category Loops.

To create the two category Loops, you need to create two separate instances of the `WP_Query` class. Copy the following code snippet into one of your template files:

```php
<?php
$query1 = new WP_Query(array('cat'=>get_cat_ID('aciform')));
if( $query1->have_posts() ) {
  ?><h1>Aciform Posts</h1><?php
  while($query1->have_posts()) {
    $query1->the_post();
    ?><h2><?php the_title(); ?></h2><?php
  }
}
echo '<hr />';
$query2 = new WP_Query(array('cat'=>get_cat_ID('Cat B')));
if( $query2->have_posts() ) {
  ?><h1>Cat B Posts</h1><?php
  while($query2->have_posts()) {
    $query2->the_post();
    ?><h2><?php the_title(); ?></h2><?php
  }
}
?>
```

The above snippet renders output that looks something like the example shown in following screenshot:

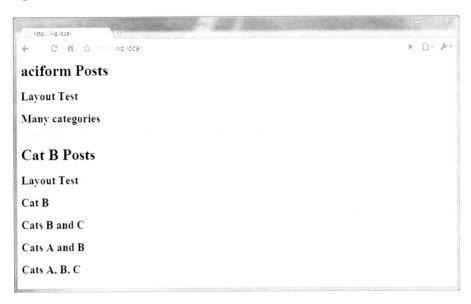

You can see in the above image that there are two major sections. The first consists of the titles of all posts with the category **aciform**. The second section consists of the titles of all posts with the category **Cat B**

How it works...

In the above code sample, two new instances of the WP_Query class are created. The first instance is created with parameters specifying that it should contain posts in the category Aciform. The second instance is created with parameters specifying that it should contain posts in the category Cat B

The parameters passed in each case direct the content of the SQL query, which is passed to the underlying WordPress database. You don't really need to know about all of that, but you can learn a lot by looking at how WordPress constructs the query inside of the WP_Query class.

After the instances are created, the basic Loop construct is used. However, you should note that all Loop functions are prefixed with the new object's name. So, when you're using the first WP_Query object that contains posts in Aciform, each Loop function call is preceded with the string $myquery1->. This ensures that the new query object's data is used instead of the global $wp_query object's data.

There's more...

The `WP_Query` constructor takes a variety of parameters as an array or formatted query string. The parameters are the same as those for the `query_posts` and `get_posts` WordPress functions, but there are far too many to even begin to dive into in this recipe. For more information on the available parameters, please see `http://codex.wordpress.org/Template_Tags/query_posts#Parameters`.

Displaying only posts in a particular category

Often there will be a category that needs to be called on specifically in your WordPress theme. If you don't know the category's ID, you can use the category name to retrieve the correct posts.

How to do it...

First, open the template file that you wish to insert the category Loop into. If you want to highlight a certain category in your theme's sidebar, for example, you would open `sidebar.php`. Insert your cursor at the appropriate spot, and then add the following code:

```php
<?php
$cat_name = 'My Category Name';
query_posts(array('category_name'=>$cat_name));
if(have_posts() ) {
  while(have_posts() ) {
    the_post();
  }
}
?>
```

How it works...

The available parameters for the `query_posts` function are varied and many. In this instance, you take advantage of the `category_name` parameter to ensure that only posts in the specified category (in this instance, `My Category Name`) are returned for the Loop. Want to use a different category? Change the value of the `$cat_name` parameter.

Styling every other post differently

Styling every other post differently is a powerful technique for creating interest in your theme and leading a visitor's eye down the page. The options for styling are endless, but some of the most popular and pervasive options include changing background images, colors, layout items, and more.

How to do it...

Open the template file in which you wish to style posts differently as they are iterated over. In general, you'll insert this functionality into a template like index.php or category.php. Place your cursor where you wish to insert *The Loop*. Insert the following code:

```php
<?php
if( have_posts() ) {
  $alt_post = 'alt-post';
  while( have_posts() ) {
    the_post();
    $alt_post = $alt_post == 'alt-post' ? '' : 'alt-post';
    ?>
    <div class="post <?php echo $alt_post; ?>">
      <h2><?php the_title(); ?></h2>
    </div>
    <?php
  }
}
?>
```

Now open your theme's stylesheet, style.css, and insert the following styles:

```css
/** Styling for alternating posts **/

.post {
  background: #990000;
  color: #ffffff;
  padding: 5px;
}

.alt-post {
  background: #000099;
}
```

Assuming that your stylesheet is linked to your theme appropriately, you should see something like the example shown in the following screenshot:

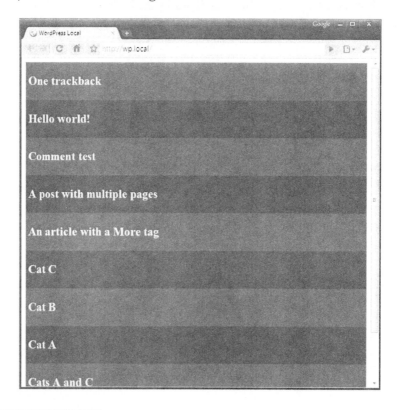

How it works...

Each time The Loop is iterated over, PHP checks to see if the `$alt_post` variable indicates whether an alternate post was rendered on the previous run. If it does, it switches the variable back to the empty string. Otherwise, it sets the variable to `alt-post`.

When the post container is being printed, it includes a class of `post` by default, and then prints out the value of the `$alt_post` variable. If the `$alt_post` variable was set, the post container then has a class of `alt-post` in addition to `post`.

In the theme's stylesheet, you can change the style for the alternate post. In this instance, the background of a regular post will be dark red whereas every alternate post will have a background of royal blue.

Styling posts in a particular category differently

In WordPress, one of the best ways to differentiate content is via the use of categories. In your theme, styling posts from different categories in unique ways will help visitors find what they want quickly and easily.

How to do it...

Decide where you want to check for a particular category. For this example, you'll be checking for the `Featured` category and appending a little snippet of text. Insert your cursor inside of your Loop, and then add the following code:

```php
<?php
$category_name = 'Featured';
if(in_category($category_name)) {
  echo '<div class="featured-icon">Featured</div>';
}
?>
```

After you detect the special category and print the extra piece of content, you can style it however you want. In this particular case, you may want to use absolute positioning to add a star icon or badge to the post's main content container. Alternatively, you could add a large header that makes the post stand out. There is no limit to what you can do.

How it works...

The `in_category` function operates on the currently-active post in The Loop. In this instance, you are checking to see if the post is in a category named `Featured`. If it is, then an extra piece of HTML markup is displayed. This piece of markup could be styled in a way that makes it readily apparent that the post is a featured piece of content.

This technique can be easily adopted for use with other content types: highlighted posts, code snippets, and more. The limit is your imagination.

Showing every post in a category on a category archive page

If you want your category pages to operate as a complete archive of all posts in that category (basically removing any type of pagination), you can make some simple changes to the basic Loop.

How to do it...

Open or create your theme's `category.php` file. This template file is used to display your category archives. Create a basic Loop by following the directions from the recipe *Creating a basic Loop*.

Above your Loop, insert the following code:

```
global $wp_query;
query_posts(
  array_merge(
    array('nopaging' => true),
    $wp_query->query
  )
);
```

How it works...

In the above code snippet, the `query_posts` function is used to modify the global query object. To ensure that all of the appropriate query parameters are preserved from the original query, the new parameters are merged with the old parameters. The old parameters are kept in the array `$wp_query->query`.

The `nopaging` parameter is set to `true` to indicate that all posts should be returned, and any post limit should be ignored.

See also

▶ *Creating a basic Loop*

4
Template Tags

In this chapter, we will cover:

- ▶ Displaying the post title
- ▶ Automatically limiting the number of words of content
- ▶ Determining if the user is on a specific page
- ▶ Determining if the user is viewing a post in a particular category
- ▶ Displaying the post date for each post
- ▶ Highlighting search terms in post content
- ▶ Displaying login/logout links
- ▶ Adding navigation through older/newer posts
- ▶ Displaying an edit link for posts
- ▶ Displaying custom field content
- ▶ Displaying a post author's avatar

Introduction

The most important part of any website is its content. Your content and its presentation is the reason people visit and stick around, the thing that search engines index, and the way you get your unique message out to the world.

Luckily for you, WordPress offers a variety of interesting ways to display content for all of the data it manages. As a theme developer, you can also modify the content before WordPress displays it, allowing you to produce some pretty interesting effects, such as search term highlighting, automatic appending of static content to all posts, or truncation of content for non-logged-in users.

In this chapter, you'll learn about some of WordPress' built-in content display functions, create your own unique content mashups, and learn how to exploit the power of WordPress to display the data that you want to display where you want to display it.

Displaying the post title

For a blog, one of the most important pieces of content that you can display is a post's title. The title should be interesting; it should grab attention, it should provide great linking material, and it should make your readers want more. In this recipe, we'll start talking about template tags by describing how you would display a post's title.

How to do it...

First, open a template file for your theme that contains a variation on The Loop. You can learn more about The Loop in Chapter 3. As a reminder, it looks something like this:

```php
<?php
if(have_posts()) {
  while(have_posts()) {
    // Display content here
  }
}
```

Inside of your instance of The Loop, insert the following code, in order to display each post's title:

```php
<?php the_title(); ?>
```

To see this in action, you can refer back to the recipe Creating a basic Loop. There you used the_title inside of The Loop, successfully displaying the title of each of the posts.

How it works...

the_title is one of a variety of functions that are used to display information about the post data currently held in the global $post object. To do this, they look at the value of the $post variable and apply the necessary filters to the appropriate content before sending it to the browser. In the function the_title, WordPress looks at the post_title property of the $post object and applies all of the filters hooked to the_title. The application of these filters allows the WordPress core code, as well as third-party plugins, to modify the title value for any post.

If you're interested in diving deeper into the template tag function definitions, you can find most of them inside a file contained in your WordPress installation at wp-includes/post-template.php. This is something that I highly recommend, as it can help you tremendously as you try to do more and more complex things with WordPress.

There's more...

WordPress defines a wide variety of PHP functions that retrieve or print information about the currently-active post. The following functions are the most frequently-used functions in any template:

- ▶ `the_ID`
- ▶ `the_title`
- ▶ `the_title_attribute`
- ▶ `the_content`
- ▶ `the_excerpt`
- ▶ `the_category`
- ▶ `the_tags`
- ▶ `next_post_link`
- ▶ `next_posts_link`
- ▶ `previous_post_link`
- ▶ `previous_posts_link`

The purpose of most of these functions is self-explanatory, but you should try each of them in a template to see what kind of output you end up with. In addition, you can see the complete list of template tags and the corresponding documentation, for posts and otherwise, at `http://codex.wordpress.org/Template_Tags/`.

See also

- ▶ *Creating a basic Loop*

Automatically limiting the number of words of content

In some instances, you may wish to display a specific number of words from a post's content, perhaps in a compact loop for older posts or as part of an asides section in a blog's sidebar. This recipe shows you how to go about it.

How to do it...

First, open or create your `functions.php` file. This file resides in your theme's root directory. You're going to create a custom template tag for your theme, and the `functions.php` file is the proper place to do so. Inside of your `functions.php` file, place the following code:

```php
<?php
function limited_the_content($number_words = 200) {
  global $post;
  $stripped_content = strip_tags($post->post_content);
  $words = explode(' ', $stripped_content);
  if( count($words) < $number_words ) {
    echo $stripped_content;
  } else {
    $words = array_slice($words, 0, $number_words);
    echo implode(' ', $words);
  }
}
?>
```

You'll use this function in place of `the_content` to display your post's content. Open one of your theme's template files (such as `index.php`) and insert the following code inside The Loop:

```php
<?php limited_the_content($number_words); ?>
```

Replace the `$number_words` variable in the above code snippet with whatever number of words you wish to display. You can check the difference between `the_content` and `limited_the_content` by using the following Loop:

```php
<?php
if( have_posts() ) {
  while( have_posts() ) {
    the_post();
    ?>
    <div class="post <?php echo $alt_post; ?>">
      <h2><?php the_title(); ?></h2>
      <h3>Content</h3>
      <div><?php the_content(); ?></div>
      <h3>Limited to 25 Words</h3>
      <div><?php limited_the_content(25); ?></div>
    </div>
    <?php
  }
}
?>
```

When viewing the output of the above snippet, you'll see something like the example shown in the following screenshot:

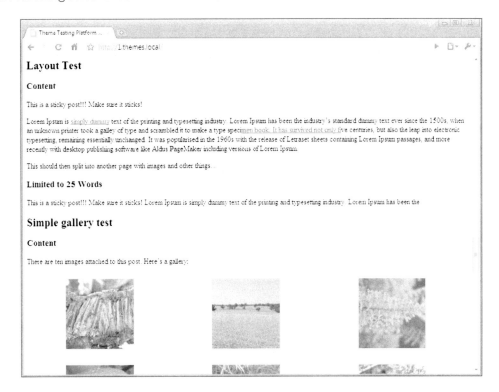

How it works...

The `limited_the_content` function accesses the currently-active post by globalizing the $post variable. The global $post variable always contains the value of the post currently being displayed in The Loop.

After that, the active post's contents are retrieved from the `$post` variable's `post_content` property, and all HTML tags are removed. Finally, the modified post contents are split apart into separate words by exploding the contents on the space character (this means that you are assuming that every time there is a space, we should break off the previously-seen characters as a new word). If the total number of words present in the post's content is less than the maximum allowed, then the tag-less content is returned intact. Otherwise, the number of words is pared down to the number allowed. The words are re-joined by replacing the spaces removed earlier, and the newly-constructed string is returned.

As seen in this chapter, almost every single instance where you're modifying PHP output involves concatenation and other string operations. If you're unfamiliar with these concepts, then you should check out the official PHP reference manual at `http://php.net/strings/`.

Again, it is important to note here that all HTML tags have been stripped out from the post's content before doing this manipulation. This is to avoid a scenario where HTML tags become mismatched, messing up the display of your carefully-constructed theme.

Determining if the user is on a specific page

There will come a time when your theme should do something special for a certain page. Maybe your **About** page should display the author biographies or avatars, or perhaps you want your **Contact** page to include your phone number and address at the top, in addition to whatever other content appears.

How to do it...

Decide on the page that you want to customize, and remember its name. Open your theme's `page.php` file. This template file is used when displaying a single page. Place the cursor in the template where you want your custom content to be displayed, and then insert the following code:

```php
<?php
if(is_page('Page Name')) {
   // Put special content code here
}
?>
```

Replace `Page Name` with the name that you previously determined. Save the file and view the special page in your browser. Whatever content you added specifically for that page should appear. However, if you navigate to a different page, then the special content will not appear.

How it works...

The `is_page` function utilizes the global `$wp_query` variable and its data to verify that a page is being viewed and that the page being viewed matches the conditions specified by the function's parameter.

By default, the `is_page` function only checks to see if a page is currently being displayed. However, by passing it a parameter, you can check to see if a specific page is being viewed. The parameter could be the page name, page slug, or page ID, whichever is most convenient. I recommend using the page slug or page name over the page ID, as the ID has little chance of being the same on your development and production installations, whereas the name and slug will almost certainly be identical between the two environments.

Determining if the user is viewing a post in a particular category

Many WordPress users utilize categories to differentiate between different types of content or to show their intent with regard to a particular post. As a theme author, it is sometimes useful to differentiate between categories by using an image or special text. To do so, you must first determine if the user is viewing a post in a special category. Then you can take the appropriate action or render the appropriate output.

How to do it...

First, decide on the category that you wish to display special content for, and remember its name. Open a template file where you are displaying posts in a Loop and you wish to add special content for posts in a certain category. Place your cursor where you want to display special output, and then insert the following code:

```php
<?php
if(in_category('Category Name')) {
  // Output appropriate code here
}
?>
```

Replace `Category Name` with the name of the category that you wish to use.

How it works...

Every post can be in many different categories. For example, a post might be about programming and more specifically about WordPress. Thus, you'd put that post into the Programming category and the WordPress category.

In this recipe, you're checking to see if the currently-active post is in the `Category Name` category. If it is, whatever output you render between the braces ({ }) will be shown. If the active post is not in that category, nothing will happen.

The parameter to `in_category` can be a category name, slug, or ID. In most cases, you'll want to use a name or slug, as those items will likely match on your development and production installations, whereas the category ID will not.

There's more...

in_category can also check multiple categories. If you have Category 1 and Category 2 on your blog, you can check to see if a post is in **either** of these categories by using the following code:

```php
<?php
if(in_category(array('Category 1','Category 2'))) {
  // Output appropriate code here
}
?>
```

If you need to check if a post is in **both** Category 1 and Category 2, then you would use the following code:

```php
<?php
if(in_category('Category 1') && in_category('Category 2')) {
  // Output appropriate code here
}
?>
```

Displaying the post date for each post

Generally speaking, blogs run chronologically. One blog post follows another and they are often sorted by date. Several similar-sounding template tags seem like they would show the date for a post, but only one does it for each post.

How to do it...

Open one of your theme's template files that contain The Loop. Inside The Loop, place your cursor at the point where you want to output the time and date on which the post was published. Insert the following code:

```php
<?php the_time( 'F j, Y' ); ?>
```

How it works...

Looking at the list of template tags, many theme developers believe that the_date will output the date for each post. However, it will only display the date once for each unique date in The Loop. That is, if you had multiple posts on a single day, the_date would only render output for the first one. To display the date for each post, use the_time with a date format string that specifies that the month, day, and year should be displayed.

You can modify the date and time components that are output from `the_time` by modifying the date format parameter. Find out more about date format strings by visiting `http://us2.php.net/manual/en/function.date.php`.

Highlighting search terms in post content

If a user utilizes the WordPress search function to scour your site for something, then you know that their query is probably pretty specific. You can make it easier on your visitors by highlighting search terms in their search results. This way, they'll be able to immediately scan to the appropriate places in your content.

How to do it...

First, open or create your theme's `functions.php` file. You'll be creating a custom filter that latches onto post content and excerpts, and the `functions.php` file is the correct place to do so. Insert the following code in this file:

```php
<?php
function highlight_search_terms($content) {
  if( is_search() ) {
    $search_term = get_query_var('s');
    $content = preg_replace( "/\b($search_term)\b/i",
    '<span class="search-result">$1</span>', $content );
  }

  return $content;
}

add_action( 'the_content', 'highlight_search_terms' );
add_action( 'the_excerpt', 'highlight_search_terms' );
?>
```

Open your theme's stylesheet (`style.css`) and insert the following style declarations:

```css
.search-result {
  background: #0000ff;
  color: #ffffff;
  padding: 0 3px;
}
```

Finally, ensure that your theme file has a search field on it somewhere. Search for a term on your site and you should see that the term is highlighted in blue in the content that is displayed. In the following example, I've searched for the string **this**:

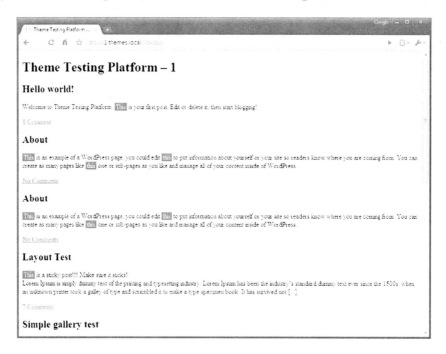

How it works...

You'll see that after you search every instance of your search term is wrapped in a new `<span>` tag that is styled by the `search-result` declaration in your stylesheet. These specially-styled tags will appear as long as the output is being rendered by using either `the_content` or `the_excerpt`.

To start, you create a new function that accepts a string of content and performs an operation on that content before returning it. In this instance, you use a conditional tag to check if a search page is being displayed. If it is, the search term is fetched (it is stored in the WordPress query variable `s`) and then the content is run through a simple regular expression.

In this instance, the regular expression seeks out each instance of the search term that appears in the $content string. When it finds one, it surrounds it in a `<span>` tag by doing a match replacement. This regular expression usage is case insensitive, so a search for **Test** will match both **Test** and **test**. Please note that this will only match whole words, so a search for **Test** will not cause the first part of **Testing** to be highlighted.

The style declaration here simply highlights the word by giving it a background of blue, making the color of the text white, and spacing it out a bit from surrounding words. The possibilities with this method are endless, however.

Displaying login/logout links

One of the most important actions that your theme's users will take is to log in and out of your WordPress installation. Many installations limit certain content to logged-in users, so **login** and **logout** links must be prominent and correct.

For security purposes, **logout** links must contain a specially-constructed nonce (basically, a secure key), so it isn't good enough to point to the login page with a specific action argument. Using the WordPress functions, you can display **login** and **logout** links with one simple function call.

How to do it...

Open a template file that you wish to insert the **login**/**logout** link into. Generally, you want login/logout functionality to be available across your entire site, so a good place for this code is in your header or sidebar. Place your cursor wherever you want the **login**/**logout** link to appear, and then insert the following code:

```php
<?php wp_loginout(); ?>
```

How it works...

This super handy utility function does a few things. First, it checks to see if a user is currently logged in. If the user is logged in, it prints a link containing a security nonce to the logout page with the text **Log out** (localized as necessary). Conversely, if a user is not logged in, a link to the login page is printed with the text **Log in** (again, localized as necessary).

There's more...

You may wish to have different text for the **login** and **logout** links than the default that is provided. Unfortunately, there is no parameter that lets you change the text directly through the wp_loginout function. As such, you need to get slightly more creative, and replace the above code with the following piece of code:

```php
<?php
if ( ! is_user_logged_in() ) {
  $link = '<a href="' . wp_login_url() . '">' . __('Log in text') .
'</a>';
} else {
  $link = '<a href="' . wp_logout_url() . '">' . __('Log out text') .
'</a>';
}
print $link;
?>
```

From there, you can replace the Log in text and Log out text as appropriate for your site.

Adding navigation through older/newer posts

If users are properly engaged, they'll want to navigate through your archives, reading old posts that you published long before the ones on the front page of your site. Luckily, WordPress has functions built in to allow you to easily print these navigation links.

How to do it...

Open a template file that you wish to add post navigation to. The most likely candidates for this are your index.php template file or any of the archive-based template files (category.php, tag.php, author.php, and so on). Place your cursor where you want the navigation links to appear, and then insert the following code:

```php
<div class="navigation">
  <div><?php
  next_posts_link('&laquo; Older Entries')
  ?></div>
  <div><?php
  previous_posts_link('Newer Entries &raquo;')
  ?></div>
</div>
```

How it works...

The `next_posts_link` and `previous_posts_link` functions each print a link that allows users to navigate through the archives of a site. Interestingly, `previous_posts_link` navigates forward through posts chronologically, whereas `next_posts_link` navigates backward through posts chronologically. While this is counterintuitive to many people, it has yet to be changed, and probably won't be, due to concerns over legacy themes.

In addition, the lone parameter to these functions allows you to customize the text that is displayed with the link. Simply change the parameter value to change the links' text in your theme.

There's more...

Archive navigation isn't just for big loops with multiple posts. Single pages can be navigated through similarly, by using functions named almost exactly the same. In `single.php` or `page.php`, insert the following wherever you want navigation links to appear:

```
<div class="navigation">
  <div><?php previous_post_link('&laquo; %link') ?></div>
  <div><?php next_post_link('%link &raquo;') ?></div>
</div>
```

Displaying an edit link for posts

After you publish a post, you'll often want to go back and update facts as more becomes available on a developing story, or to correct spelling and grammar errors that you've noticed after reading through it. Rather than force your theme's users to log in and search to find the post to edit, you can provide a link to the editing page directly in your theme.

How to do it...

Open a template file where you are displaying posts in the The Loop. Decide where you want the edit link to appear. It can appear anywhere inside The Loop. Place your cursor at that point and insert the following code:

```
<?php edit_post_link('Edit this entry','','.'); ?>
```

How it works...

The `edit_post_link` function detects the currently logged in user's role and capabilities. If the user is logged in and he or she has the ability to modify the post that is currently being displayed, then the **Edit** link appears.

Three parameters are used to format the link. The first parameter allows for customization of the text of the link. The second parameter is displayed before the link and the third parameter is displayed after the link.

Use this function in your theme! Your users will thank you for it when they don't have to go searching for an old post in the admin system.

Displaying custom field content

As WordPress is used for an increasingly varied array of content, users often add extra meta information to posts that should be displayed in a theme. This metadata includes things like post thumbnail URLs, ratings, or even entirely new blocks of content like callouts or something similar.

How to do it...

First, you need to determine the name of the meta information that the user has entered via the Write Post or Write Page interface. As a theme developer, you'll probably want to give some instructions to your users on what custom meta keys are supported. The meta information entry interface looks like the following example to WordPress users:

Custom Fields

Add new custom field:

Name	Value

Cancel

Add Custom Field

Custom fields can be used to add extra metadata to a post that you can use in your theme.

You can see the meta key field on the left and the **Value** field on the right. The meta key is generally more important to you as a theme developer, so instruct your users on what to enter there. If they had previously used a meta key, it will appear in a drop-down list as shown in the following:

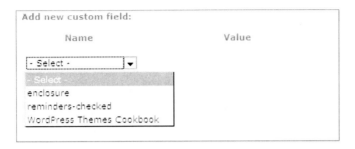

After you've determined what meta key you want to display on the blog's frontend, it is simple to make it appear. Open a theme file that contains The Loop and place your cursor where you want to display the meta information. Insert the following code:

```php
<?php
echo get_post_meta(get_the_ID(), 'meta_name', true);
?>
```

Replace the string meta_name in the above code sample with the name of the meta key field that you wish to display the value for.

How it works...

WordPress stores meta information in the post meta table in the WordPress database. When you call get_post_meta in your theme, it looks for metadata named by the string passed as the second parameter to the function related to the post specified by the ID passed in the first parameter. The third parameter tells WordPress to return only one result, so that you can print it immediately.

There's more...

A user can enter multiple post meta values for a single key. In order to retrieve and fetch all of these, use the following code:

```php
<?php
global $post;
$post_meta = get_post_meta( $post->ID, 'meta_name' );
foreach( $post_meta as $meta_item ) {
  echo $meta_item . '<br />';
}
```

Replace the string 'meta_name' in the above code sample with the name of the meta key field that you wish to display the value for.

Here the omission of the third parameter instructs WordPress to return all post meta with the key `meta_name` as an array. After that, you iterate over each post meta item and print it, followed by a line break.

Displaying a post author's avatar

Visitors are more likely to engage with your post authors if they can identify them quickly and easily. One of the best ways to allow this is to build support for displaying avatars directly into your theme.

This technique is best for multi-author blogs where authors for different posts vary. If your blog expects only a single user to be writing, then this tip might not be for you.

How to do it...

Open a theme file that contains The Loop. Place your cursor inside the loop where you want the author's avatar to appear, and then insert the following code:

```php
<?php
global $post;
echo get_avatar($post->post_author);
?>
```

This code will produce markup like the following:

```html
<img
width="96"
height="96"
class="avatar avatar-96 photo"
src="http://www.gravatar.com/avatar/
252ed115afcb3c69546ed891b8eddddf?s=96&amp;d=http%3A%2F%2Fwww.gravatar.
com%2Favatar%2Fad516503a11cd5ca435acc9bb6523536%3Fs%3D96&amp;r=G"
alt=""/>
```

This markup will display as a small image like the following:

How it works...

When you pass a user ID to the `get_avatar` function, it recognizes the numeric value and looks up the user in the WordPress database. It then assigns the e-mail to use for Gravatar retrieval as the e-mail set for that user in the WordPress back-end. By default, the function then contacts Gravatar to fetch the appropriate image for the user (although this functionality can be overridden by plugins).

5
Comments

In this chapter, we will cover:

- ▶ Displaying a comment form on a post
- ▶ Displaying comments on a post
- ▶ Displaying the latest comments on your blog
- ▶ Highlighting the post author's comments
- ▶ Alternating the style for comments
- ▶ Displaying threaded comments properly

Introduction

Comments are one of the most important parts of blogging. In fact, some say that a blog isn't really a blog without comments. As such, it is very important to pay attention to the way that comments are styled and the way that they function in your theme.

This chapter starts with the basic tenets of comment display and formatting, and later expands on some really interesting things that you can do with the WordPress comment system.

Displaying a comment form on a post

Because comments are so important on a blog, it stands to reason that the best place to start is with how to display an appropriate comment form on each post. The comment form allows the appropriate visitors to leave comments with their name, e-mail address, and URL. The form presented in this recipe is the standard comment form that the default WordPress theme uses.

How to do it...

The first thing you need to do here is to open your single content template, either `single.php` or `page.php`, and insert the appropriate template tag. Scroll to the end of your post display code, and insert the following function call:

```php
<?php comments_template(); ?>
```

Open up your site and browse to a single post. Upon arriving there, you should see one of two things. If you are logged in, you'll see a notice indicating your username and a **Log out** link, as well as the comment input box. This is shown as follows:

If you are not logged in, you'll see a **Name**, **Mail**, and **Website** field, in addition to the comment input box. You can see an example here:

How it works...

The code above is quite simple. It consists of a single template tag, but produces a whole boatload of content. Where does this content come from? Well, you haven't created a comments template yet, so this output comes from the default theme, and is contained in a file called comments.php. This comments.php contains all of the proper inputs, checks for comment registration requirements, and ensures that comments are rendered in an appropriately semantic and purposeful manner.

In addition to rendering the appropriate output, the comments_template function also does some behind-the-scenes work that determines the comments to display, whether to display comments and trackbacks separately, and gets the information for the current commenter. This is the reason you use the comments_template function instead of including comments.php directly.

There's more...

The base `comments.php` file is great for most purposes, and very rarely needs to be changed. If you do want to display your comments in a vastly different way, you can do so quite easily. First, copy the `comments.php` file from the default WordPress theme to your custom theme. Then make the modifications that you need to the output in your local file. WordPress will automatically use your new `comments.php` file instead of the default theme's `comments.php` file.

Displaying comments on a post

After users leave comments on your posts, you'll obviously want to display them. The most frequent use case for displaying comments is to list all of the comments on a single post, and there is a template tag that does this quickly and easily. In this recipe, we'll take a look at the template tags used to display comments and where you would use them.

How to do it...

First, you'll need to decide where you want to display your comments. The most obvious place to use comment template tags would be in a custom comments template. Alternatively, you could just list comments directly on a post without concern for the other things that a comments template provides (appropriate inputs and more).

Here we'll use the default `comments.php` file as an example. Copy the `comments.php` file from the default theme to your custom theme's directory. Scroll down to line 28 (as of WordPress 2.9) of the file and see that the following code is present:

```
<ol class="commentlist">
<?php wp_list_comments(); ?>
</ol>
```

Here you're using the `wp_list_comments` function, which iterates over the comments on a post and renders the appropriate output based on the comment display callback. A default callback is used if you do not explicitly pass one.

How it works...

`wp_list_comments` is a special template tag that looks at the comments for the current post and displays them by using a special callback function. Calling the template tag without any parameters tells it to use the default options, which will generally produce markup compatible with your theme. The output is, by default, a list of `<li>` elements containing various comment metadata as well as the comment author's avatar. You can see an example of a few comments in the following screenshot from the default theme:

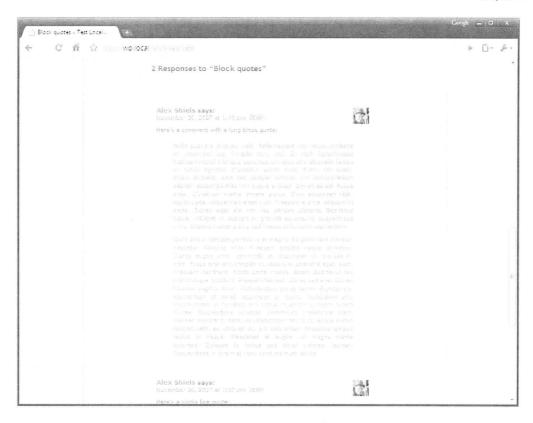

There's more...

The number of parameters available to customize your comment's display is vast and varied. Let's look at some of the important ones and the interesting things you can do with only a few characters of code.

Separating comments and trackbacks

Comments on blog posts are generally left by a person with an opinion on the post in question. Trackbacks occur when another blog links to a particular post or page. By default, WordPress displays these different types of post commentary together, with comments and trackbacks occurring side by side.

One of the easiest and most useful modifications to make to your post comment listings is to separate these two items. You can do this using only one parameter. Replace the code from the recipe above with the following:

```
<h3>Trackbacks</h3>
<ol class="commentlist">
<?php wp_list_comments(array('type'=>'pings')); ?>
```

```
</ol>
<h3>Comments</h3>
<ol class="commentlist">
<?php wp_list_comments(array('type'=>'comment')); ?>
</ol>
```

You can see here that you're using the `type` parameter for the `wp_list_comments` function to only output comments of a certain type in each list. You also added some headers to indicate the type of content to follow. You can see the resulting output as follows:

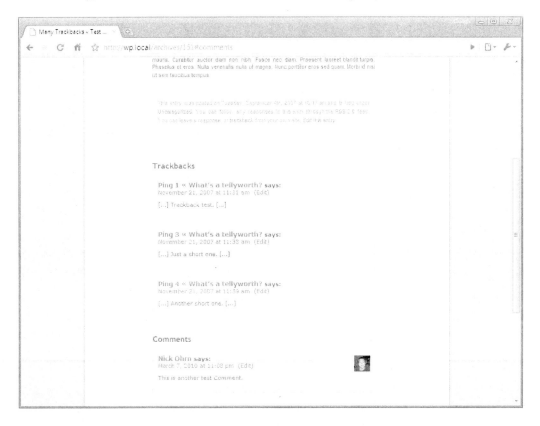

Changing the Avatar size

One of the things that you'll want to customize is the avatar size displayed next to comments. By default, the size is set to 32 pixels square. For a lot of themes, this is just not enough. To change the size of the avatar, you simply change the `avatar_size` parameter as follows:

```
<ol class="commentlist">
<?php wp_list_comments(array('avatar_size'=>80)); ?>
</ol>
```

When you refresh your comments list, you'll see that all of your avatars have been resized to 80 pixels square.

Available parameters

Although we've touched on a couple of the available parameters for wp_list_comments, there are many more available. You can find the complete list of all wp_list_comments parameters at http://codex.wordpress.org/Template_Tags/wp_list_comments.

Displaying the latest comments on your blog

Sometimes you might want to display the latest comments on the blog regardless of post. This could be useful in an expanded footer or the sidebar of a blog that receives a lot of comments. You might even put an excerpt from the latest comment near the header, in order to provide something for frequent visitors to observe.

Regardless of how you want to display the latest comments, actually doing it couldn't be easier.

How to do it...

First, open any theme file and place your cursor where you want the latest comments to appear. You could do this in sidebar.php, footer.php, or anywhere else where secondary content could be expected.

In your chosen theme file, insert the following code:

```php
<?php
$number_comments = 5;
$comments = get_comments( array( 'number' => $number_comments ) );
?>
<ol class="commentlist">
<?php wp_list_comments( array(), $comments ); ?>
</ol>
```

How it works...

The get_comments function fetches a number of different comments from the database, based on the parameters passed to it. In the previous example, five comments are being requested, and get_comments is allowed to otherwise use the default options for the function. This leads to the five latest comments being fetched, regardless of the post on which they were made.

wp_list_comments, described in the previous recipe, takes an optional second parameter, which must be an array of comment objects. Here we are passing the comments returned from get_comments along with an empty array, in order to ensure that wp_list_comments uses its default display parameters.

There's more...

The `get_comments` function takes a wide variety of parameters that can be used to affect the comment results that are returned. You should be familiar with some of the most commonly-used ones, which are outlined in the following sections.

Getting only certain comment types

By default, `get_comments` returns comment objects regardless of type. However, you can easily change this by passing a single parameter. This might be useful when you want to get the last five trackbacks, or if you're using a custom comment type to represent some information (like user reviews or something similar).

```php
<?php $trackbacks = get_comments(array('type'=>'pings')); ?>
```

Getting only comments for a particular post

If you specify a `post id` when calling `get_comments`, you can retrieve comments for that post only. The following code will do just that, specifying a `post` ID of 34:

```php
<?php
$post_34_comments = get_comments(array('post_id'=>34));
?>
```

Available parameters

While we've touched on a couple of the available parameters for `get_comments`, there are many more available. You can find the complete list of all of the `get_comments` parameters at `http://codex.wordpress.org/Function_Reference/get_comments`.

Highlighting the post author's comments

Because of their authority on the subject (they wrote the post in the first place, after all), it is often reasonable to assume that an author's opinions in the comments of a post are more important or pertinent than others'. As such, it is beneficial to readers of a blog for a theme for the author's comments to be highlighted in a noticeable way.

While there are many ways to make an author's comment stand out, the most common way is to have the background color be different for the author's comments.

How to do it...

First, you need to make sure that comments are being displayed for your posts. As such, follow the recipe *Displaying comments on a post* and add a comment loop to your theme for your `single.php` or `page.php` template files. This makes sure that the appropriate HTML code is output so that your browser can render the comments on your site.

Next, you need to style your theme's comments in a way that makes it apparent when an author is commenting on your site. To do so, open your theme's stylesheet (`style.css`) and insert the following CSS:

```
.comment { background: #fff; color: #000; }
.comment.bypostauthor { background: #000; color: #fff }
```

How it works...

The default comment display callback assigns special classes to the containing element for a comment. Examples of these classes include `comment`, `odd`, `byuser`, `alt`, and many more. The following is a sample of code showing the containing elements that WordPress outputs for comments. This sample shows many of these different identifying classes:

```
<ol class="commentlist">
  <li class="pingback even thread-even depth-1"
      id="comment-45">
    <!-- Comment Content -->
  </li>
  <li class="pingback odd alt thread-odd
      thread-alt depth-1"
      id="comment-48">
    <!-- Comment Content -->
  </li>
  <li class="pingback even thread-even depth-1"
      id="comment-47">
    <!-- Comment Content -->
  </li>
  <li class="comment byuser comment-author-admin
      bypostauthor odd alt thread-odd thread-alt
      depth-1"
      id="comment-59">
    <!-- Comment Content -->
  </li>
</ol>
```

If a comment is made by the post author, then the containing element is assigned a class of `bypostauthor`. In the above CSS snippet, elements with both the `comment` and `bypostauthor` classes are assigned a different background color and text color than the regular comment containers. You can see this in action in the following screenshot:

See also

► *Displaying comments on a post*

Alternating the style for comments

Comments are often displayed in a list form, with each comment being displayed one after another. Each comment includes the same title, a similar-looking avatar, and paragraphs of comment content. The format can get monotonous and cause eye strain and confusion in users who find it hard to differentiate between comments. Luckily, reconciling this issue is a simple matter of adding a small amount of styling using CSS. Due to the semantic nature of comment HTML output by WordPress, this is a snap.

How to do it...

First, you need to make sure that comments are being displayed for your posts. As such, follow the recipe *Displaying comments on a post*, and add a `comment` loop to your theme in your `single.php` or `page.php` template files. This makes sure that the appropriate HTML code is output so that your browser can render the comments on your site.

Next, you need to style your theme's comments in a way that makes it apparent when a new comment begins in the comment list. To do this, open your theme's stylesheet (`style.css`) and insert the following CSS:

```
.comment { background: #fff; color: #000; }
.comment.alt { background: #eee; color: #000; }
```

How it works...

As with the method used to style a post author's comments separately, here you rely on a class that is automatically assigned by WordPress to comments, based on their position in the list. Every other comment has the class `alt` assigned to it. As you can see, it is a simple matter to declare some new styles that help differentiate between subsequent comments.

In this particular instance, the effect that you implemented was subtle. You provide a light grey background for every other comment, while the rest have plain white backgrounds. A screenshot of this can be seen below:

See also

▶ *Displaying comments on a post*

Displaying threaded comments properly

Comments provide a way for a conversation to develop between the post author and visitors. Sometimes, visitors to the blog engage in discussions with each other directly.

In older versions of WordPress, displaying these discussions was something that couldn't be done without the help of plugins. In newer versions of WordPress, however, threaded comments are something that is provided right out of the box. Given this, it is easy and straightforward to implement the correct display of comment threads.

How to do it...

First, you must enable comments on a post and display them properly. Follow the *Displaying a comment form on a post* recipe to make sure that your comment form shows up and that comments on particular posts are displayed in a list.

Next, open your theme's `header.php` file and place the following code above your call to `wp_head`. This code enables the comment reply JavaScript functionality, allowing your users to easily and quickly form threaded conversations.

```php
<?php
if( is_singular() ) {
  wp_enqueue_script( 'comment-reply' );
}
?>
```

Next, you need to add the appropriate styles that will effectively display your conversations. Open your theme's stylesheet, `style.css`, and insert the following style declaration:

```css
.children {
    margin-left: 10px;
}
```

Now refresh a single post view on your blog and add a threaded comment by clicking on the reply button for a comment and filling in the appropriate information. After you submit the comment, you should see something that looks like the following, depending on your styles:

How it works...

The default `wp_list_comments` function displays threaded comments to a depth specified in the WordPress administrative back-end. The markup technique used is to nest lists inside of list items in order to produce the threaded effect.

By enqueuing the appropriate JavaScript file, you're allowing WordPress's built-in comment reply ability to be used by anyone visiting the blog. The style declaration that you added simply says that child comments should be indented to the right by 10px when they are being displayed. This provides a distinct visual hierarchy.

See also

▶ *Displaying a comment form on a post*

6
Sidebars

In this chapter, we will cover:

- ► Using the Text widget for custom sidebar content
- ► Including a dynamic sidebar in your theme
- ► Including multiple dynamic sidebars in your theme
- ► Setting the default widgets for a sidebar in your theme
- ► Positioning multiple sidebars in your theme by using CSS
- ► Styling the appearance of sidebars in your theme by using CSS
- ► Displaying different widgets on different pages by using the Widget Logic plugin and conditional tags
- ► Showing asides in the sidebar by using the Miniposts plugin
- ► Adding an interactive Facebook-style wall to a sidebar by using jQuery

Introduction

Most WordPress themes follow a fairly standard structure: there is a header with some type of navigation, a main content area where post contents are read, and one or more sidebars that display auxiliary information about the post being displayed or about the blog as a whole.

WordPress has quite a bit of functionality built in that supports the sidebar paradigm. Dynamic sidebars and widgets are included in many of the most popular themes. The power for end users to change the content displayed in the theme's sidebar without involving a programmer is one of the best developments in the history of the WordPress platform.

In addition to widgets provided by WordPress core and various plugins, sidebars can be created to display various data, including posts, comments, or links. Anything that isn't a main piece of content, but that you want to show to your site's visitors, is a great item to put in a sidebar.

Using the Text widget for custom sidebar content

Sometimes you need to include code from a Facebook badge, or promote your latest book if you happen to be a book author. Whatever it may be, if a block of HTML or text is provided, you can probably use it in the versatile Text widget.

Getting ready

For this recipe, you'll need to have a basic theme installed, preferably a default theme or one that has a **Widgets** panel underneath the **Appearance** section of your WordPress admin control screen. If you don't, a recipe for adding one is given in just a few pages. Oh, and make sure that the theme that you download or create has a place set aside for your sidebar on the left or right side of your design. You could also place it at the top or bottom of the design—I'm not judging. Lost? Download the companion code for this book at Packt Publishing's website to follow along.

How to do it...

Log into your Wordpress admin area, and then click on the **Appearance** tab on the left side of the screen. Select **Widgets** from the menu that appears. You will now see a whole lot of available widgets. Drag the **Text** widget to your **Sidebar** panel, as shown in the next screenshot:

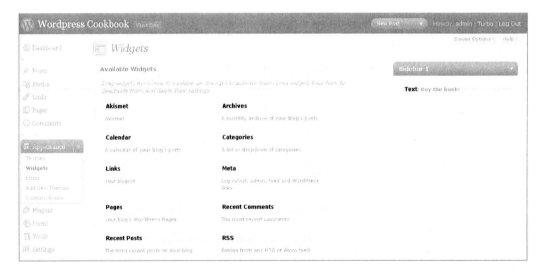

For the **Title** of the widget, enter **Shameless Plug**. Type the following code into the big text area as shown in the following screenshot:

```
The Wordpress Themes Cookbook is now available for preorder!
<a href ="http://www.packtpub.com/wordpress-2-8-themes-cookbook/book">
<img src =http://wordpressbook.leesjordan.net/wp-content/
uploads/2010/03/wordpress-themes-book.png alt="wordpress cookbook
cover"/><br />
Preorder now or learn more &gt;&gt;</a>
```

Place a checkmark in the **Automatically add paragraphs** checkbox, and then click on the **Save** button, as shown in the next screenshot:

View your blog to admire the snazzy new sidebar widget. You can see a screenshot of what it should look like, in the following screenshot:

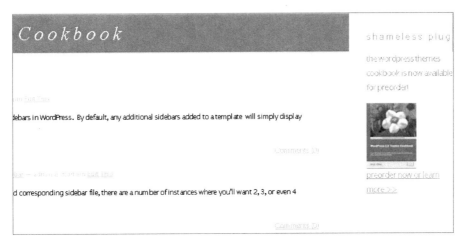

Including a dynamic sidebar in your theme

If you are creating your own custom theme for a more recent version of WordPress, or are updating an old theme, then you will need a dynamic sidebar to take advantage of WordPress' visual widget administration features.

Getting ready

For this recipe, you'll need to have a basic theme installed, or be in the process of building your own theme. Oh, and make sure that the theme that you downloaded or created has a place set aside for your sidebar on the left or right side of your design. You could also place it at the top or bottom of the design—you decide. Lost? Download the companion code for this book at Packt Publishing's website to follow along.

How to do it...

First, download and open up the `index.php` file of your theme. Paste the code, `<?php get_sidebar(); ?>`, just above the footer code, near or at the end of your `index.php` file, so it should now look like:

```php
<?php get_sidebar(); ?>
<?php get_footer(); ?>
```

Save your changes to the `index.php` file.

Next, we need to create a `sidebar.php` file, and as a bonus, we will add a search box at the same time. Create a new file in your favorite PHP or HTML editor. Save the file as `sidebar.php`. You need the same basic information at the top of this file as you do for all other WordPress theme files, so paste the following code into your `sidebar.php` file:

```php
<?php
/**
 * @package WordPress
 * @subpackage MyAwesome_Theme
 */ ?> <!-- begin sidebar -->
<!-- begin sidebar -->
<div id="menu">
  <ul>
  <?php   /* Widgetized sidebar, if you have the plugin installed. */
    if ( !function_exists('dynamic_sidebar') || !dynamic_sidebar() ) :
?>

  <li id="search">
    <label for="s"><?php _e('Search:'); ?></label>
```

```
    <form id="searchform" method="get" action="<?php bloginfo('home');
?>">
    <div>
      <input type="text" name="s" id="s" size="15" /><br />
      <input type="submit" value="<?php esc_attr_e('Search'); ?>" />
    </div></form></li>
<?php endif; ?></ul></div>
<!-- end sidebar -->
```

Save the changes. Next, look in your theme folder for a file called `functions.php`. If it exists, the code for the sidebar function should look like this:

```php
<?php
/**
 * @package WordPress
 * @subpackage My_Awesome_Theme
 */
if ( function_exists('register_sidebar') )
  register_sidebar(array(
    'before_widget' => '<li id="%1$s" class="widget %2$s">',
    'after_widget' => '</li>',
    'before_title' => '',
    'after_title' => '',
  ));?>
```

If you don't have a `functions.php` file, paste the previous code into an empty file and name it `functions.php`. Save the files, and then upload them to your theme folder.

How it works...

The `get_sidebar` function is a special template tag that, just like `get_header` and `get_footer`, calls a specific template file in the current theme. When the main theme file, such as `index.php`, loads in a browser, all of the functions within it are called. The `functions.php` file is checked as a part of the process. The code that we placed in the `functions.php` file notifies the theme and WordPress that if it finds a `sidebar.php` file with the correct sidebar code, to go ahead and load it. WordPress then looks in the current theme folder for a file named `sidebar.php`, and if it is found, includes the content specified within `sidebar.php` in place of the `get_sidebar()` template tag.

 Unlike a regular PHP include, you will not have access to local variables inside your sidebar when including it by using `get_sidebar`, because of a scope difference.

There's more...

Because of the standard header, content, sidebar, and footer format, WordPress supplies theme authors with a standard function to quickly and easily include a separate sidebar template into your main design. You can also search for themes with sidebars similar to what you want, for inspiration.

Finding inspiring sidebars for your theme design

We are using the *Thematic* theme as our inspiration in this chapter, and as you can see in the following screenshot, it contains a lot of default sidebars. It can be freely downloaded from the WordPress.org theme repository at `http://wordpress.org/extend/themes/thematic/` if you want all of the sidebars and none of the sweat equity, If you are determined to add your own sidebars, check out the next recipe for more details.

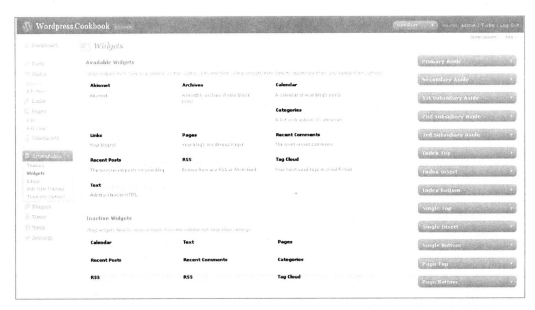

Including multiple dynamic sidebars in your theme

Although many themes are two-column, with only a single sidebar and corresponding `sidebar.php` file, there are a number of instances where you'll want two, three, or even four sidebars surrounding your main content. Visit sites such as `http://divitodesign.com/` for inspiration on how to use multiple sidebars with your theme.

In older versions of WordPress, having multiple sidebars meant resorting to using PHP's `include` function, or in-lining the sidebar's contents into your main template files. Luckily, with newer versions of WordPress, you can specify the name of the sidebar to include, by using the `get_sidebar` function.

Getting ready

We are using a basic template based on the *Classic* WordPress theme. You should already have a `sidebar.php` file, and your theme layout should support at least one sidebar.

How to do it...

We're going to give our current sidebar, which was created in the first recipe of this chapter, a name, and then create additional sidebars in which to store WordPress widgets.

Create a file for each sidebar, naming them by appending a descriptor to the string `sidebar-`. For this example, let's go ahead and plan to have two sidebars: `sidebar-one.php` and `sidebar-two.php`. Start by renaming your current `sidebar.php` file to `sidebar-one.php`. Copy that file, and name the new file `sidebar-two.php`.

Open up the `index.php` file of your current theme, and then insert the following code above the `get_footer` tag:

```php
<?php get_sidebar( 'one' ); ?>
<?php get_sidebar( 'two' ); ?>
```

Save the `index.php` file, and then open up your `functions.php` file. If you don't have one, refer to the last recipe. You will see the code:

```php
if ( function_exists('register_sidebar') )
  register_sidebar(array(
    'before_widget' => '<li id="%1$s" class="widget %2$s">',
    'after_widget' => '</li>',
    'before_title' => '',
    'after_title' => '',
  ));?>
```

Replace it with:

```php
if ( function_exists('register_sidebars') )
  register_sidebars(2);
?>
```

Don't worry about the extra widget or style code; we will work on that in another recipe. Save the file and then open your `sidebar-one.php` file:

```
<!-- begin sidebar -->
<div id="menu"><ul>
<?php   /* Widgetized sidebar, if you have the plugin installed. */
    if ( !function_exists('dynamic_sidebar') || !dynamic_sidebar(1) )
: ?>
  <li id="search">
   <label for="s"><?php _e('Search:'); ?></label>
   <form id="searchform" method="get" action="<?php bloginfo('home');
?>">
   <div><input type="text" name="s" id="s" size="15" /><br />
     <input type="submit" value="<?php esc_attr_e('Search'); ?>" />
   </div></form></li>
<?php endif; ?>
</ul></div>
<!-- end sidebar -->
```

Save the `sidebar-one.php` file and open up the `sidebar-two.php` file. Paste the following code into the file, replacing the existing content:

```
<!-- begin sidebar -->
<div id="menu">
<ul>
<?php   /* Widgetized sidebar, if you have the plugin installed. */
 if ( function_exists('dynamic_sidebar') && dynamic_sidebar(2) ) :
else : ?>
<?php endif; ?>
</ul></div>
<!-- end sidebar -->
```

Save the `sidebar-two.php` file. Back up your current theme folder, and then upload the files `index.php`, `functions.php`, `sidebar-one.php`, and `sidebar-two.php` into your current theme folder on your server. Delete the old `sidebar.php` file from the server.

You should now have two sidebars showing up when you select **Appearance | Widgets** in your control panel, as shown in the next screenshot:

Now, if you view your site, you should see two sidebars. By default, they will usually appear on the right and the bottom without any extra CSS styles applied, as shown in the following screenshot. We will adjust the layout of our theme by using CSS styles in a later recipe.

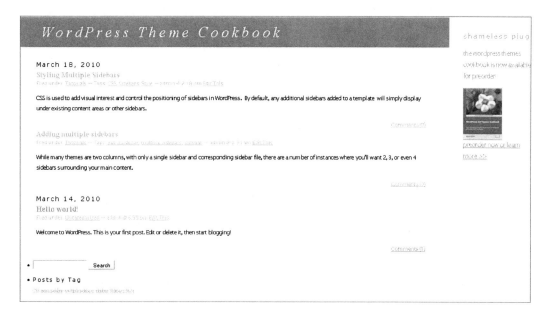

How it works...

WordPress will automatically look for a file named `sidebar-one.php` in the theme folder when it encounters `<? get_sidebar('one');?>` in the `index.php` file. WordPress will check the `functions.php` file for a `register_sidebars` function, and use it to determine how many sidebars should be available. WordPress will then examine `sidebar-one.php` and include the content of `sidebar-one.php` if it exists. If you use the name of a sidebar that does not exist, the theme's code will either throw an error message or the WordPress back-end code will detect the sidebar hook and substitute an automatically-generated sidebar.

Notice that we've gone ahead and used dynamic sidebars, as most WordPress 2.8 and 2.9 themes will have them.

There's more...

You can set defaults for sidebar names, and affect the appearance of widgets in a particular sidebar, by using parameters when you register your sidebar.

Sidebar parameters

When calling `register_sidebar`, there are a number of different parameters that you can pass in the following form:

```php
<?php
dynamic_sidebar(
  array( 'parameter_name' => 'parameter_value' )
);
?>
```

The important parameters are as follows:

- Name—allows you to change the name of the sidebar that is displayed in the admin interface on the widgets management page. In themes with multiple sidebars, the use of the name parameter can really help your theme's end users.
- ID—the ID assigned to the sidebar, mostly for styling use. You can generally leave this parameter with its default setting.
- before_widget—the HTML to display before printing the contents of a widget. You can use two placeholders here:
  - `%1$s` will be replaced by the widget's ID.
  - `%2$s` will be replaced by the widget's class name.
- after_widget—the HTML to display after printing the contents of a widget.
- before_title—the HTML to display before the title of the widget.
- after_title—the HTML to display after the title of the widget.

Although the defaults are fairly well thought out, they assume a certain structure to your sidebar and your theme. It is good to examine the `register_sidebar` function for yourself, and decide if the defaults are okay. If not, change them to make it easier for you to style by adding different class tags or removing list item tags.

Default content

If your user has not added any widgets to their sidebars, your theme may look extraordinarily blank. For this reason, it is a good idea to include default content that will be displayed if the sidebar does not have any active widgets. If you noticed in the last example, we went ahead and placed search box code in `sidebar-one.php`.

You can add your own placeholder content or default widgets by adding the relevant code just below the `dynamic_sidebar` function in a `sidebar.php` file. In the following example, the `Archives` widget has been added as a default widget, and will show the 15 most recent posts:

```
<ul>
<?php if( !dynamic_sidebar(1) ); ?>
  // Insert default content here
<li id="archives"><?php _e('Archives:'); ?>
<ul>
<?php wp_get_archives(type=postbypost&limit=15'); ?>
    </ul> </li>
</ul
```

> Learn more about parameters and options for sidebars at the WordPress codex
> `http://codex.wordpress.org/Customizing_Your_Sidebar`.

Setting the default widgets for a sidebar in your theme

Your theme may have a particular purpose, or serve a certain niche group. You may bundle a number of different widgets with your theme that provide the best possible experience when using it. If so, you'll likely want to have these widgets inserted into your sidebars when the theme is activated.

Getting ready

You need to have a theme with a `sidebar.php` template, and at least one of your main theme files must use the `get_sidebar` function to include the sidebar. In addition, your sidebar must be dynamic. Finally, you must know the unique IDs of your sidebars and of the widgets that you wish to pre-set in those sidebars. To make your sidebar dynamic, see the earlier recipes in this chapter. Back up your current theme, and be aware that using this recipe will reset the widgets of the active theme.

How to do it...

Open or create your theme's `functions.php` file. In this example, we will be inserting default widgets for default search, pages, categories, and recent comments. Insert the following block of code immediately before the closing `?>` tag within the file:

```
$current_theme = get_option( 'template' );
$target_theme = 'Widgety_Theme';

if ( is_admin() &&
    current_user_can( 'switch_themes' ) &&
    isset( $_GET['activated'] ) &&
    $current_theme == $target_theme
    ){
$preset_widgets = array ( 'sidebar-one' => array(
                          'widget-search-2', 'widget-pages-3' ),
                          'sidebar-two'=> array('widget-categories-4',
                          'widget-recent-comments-3'));
    update_option( 'sidebars_widgets', $preset_widgets );}
```

You will need to substitute the correct values for the following variables before the code will work with your theme:

- `$target_theme`—replace `Widgety_Theme` with the name of the folder in which your theme resides
- `$preset_widgets`—replace the array with a multidimensional array in which each of your sidebar IDs is a key to an array of widget IDs that you wish to have in the sidebar, as shown in the example above

Save the `functions.php` file. Remember, this code only works when a theme is activated; so deactivate this theme if it is your current theme, then upload the updated `functions.php` file and reactivate your theme, or install it on a test site to see the changes to the sidebars in the **Widgets** area of the admin panel as seen in the next screenshot:

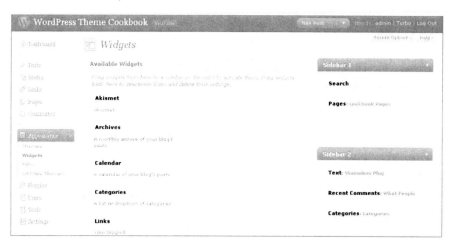

Now that you have the basic idea down, you can create your sets of default widgets for the sidebars of your theme.

How it works...

You accomplished a lot in this example! Let's take a closer look at what happened. First, the name of the currently-active template is stored in a variable. Then, the name of the target template (the name of the folder that your theme is stored in) is stored in another variable.

Following this, a comparison is made. A check is performed to confirm that an administrative interface page is being displayed. Next, the code confirms that the currently logged-in user has the ability to switch themes and manage widgets. Without these two checks, any anonymous user would be able to reset all of your widgets.

The next two parts of the conditional are equally important. The third condition checks that a new theme is being activated. Obviously, the widget reset should only happen when the theme has been switched to. The final condition checks that the currently-active theme is the same as the target theme (your theme, in this case).

If all of these conditions hold true, then it is time for the real work of setting the predefined widgets. First, an associative array is defined. Looking at this in more detail may be helpful:

```
$preset_widgets =
  array
( 'sidebar-one'  => array( 'widget-search-2', 'widget-pages-3'
),'sidebar-two'=> array('widget-categories-4', 'widget-recent-
comments-3'));
```

In this example, the assumption is made that a sidebar with the ID `sidebar-one` exists in your theme and that there are at least two widgets present, one with the ID `search-2` and one with the ID `pages-3`. This array basically says that the sidebar `sidebar-one` should have the widget `search-2` and `pages-3` inside of it, and that the sidebar `sidebar-two` should have the widgets `categories-4` and `recent-comments-3` without any further configuration from the user.

The next line updates the `sidebars_widgets` option in the WordPress database, where information regarding the content of dynamic sidebars is stored. After that is done, the widgets will be set appropriately.

There's more...

Widget IDs can be found in several ways. Read on for two options on how to discover the IDs of your widgets.

Widget IDs

To find the ID of a particular widget, you have a few options. The first option is to look at the code of the plugin that provides the widget (if it comes from a plugin) or examine the WordPress source for plugins that come with the default distribution.

The second option may be easier. Install a test blog and use the WordPress *Classic* theme, adding the widgets that you want to know the IDs for, to the only sidebar available. Then, view the source of the front page of the blog and look for the sidebar HTML. Each widget's ID will be displayed as the `id` attribute of a list item in the sidebar, as follows:

```
<li id="widget-id">
```

Make a note of the IDs of the widgets that you want to use and you're all set.

Positioning multiple sidebars in your theme by using CSS

As you may have seen previously in this chapter, just because you add a second or third sidebar to your theme does not mean that it will be placed where you want it in your layout. We will adjust the layout of a two-column theme to a three-column theme with a sidebar on each side, by using only CSS, in your `style.css` file.

Getting ready

We will be using a basic theme customized from the WordPress *Classic* theme. If you are already using the *Classic* theme, the measurements should work precisely. You may have to adjust the width, padding, or margins from the examples in this recipe to fit your layout. We will be spending most of our time in the `style.css` file of the theme, so if you are unfamiliar with CSS, you may want to visit www.w3schools.com to learn more about it, as this recipe assumes a basic knowledge of CSS and stylesheets.

How to do it...

First, open up the `sidebar-two.php` file, or whatever file is your secondary sidebar file, in your editor. It may already have a `div` tag wrapped around the sidebar code that looks like: `<div id="menu">`. Rename the id to `<div id="menu-left">` and make sure there is a closing div tag `</div>` at the end of the file. Save the file.

Next, we will begin adding the positioning information to the `styles.css` file, so open that file up. Find the `#menu{}` rule and copy it and all the others below it that have `#menu`. The last one should be `#menu ul ul ul.children {font-size: 142%;padding-left: 4px;}`. There are too many to list here, but you can refer to the `styles.css` file included in the companion code of this book.

Paste the #menu{} rules below the closing bracket of the last #menu ul ul ul.children{} style. Add -left to each of the newly pasted #menu style rules so that they all begin with #menu-left.

Now adjust the declarations within #menu-left{} to add more padding, set the width and height, and align sidebar-two to the left , so that your CSS looks like the following:

```
#menu-left {
    position: absolute;
    background: #fff;
    border-left: 1px dotted #ccc;
    border-right: 1px dotted #ccc;
    border-top: 10px solid #e0e6e0;
    padding: 20px 0 10px 10px;
    color:#333;
    left: 2px;
    top: 0;
    width: 12.5em;
    height:75%;
}
```

We now need to adjust the height, padding, right alignment amount, and width of the #menu rule that controls the positioning of the main (right) sidebar:

```
#menu {
    position: absolute;
    background: #fff;
    border-left: 1px dotted #ccc;
    border-top: 10px solid #e0e6e0;
    padding: 20px 0 10px 30px;
    margin:0;
    right: 1px;
    top: 0;
    width: 12.5em;
    height:75%
}
```

We do not need to adjust any of the other #menu or #menu-left style rules at this time. The body, #header, and #content rules will need their declarations adjusted to make room for the two sidebars. Scroll up to the body selector. Add the declaration width:100%; to the bottom of the styles, just before the closing bracket so that the body style rule now looks like the following code:

```
body {
    background: #fff;
    border: 2px solid #565;
```

```
    border-bottom: 1px solid #565;
    border-top: 3px solid #565;
    color: #000;
    font-family: 'Lucida Grande', 'Lucida Sans Unicode', Verdana, sans-
serif;
    margin: 0;
    padding: 0;
    width:100%;
}
```

The #content styles now need their padding, margin, and width adjusted. Adjust the margins and padding, and add a width declaration as shown in the next block of code:

```
#content {
    margin: 5px 13em 0 13em;
    background:transparent;
    padding-right:30px;
    padding-left:30px;
    width:46em;
}
```

The #header styles are in the last section of the style sheet that needs adjusting, in order to control the positioning of the sidebars. Add a width selector of 25.5em, change the border-top to none and set the padding declaration to 20px 40px 20px 60px as shown in the code example below:

```
#header {
    background: #333;
    font: italic normal 230% 'Times New Roman', Times, serif;
    letter-spacing: 0.2em;
    margin: 0 6em 0 5em;
    padding: 20px 40px 20px 60px;
    width:25.5em;
    border-bottom: 3px double #aba;
    border-left: 1px solid #9a9;
    border-right: 1px solid #565;
    border-top: none;
}
```

Save and then upload the secondary sidebar file (`sidebar-two.php`) and the `style.css` file. When you view the result in your browser, the blog should now look like the next screenshot:

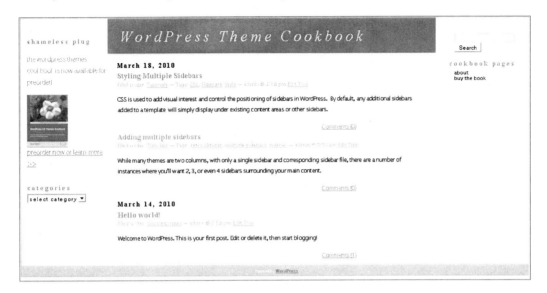

How it works...

In a basic WordPress theme, the `#menu` or `#sidebar` styles control the positioning of the sidebar on the screen. Adding a secondary `div` to control the secondary sidebar, and making adjustments to the layout creates an area for the secondary sidebar, and gives the theme user greater control over the layout. The `style.css` file controls the presentation and positioning of the objects within the screen, including the posts, widgets, header, footer, and sidebars. First, we added a new div style to the secondary sidebar in its sidebar file, assigning that CSS style to the sidebar. Then, the new style rule was created in the `style.css` file that told WordPress the height, width, and location of the sidebar within the layout. The positioning for the other key elements, primary sidebar, header, and content area, also had to be adjusted.

There's more...

You can make room for additional sidebars, or have one sidebar be wider than the other, depending on how you adjust the width, margins, and padding of the styles in your `styles.css` file, and how you apply them in the other files of your theme. Also, check the `.feedback` class and `.story` class in your stylesheet, as you may have to adjust padding in those as well.

Position: absolute versus float

We kept the sidebar styles set to absolute positioning in order to keep this recipe focused on its core purpose: adjusting the layout of the sidebars. In most cases, you will want to explore using the float property, as this gives you more options as a designer, and allows your layout to be flexible instead of fixed.

Doing more with design and layout

If this recipe sparked your interest in doing more positioning actions through the use of CSS in your theme, you will want to visit the *Blog Design and Layout* section of the WordPress codex, at http://codex.wordpress.org/Blog_Design_and_Layout.

Styling the appearance of sidebars in your theme by using CSS

WordPress themes use the style.css file to control both the layout (positioning) of objects as well as how they look (appearance). We will create a different appearance for each sidebar of the theme, by using the color and background declarations of each sidebar selector.

Getting ready

We'll be using a variation of the *Classic* Wordpress theme in this example. You can use any theme you like, but the names of the selectors (such as #sidebar instead of #menu) may vary depending on the theme.

How to do it...

Open up your style.css file and find the #menu{} style. Change the background color to #ff9966, a peachy pink color. Next, change the border-top declaration to none, and the border-left declaration to 5px dotted #ff3333;. The #ff3333 hexidecimal code is a dark orange. Add the declaration color:#333; to the #menu style. Your style should now look like the example shown below:

```
#menu {
    position: absolute;
    background: #FF9966;
    border-left: 5px dotted #FF3333;
    border-top: none;
    padding: 20px 0 10px 30px;
    margin:0;
    right: 1px;
    top: 0;
    width: 12.5em;
    height:100%;
    color:#333; }
```

Upload the `style.css` file, and then view the change in your browser window. It should look as shown in the following screenshot:

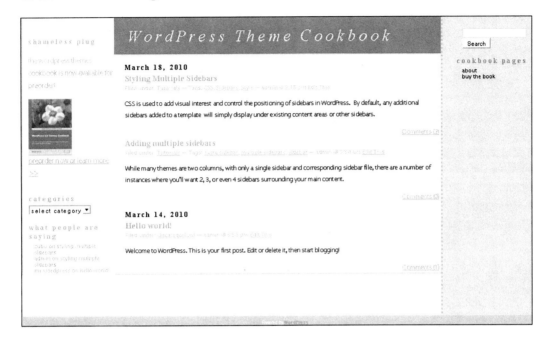

How it works...

WordPress relies heavily on the `style.css` file to control the appearance of widgets, pages, and other objects in a theme. When a page or other object is loaded, Wordpress checks the `style.css` file for any special instructions regarding text color, background color, borders, and so on. Starting with the larger default tags such as `body`, WordPress then moves down the stylesheet from larger to smaller elements.

For example, it will check the `body` statement first for any background color declarations, then moves on to custom style rules like #menu. If menu declares a different background color, as it did in our recipe, then WordPress will display that color when the sidebar is called. If there are no smaller elements such as custom widget style rules with specific background color declarations, WordPress stops there and you now have a peachy colored default sidebar instead of a white one.

There's more...

There is much more that you can do to change the appearance of your sidebars. Adding background images and customizing list items with graphics or other list-style-types (circles, squares, and so on) is just the beginning. Going more in-depth about the possibilities of CSS is beyond the scope of this book, but in the paragraphs below you will find additional resources to take it further.

Design and Layouts: The WordPress codex

There is a wealth of information about WordPress theme design in the WordPress codex. Start with `http://codex.wordpress.org/Developing_a_Colour_Scheme` to begin your journey into altering the appearance of the sidebars in your theme.

Sandbox: The theme for maximum appearance options

The *Sandbox* theme comes with multiple layout options and examples, and is a very clean theme to use when you want to focus on styling its appearance without touching anything in the theme other than the stylesheet. It was also featured in *"WordPress for Business Bloggers", Paul Thewlis, Packt Publishing*. You can download the theme from: `http://www.plaintxt.org/themes/sandbox/`.

Displaying different widgets on different pages by using the Widget Logic plugin and conditional tags

Given the different contexts for different page displays, you may wish to display different widgets in sidebars for places like the home page, category archive, or single-post display pages. With dynamic sidebars and the Widget Logic plugin, this is easy to accomplish.

Getting ready

You need to have a theme that uses dynamic sidebars with a `sidebar.php` template, and at least one of your main theme files must use the `get_sidebar` function to include the sidebar.

How to do it...

Download the Widget Logic plugin from `http://wordpress.org/extend/plugins/widget-logic/`. Upload the `widget_logic.php` file to the plugins directory of your theme's folder.

Log into your WordPress administration panel, and then click on **Plugins**. The **Widget Logic** plugin should appear in the **Manage Plugins** list. Click on the **Activate** link for this plugin. A message should appear at the top of the page verifying that the plugin is now activated. Now, if you visit the **Active** area of your **Manage Plugins** screen, you should see it listed, as seen in the next screenshot:

Next, go to **Appearance | Widgets**, in order to add an **Archives** widget that will only display on single-post pages. Drag an **Archives** widget over to **Sidebar 1**, then enter the relevant information in the widget. For example, for the **Title**, enter the text **Recipes by Date**, place a checkmark in the **Show post counts** checkbox, and type the conditional statement **is_single()** in the **Widget logic** text field. Click on the **Save** button in the widget form.

The **Archives** widget should now look like the screenshot below:

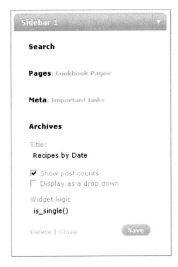

When we view the blog, we should now see this **Archives** widget only on our single posts page, as shown in the next screenshot:

How it works...

Here you are using the various conditional tags supplied by WordPress to check for the context of the current page. Then, depending on the context, a specified widget is displayed in the dynamic sidebar, without you creating any additional sidebar files. Instead, the Widget Logic plugin allows you to use existing sidebars and add conditional behaviours to the widgets that you assign to them with the convenience of using the existing widgets panel.

This allows your theme's users to display widgets conditionally depending on their needs given the different contexts. Erring on the side of giving your users more control is always a great way to go.

 Find the category ID (or a post ID, and so on) by hovering your mouse over the **Edit** link of your category or other item. The category ID will appear in the status bar of your browser.

There's more...

In this recipe, we focused on controlling the content that appeared in existing sidebars, by using a plugin that accepted conditional tags. This is an area of WordPress that you can dive into and customize the display of widgets in your sidebars as much as you like.

Getting more out of conditional tags

There is much more that you can do with both the Widget Logic plugin and conditional tags. To learn more, visit:

- http://codex.wordpress.org/Conditional_Tags/
- http://wordpress.org/extend/plugins/widget-logic/faq/

Specific sidebars for custom theme pages

An alternate method in cases where you want to explicitly use specific pages in your theme pack and provide them to users (such as a gallery, table of contents, and so on) is to create a unique sidebar page for each corresponding template page, and then call the sidebar in the appropriate page. You may also want to assign default widgets to the different sidebars, as well.

For example, create a sidebar page called `sidebar-toc.php`, adding a dynamic sidebar function call:

```php
<?php if ( function_exists ( dynamic_sidebar(1) ) ) : ?>
<div id="my-sidebar-div">
<ul id="my-sidebar-ulstyle">
<?php dynamic_sidebar (1); ?>
<li>
//table of contents conditional statements or other content here
</li>
</ul></div>
<?php endif; ?>
```

The 1 in `dynamic_sidebar(1)` is the number that WordPress uses to identify the sidebar. It considers the default sidebar (`sidebar.php`) to be sidebar(0). If you already have other sidebars before adding one, like in this example, you will need to number it appropriately.

In `functions.php`, you register the sidebar by the name `toc`:

```php
<?php if ( function_exists ('register_sidebar')) {
  register_sidebar ('toc');
} ?>
```

Finally, open the `table-contents.php` (or whatever you name that page) and place a `get_sidebar` tag:

```
<? get_sidebar('toc'); ?>
```

Save all files, and then upload them to your theme. Visit `http://codex.wordpress.org/Customizing_Your_Sidebar` to learn more.

Showing asides in the sidebar by using the Miniposts plugin

Asides are a concept unique to blogging. When a blogger wants to say something, but there isn't enough content to constitute an entire post, they can put it in a special "Aside" category that is displayed in the sidebar, or use a plugin to assign posts as "asides".

Getting ready

You will need a theme that contains a `sidebar.php` file, or else you can create one using earlier recipes in this book. We will be using a variation of the *Classic* WordPress theme in this recipe.

How to do it...

Download the Miniposts plugin from `http://wordpress.org/extend/plugins/miniposts/`, and unzip the folder. Look for the `miniposts` folder inside the wrapper folder, and upload it to the `plugins` folder of your theme. Log into your WordPress administration panel, and then click on **Plugins**. Click on the **Activate** link to activate the **Miniposts plugin**.

Next, go to **Appearance | Widgets** and drag the **Miniposts** widget to the main sidebar. There is no additional default configuration for this widget.

Finally, go to the **Posts** panel and create a new post to be an aside. Place text in the main post and the excerpt textfield. Place a check against any categories that you like. The most important step at this point is to place a check in the Miniposts **This is a mini post** checkbox.

You can see an example post in the following screenshot:

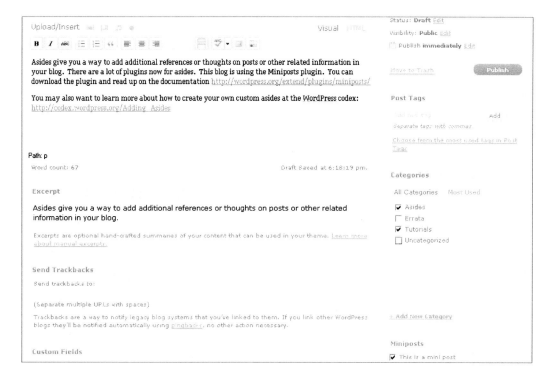

Any posts that you create and mark as Miniposts will now appear in your sidebar. The next screenshot shows an example of how an aside post will appear in a sidebar:

How it works...

Miniposts singles out any post that you identify as a minipost from the regular posts on your blog and causes them to be displayed in your sidebar. Read more about the Miniposts plugin at http://www.piepalace.ca/blog/projects/miniposts/.

There's more...

You can also create your own custom asides.

Creating custom asides

Back in the dark ages of WordPress, before version 2.8, creating asides often meant hacking into code. If you are interested in asides and want to customize them for your theme, you can learn more about them at http://codex.wordpress.org/Adding_Asides.

Adding an interactive Facebook-style wall to a sidebar by using jQuery

Visitors love interactive features on blogs. This recipe will help you create a Facebook-style interactive wall so that you can communicate quickly, in a sidebar.

Getting ready

You will need a WordPress theme that uses a widgetized sidebar, meaning that you should be able to manage your widgets under the **Appearance** panel of your administration area.

How to do it...

Download WP Wall from http://www.prelovac.com/vladimir/wordpress-plugins/wp-wall. Unzip the folder, and then upload the wp-wall folder (be careful to upload the inner wp-wall folder and not the outside download wrapper folder, in which also named wp-wall) to your /wp-content/plugins/ folder.

Log in to your administration panel and go to the **Plugins** page. Click on the **Activate** link for the plugin to activate it. Add the widget to a sidebar, and then expand the widget to view the **Options** link (you can also find the options for WP Wall in your administration panel under **Settings | WP Wall**). Click on it to view the options page.

Next, we set the options. There is a long list of options for this plugin, so we will focus on the most important ones. Under the **General Options** heading, set the **Title for the widget** to **Say What?** and change the **Leave a reply text** to **Say it**. Next, enter **10** in the **Number of comments to show** box. Finally, place a check in the following checkboxes: **Show 'All' link**, **Show email field in the form**, **Show gravatar images**, **Show post comment box expanded by default**, and **Reverse order of displayed comments**. Select two checkboxes in the **Comments** heading: **Only registered users can post** and **Treat admin deleted comments as spam**.

An example of how many of the settings for WP Wall should appear is shown in the following screenshot:

WP Wall

General Options

WP Wall allows you to have a comments 'wall' on your blog.

Say What?	Title for the widget
Say it	Leave a reply text
10	Number of comments to show (max 25)

☑ Show 'All' link - Shows the link to your wall guestbook page. You need to publish your Wall page (go there). If you do not see any comments, your theme does not show comments on pages and needs to be modified

☑ Show email field in the form

☑ Show gravatar images (requires email field option checked)

☐ Allow HTML in comments (use with CAUTION)
   ☐ Make links clickable ('www.prelovac.com' would become clickable link)

☑ Show post comment box expanded by default

☑ Reverse order of displayed comments

Comments

☐ Disable new comments
☑ Only registered users can post
☑ Treat admin deleted comments as spam

Save your settings, and then go back to your widgets panel to verify that the widget has been placed on your preferred sidebar and that the title is correct. Save the widget, and then view it in your browser window. Add a comment or two (invite a few friends over to try it out as well), and you should see something similar to the next screenshot:

How it works...

The WP Wall creates a site-wide comments system for your blog. When you install and activate the plugin, it creates additional hooks into the existing WordPress comments by adding additional functions. Configuring a WP Wall widget allows you to leverage the security features of WordPress comments and the flexibility to add the wall to all of the pages of your blog, or restrict it to specific sidebars or areas.

There's more...

WP Wall allows you to create a simple wall to define complex options and behaviours.

Doing more with WP Wall

Read up on the many additional options and discover more ways to use WP Wall with your blog by visiting http://www.prelovac.com/vladimir/wordpress-plugins/wp-wall.

7
Custom Page Templates

In this chapter, we will cover:

- ▶ Creating a simple page template
- ▶ Creating an archives page template
- ▶ Creating a taxonomy navigation template
- ▶ Displaying author avatars and descriptions
- ▶ Creating a table of contents page template
- ▶ Showing your pictures from Flickr
- ▶ Displaying a special template for a specific category

Introduction

One of the most important reasons for the proliferation of WordPress-based sites is the ease with which the software allows web developers and designers to display different content in a myriad of different ways. This starts in the core and extends to the theming system.

First, there is the concept of core template files. Out of the box, WordPress will attempt to load predetermined template files for different types of content. For example, the `author.php` file, if it exists, is used when a user visits an author's post listing page. Likewise, the `home.php` file is used when a visitor happens upon the root of the site.

On top of this base system, there is a whole additional level available to theme developers. The developers can create specific page templates that display a variety of content in a very specific way. The templates are created individually when the theme is being developed, and they may or may not rely upon user-supplied content. These types of templates are activated, per page, by the user, from the WordPress administrative area. These types of template files are particularly useful for static page content or when you need to completely override the appearance of a particular piece of content.

Creating a simple page template

The first thing that we'll cover in this chapter is creating a simple page template. This recipe shows the specific markup that you need to include in a PHP file in order to make sure that WordPress recognizes it as a page template. In addition, we'll demonstrate how to choose a page template when creating a page. When you get to the end of this recipe, you'll be fully equipped to create and use new page templates with your custom themes.

Getting ready

To properly use the techniques in this recipe, you'll need to be working with a theme that you previously acquired or developed. If you haven't started developing a custom theme yet, I recommend using the Thematic theme. It can be freely downloaded from the WordPress.org Theme Repository at `http://wordpress.org/extend/themes/thematic/`.

How to do it...

To create a custom page template, you start by creating a single file. In general, the filename should be descriptive of its content or purpose and should clearly delineate it as a page template. Open your theme's directory and create a new file called `hello-world-page-template.php`.

Next, you need to add the appropriate markup that lets WordPress recognize the file as a page template. Open the file that you just created (`hello-world-page-template.php`) for editing, and insert the following code at the very top of the file:

```php
<?php
/*
Template Name: Hello World
*/
?>
```

If you've worked with PHP before, you'll immediately recognize this as a standard comment block. Inside of the comment block is a specially-formatted string that tells WordPress that this is a page template. We'll go over the details of how WordPress works with this file later, but for now let's move on to displaying content.

For the sake of remaining simple, this page template will only display a simple string. Directly after the piece of markup that you added earlier, insert the following code:

```
<!DOCTYPE HTML PUBLIC "-//W3C//DTD HTML 4.01//EN"
"http://www.w3.org/TR/html4/strict.dtd">
<html>
  <head>
    <title>
    Hello World!
    </title>
  </head>
  <body>
    <h1 style="text-align:center;">Hello World!</h1>
  </body>
</html>
```

This simple piece of markup defines a standard HTML document with appropriate head and body elements. Inside of the body is a single heading element that reads `Hello World!`. Save your file at this point to make sure that WordPress will be able to detect it for the next few steps.

Pat yourself on the back! You've just created your first custom page template. Although it may be simple, the new page template will serve well for demonstration purposes. Now you just need to see it in action, by creating a new page.

Open the WordPress administrative area, and navigate to the **Add New Page** interface. Once there, add a title of some sort (it doesn't matter what, but you need to have a title). Next, locate the **Attributes** meta box. It looks like the following:

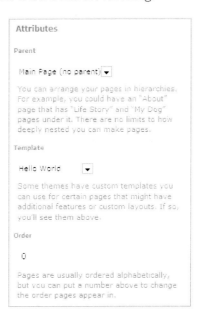

As you can see, this meta box allows you to change the page template for the page that you are editing. Select the page template **Hello World** from the drop-down menu underneath the **Template** heading.

 If you can't find the **Attributes** meta box, then it may be hidden from the screen. At the top right, click on the **Screen Options** link and make sure that the checkbox next to **Attributes** is selected.

After selecting the appropriate page template from the drop-down menu, publish your page by clicking on the **Publish** button in the **Publish** meta box. After a few brief moments, your page should refresh, and you'll be greeted with a **View Page** link at the top of the screen. Click on this link and your browser will navigate to and display your new page, showing off your custom page template. Your page should look like the example shown in the following screenshot:

How it works...

You created a simple page template that displays the text **Hello World!**, and immediately after creating your new file, WordPress made it available as an option in the **Template** drop-down menu in the **Attributes** meta box. How did WordPress know about your new page template and how did it know to display it for your newly created page?

It all starts with the comment header that you added at the very beginning of this recipe. That header looked like the following:

```php
<?php
/*
Template Name: Hello World
*/
?>
```

When it comes down to it, this header is the only thing separating your custom page template from any other WordPress template file. When you visit the **Edit Page** interface in the WordPress administrative area, the Attributes meta box dynamically populates the **Template** drop-down menu by following a multistep process.

First, a list of all files contained in the currently-active theme's directory is generated and returned from the `get_current_theme` function. Next, WordPress iterates over each file, reading its contents and attempting to find the `Template Name:` header. If such a header is found in a file, then the file is stored as an available page template that can be chosen from the drop-down menu on the **Edit Page** interface.

Once a page has been saved, the selected page template is stored as a meta item for the post, with a key of `_wp_page_template`. When WordPress displays a page, it checks to see if a custom page template was selected. If so, then WordPress attempts to fetch and display the specified template file. If that file cannot be loaded for some reason, WordPress reverts to the default display hierarchy.

Creating an archives page template

After learning how to create a simple page template in the recipe *Creating a simple page template*, you're probably brimming with ideas for custom page templates that you can provide for your theme. However, if you're going to take the time to create any page templates at all, you should make sure that you provide your users with a useful Archives template.

The Archives template can contain many things, but its main purpose is to help your users navigate around your blog in a way that makes sense to them. As such, it should almost always include a post archive by month, and a list of the categories on your blog. In this recipe, we'll be providing just that.

Getting ready

To properly use the techniques in this recipe, you'll need to be working with a theme that you previously acquired or developed. If you haven't started developing a custom theme yet, I recommend using the Thematic theme. It can be freely downloaded from the WordPress.org Theme Repository at `http://wordpress.org/extend/themes/thematic/`.

How to do it...

First, follow the steps in the recipe *Creating a simple page template* until you reach the point at which you start adding custom content. While following that recipe, modify the filename from `hello-world-page-template.php` to `archives-page-template.php` and change the value of the `Template Name:` header from `Hello World` to `Archives`.

Now, you're ready to start adding the appropriate content. After the page template comment header, add the following markup to your page template, and then save the file:

```php
<?php get_header(); ?>
<div id="container">
  <div id="content">
    <h2>Archives by Month</h2>
    <ul>
    <?php
    wp_get_archives(array(
    'type'=>'monthly',
    'show_post_count'=>true
    ));
    ?>
    </ul>

    <h2>Archives by Category</h2>
    <ul>
    <?php
    wp_list_categories(array(
    'title_li'=>'',
    'show_count'=>true
    ));
    ?>
    </ul>
  </div>
</div>
<?php get_sidebar(); ?>
<?php get_footer(); ?>
```

At this point, your Archives page template is ready for use. Go and create a new page in the WordPress administrative area and make sure that it uses the **Archives** page template. If you need more information on how to do this, see the recipe *Creating a simple page template*. Visit your newly-created page. You should see output similar to the example shown in the following screenshot:

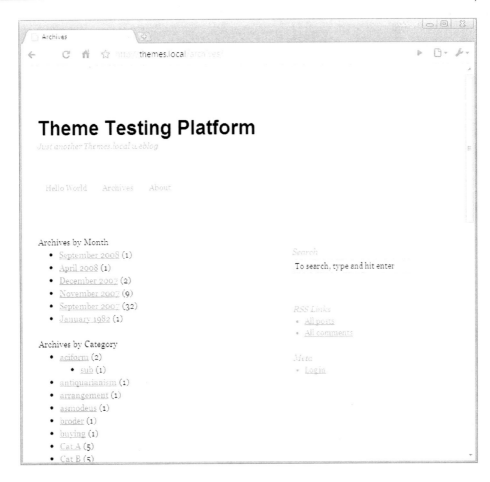

Here you can clearly see the month and category archives produced via your custom Archives page template.

How it works...

To learn more about the ways in which WordPress stores and displays custom page templates, see the *How it works...* section in the recipe *Creating a simple page template*.

Here, you're using two new functions that are particularly valuable in an Archives page template. The functions are `wp_get_archives` and `wp_list_categories`. Both of these functions are great because they:

▶ Automatically produce a list of sorted links

▶ Provide a means for visitors to browse content in a way that makes sense to them

▶ Shield you, as a theme developer, from future WordPress API changes

There's more...

Both of the new functions that you are using, `wp_get_archives` and `wp_list_categories`, take a variety of parameters that can be used to modify their output. Let's look at some of these parameters in detail.

Listing archive links

`wp_get_archives` supports a wide variety of parameters that greatly change the way that the output is produced. The most important parameter is definitely `type`, as this completely modifies the output by providing a different level of granularity for the archive.

The values available to be used for `type` are:

- monthly
- yearly
- daily
- weekly
- postbypost
- alpha

Each of the time-based values for `type` produces a list that contains an item for each of those timeframes that contains a post. For example, you can see the output for a `weekly` list as follows:

On the other hand, `postbypost` and `alpha` produce a list of each post on the blog, sorted alphabetically. You can see a partial list in the following screenshot:

For a full list of parameters supported by `wp_get_archive`, visit the WordPress Codex page for the function, at `http://codex.wordpress.org/Template_Tags/wp_get_archives`.

Listing Categories

One of the best ways to browse a site's archive and really find what you want is to follow the categories that interest you. The `wp_list_categories` function makes it easy for you, as a theme developer, to provide this capability. The wide array of parameters that `wp_list_categories` allows you to modify the output from the function in many different ways.

Some of the most used parameters for `wp_list_categories` are `number`, `show_count`, and `child_of`. The `number` parameter limits the number of items output in the category list. The `show_count` parameter is a Boolean value that determines whether the number of posts in a particular category should be output as a part of the list items produced for that category. Finally, the `child_of` parameter indicates which categories should be retrieved and displayed based on their parent category. If you wanted to display four child categories of the category with ID 3 and show the number of posts in each category, you'd use something like the following code:

```
<ul>
<?php
wp_list_categories(array(
'title_li'=>'',
'show_count'=>true,
'number'=>4,
'child_of'=>3
));
?>
</ul>
```

This code would display output very similar to the example shown in the following screenshot:

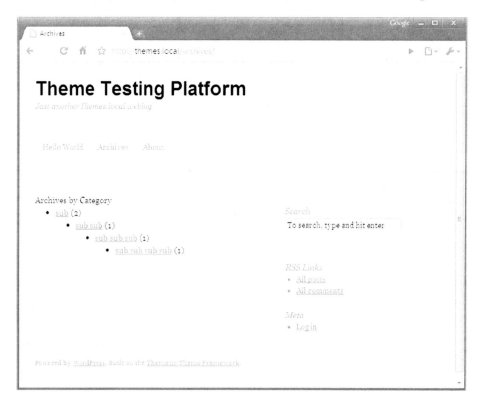

For a full list of parameters supported by `wp_list_categories`, visit the WordPress Codex page for the function at http://codex.wordpress.org/Template_Tags/wp_get_archives.

See also

▶ *Creating a simple page template*

Creating a taxonomy navigation template

Similar to the Archives page template created in *Creating an archives page template*, a Taxonomy Navigation page template can be very useful to your site visitors. With the introduction of custom post taxonomies in WordPress 2.8, WordPress users have more options than ever when it comes to classifying their content. A car enthusiast's site may have posts classified by Make, Model, or Transmission Type. Wouldn't it be useful to be able to navigate by those things in addition to the standard post tags and categories?

 Custom taxonomies are amazingly powerful and quite easy to put in place. We'll use a small snippet of code for testing purposes later, but if you want more information on how to use them, see Justin Tadlock's excellent post about custom taxonomies at http://justintadlock.com/archives/2009/05/06/custom-taxonomies-in-wordpress-28.

In this recipe, you'll learn how to create a page template that allows visitors to browse by any taxonomy that the system has in place. The best part is that you don't need to know ahead of time what taxonomies are available.

Getting ready

To properly use the techniques in this recipe, you'll need to be working with a theme that you previously acquired or developed. If you haven't started developing a custom theme yet, I recommend using the Thematic theme. It can be freely downloaded from the WordPress.org Theme Repository at http://wordpress.org/extend/themes/thematic/.

In addition to properly testing the custom taxonomy navigation for this recipe, we need to add a new taxonomy. Open up your theme's `functions.php` file and insert the following:

```php
<?php
add_action( 'init', 'wptc_taxonomies' );
function wptc_taxonomies() {
  register_taxonomy(
    'genres',
    'post',
```

```
      array(
        'hierarchical'=>false,
        'label'=>'Genres',
        'query_var'=>true,
        'rewrite' => true
      )
    );
}
```

This little snippet adds a new taxonomy for Genres, something that might be right at home on a book or movie review site. Go to the WordPress administrative interface and navigate to the **Add New Post** interface, and then make sure that the new **Genres** meta box appears. It should look like the following:

Now go ahead and add some genres to a post and publish it, to ensure that there is data to pull for your custom taxonomy.

How to do it...

First, follow the steps in the recipe *Creating a simple page template* until you reach the point at which you start adding custom content. While following that recipe, modify the filename from `hello-world-page-template.php` to `taxonomies-page-template.php`, and change the value of the `Template Name:` header from `Hello World` to `Taxonomies`.

Now you're ready to start adding the appropriate content. After the page template comment header, add the following markup to your page template, and then save the file:

```php
<?php get_header(); ?>
<div id="container">
  <div id="content">
    <?php
    $taxonomies = get_object_taxonomies('post');
    foreach($taxonomies as $tax) {
      $obj = get_taxonomy($tax);
      ?>
      <h2><?php echo esc_html($obj->label); ?></h2>
      <?php
```

```
        wp_tag_cloud(array(
        'number'=>3,
        'unit'=>'',
        'format'=>'list',
        'orderby'=>'count',
        'order'=>'DESC',
        'taxonomy'=>$tax
        ));
    }
    ?>
  </div>
</div>
<?php get_sidebar(); ?>
<?php get_footer(); ?>
```

You can now use your Taxonomies page template. Go and create a new page in the WordPress administrative area, and make sure that it uses the **Taxonomies** page template. If you need more information on how to do this, see the recipe *Creating a simple page template*. Visit your newly-created page. You should see output similar to the example shown in the following screenshot:

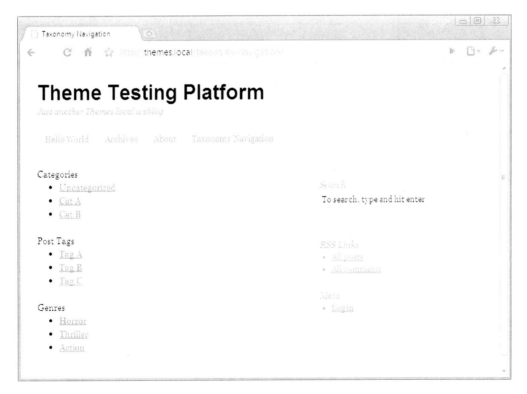

How it works...

By this time, you should have a pretty good idea of the way in which custom page templates work. If you need a refresher, see the *How it works...* section of the *Creating a simple page template* recipe.

Here you're taking advantage of the taxonomy system that has been built into WordPress since Version 2.3, as well as the custom taxonomy capabilities built into WordPress since Version 2.8. The taxonomy system essentially lets you classify objects in your system in ways that makes sense for your particular content. If you're reviewing movies, it makes sense to classify them in Genres. If you're looking at art, it makes sense to classify them by Periods.

After you've classified your content, you need to somehow let visitors navigate according to your custom taxonomies. That is where this recipe comes into play. In this recipe, you use a couple of new functions. First, you take advantage of the `get_object_taxonomies` function. This function takes a single parameter that indicates the type of object that you want to retrieve taxonomies for, and returns an array of registered taxonomy names for that object type. Next, you iterate over each taxonomy name, retrieve the appropriate taxonomy object, and then display the taxonomy label, and a list of all items in that taxonomy that have been used to classify objects.

The function that you use to display the items in taxonomy is `wp_tag_cloud`. Most people don't realize the full potential of this function, believing that it is only used for displaying post tags. However, you can use `wp_tag_cloud` to display items from any taxonomy, by passing a taxonomy name in as a parameter.

You pass other parameters as well, and it is important to know why you provide the values that you do:

- ▶ `number`—used to limit the number of taxonomy items present in the list output
- ▶ `unit`—setting this parameter to an empty string ensures that all items are the same size
- ▶ `format`—setting this parameter to the value `list` causes the output to be an unordered list
- ▶ `orderby`—you can use different values here, but using `count` ensures that your taxonomy items are sorted by the number of objects they are assigned to
- ▶ `order`—setting this to `DESC` makes the taxonomy items order themselves from high to low
- ▶ `taxonomy`—the value here determines which object classification will be looked at inside of the function

Internal to `wp_tag_cloud` is a complicated SQL query that looks at different taxonomy tables and the posts table, applies the options that you pass, and generates the appropriate output. An investigation into the internals of this function is beyond the scope of this book.

- ▶ *Creating an archives page template*
- ▶ *Creating a simple page template*

Displaying author avatars and descriptions

Multi-author blogs are gaining momentum in the professional and business blogging world. As such, if you're producing a business theme for WordPress, you might want to take special care to produce a page template that displays information about each of the authors on a blog.

In this recipe, you'll create such as page template. This will show the author's display name, avatar, biography, and the number of posts that they've written for the site. It will also contain a link to that author's posts.

Getting ready

To properly use the techniques in this recipe, you'll need to be working with a theme that you previously acquired or developed. If you haven't started developing a custom theme yet, I recommend using the Thematic theme. It can be freely downloaded from the WordPress.org Theme Repository at `http://wordpress.org/extend/themes/thematic/`.

How to do it...

First, follow the steps in the recipe *Creating a simple page template* until you reach the point at which you start adding custom content. While following that recipe, modify the filename from `hello-world-page-template.php` to `authors-page-template.php`, and change the value of the `Template Name:` header from `Hello World` to `Authors`.

Now you're ready to start adding the appropriate content. After the page template comment header, add the following markup to your page template, and then save the file:

```php
<?php get_header(); ?>
<div id="container">
  <div id="content">
    <?php
    $authors = get_users_of_blog();
    foreach($authors as $author) {
      $num_posts = get_usernumposts($author->ID);
      if($num_posts>0) {
        $id = $author->ID;
        $author = new WP_User($id);
        ?>
```

```php
                <div class="author" id="author-<?php echo $id; ?>">
                  <h2 class="author-name">
                    <?php
                    the_author_meta('display_name',$id);
                    ?>
                  </h2>
                  <div class="author-gravatar">
                    <?php
                    echo get_avatar($id);
                    ?>
                  </div>
                  <div class="author-description">
                    <?php
                    the_author_meta('description',$id);
                    ?>
                  </div>
                  <div class="author-posts-link">
                    <a href="<?php
                            echo get_author_posts_url($id); ?>">
                      <?php
                      printf(
                        '%s has written %d posts.  Check \'em out!',
                        get_the_author_meta('display_name'),
                        $num_posts
                      );
                      ?>
                    </a>
                  </div>
                </div>
              <?php
            }
          }
          ?>
      </div>
  </div>
  <?php get_sidebar(); ?>
  <?php get_footer(); ?>
```

You can now use your Authors page template. Go and create a new page in the WordPress administrative area, and make sure that it uses the **Authors** page template. If you need more information on how to do this, see the recipe *Creating a simple page template*. Visit your newly-created page. You should see output similar to the following, depending on the authors that you have on your site:

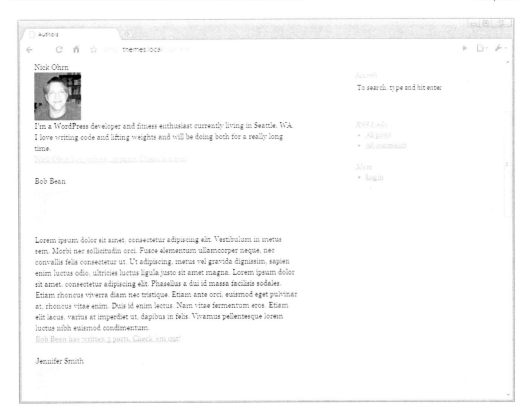

In the above screenshot, you see numerous authors with their name, description, avatar, and a link to their posts. The information could be expanded upon, but this is a good starting point.

How it works...

By this point you should have a pretty good idea of the way that custom page templates work. If you need a refresher, see the _How it works..._ section of the _Creating a simple page template_ recipe.

There are a few functions of note in this recipe, nearly all of them dealing with the retrieval of author data. The code listing starts with the `get_users_of_blog` function. This function returns an array of user objects, one for each user currently in the system. Next, you iterate over the array of users, checking to see whether they have published any posts or not. If an author has published at least one post, then you proceed with displaying various user data.

Here, user data is displayed by using the `the_author_meta` function with different parameters and the value of the user ID for the author currently being iterated over. In addition, the `get_avatar` function is used to display the appropriate image for each author. All of the data for each author is wrapped in a nice set of HTML tags that provide proper formatting and display.

There's more...

If you're going to display information for each author on a dedicated page, you should probably redisplay that information on their individual author listings as well. You already have the proper markup, so this will be a piece of cake.

First, separate out the display code for an author into its own file. You could call this file something like `author-expanded.php`. It will contain the following code:

```php
<div class="author" id="author-<?php echo $id; ?>">
  <h2 class="author-name">
  <?php
  the_author_meta('display_name',$id);
  ?>
   </h2>
  <div class="author-gravatar">
  <?php
  echo get_avatar($id);
  ?>
  </div>
  <div class="author-description">
  <?php
  the_author_meta('description',$id);
  ?>
  </div>
  <div class="author-posts-link">
    <a href="<?php echo get_author_posts_url($id); ?>">
    <?php
    printf(
    '%s has written %d posts.  Check \'em out!',
    get_the_author_meta('display_name',$id),
    $num_posts
    );
    ?>
    </a>
  </div>
</div>
```

Now go back to your `authors-page-template.php`, and change it to use the newly-created file, leaving you with something like the following:

```
<div id="container">
  <div id="content">
    <?php
    $authors = get_users_of_blog();
    foreach($authors as $author) {
      $num_posts = get_usernumposts($author->ID);
      if($num_posts>0) {
       $id = $author->ID;
       $author = new WP_User($id);
          include(STYLESHEETPATH.'/author-expanded.php');
      }
    }
    ?>
  </div>
</div>
```

After that, open up your theme's `author.php` file (if you don't have one, just create one and copy the contents of `index.php` into the new file). Immediately before the posts listing, insert a call for the expanded author information. Your code should look something like the following example:

```
<?php
    global $wp_query;
    $id = $wp_query->get_queried_object_id();
    $author = new WP_User($id);
    $num_posts = get_usernumposts($id);
    include(STYLESHEETPATH.'/author-expanded.php');
    if(have_posts()) { while(have_posts()) {
        the_post();
```

Call up an author's post page, and you'll see the expanded author information, followed by a list of that user's posts:

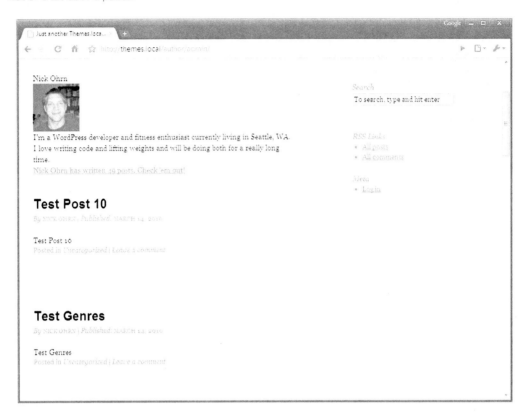

See also

▶ *Creating a simple page template*

Creating a table of contents page template

Let's say you're writing a book where you publish each chapter as it is finished. You're going to use WordPress pages for your content organization, with a top-level page describing the book and then a subpage for each of the chapters in your book.

On the top-level page, in addition to the book title and description, you want to display links to each of the chapters, and a brief description of their content. This task would be difficult with a lot of other content management systems, but not with WordPress.

Getting ready

To properly use the techniques in this recipe, you'll need to be working with a theme that you previously acquired or developed. If you haven't started developing a custom theme yet, I recommend using the Thematic theme. It can be freely downloaded from the WordPress.org Theme Repository, at `http://wordpress.org/extend/themes/thematic/`.

How to do it...

First, follow the steps in the recipe *Creating a simple page template* until you reach the point at which you start adding custom content. While following that recipe, modify the filename from `hello-world-page-template.php` to `toc-page-template.php` and change the value of the `Template Name:` header from `Hello World` to `Table of Contents`.

Now you need to create the appropriate content that will be displayed when using this page template. Create a top-level page for your book with the work's title as the post title, and choose the **Table of Contents** template from the **Template** drop-down menu in the **Attributes** meta box. Then create several child pages, using the chapter's title as the post title. For each child page, make sure that you choose your main book page from the **Parent** dropdown and the **Table of Contents** option from the **Template** dropdown. When you're done, visit the **Edit Pages** interface, and you should see something like the example shown in the following screenshot:

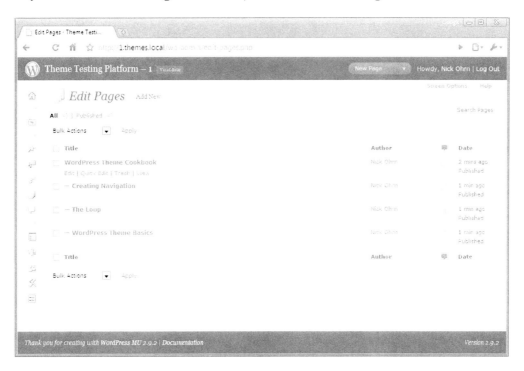

Chapter order

When you're creating your book's chapters, make sure that you set the **Order** property in the **Attributes** meta box (the same place that you change the page template) to the number of the chapter. This ensures that your chapters appear in the correct order.

Now you're ready to write the code to generate your table of contents. After the comment header, add the following markup to your page template, and then save the file:

```php
<?php get_header(); ?>
<div id="container">
  <div id="content">
  <?php
  if(have_posts()) {
   while(have_posts()) {
     the_post();
     ?>
      <h2 class="book-title"><?php the_title(); ?></h2>
      <div class="book-description">
      <?php the_content(); ?>
      </div>
      <h2>Chapters</h2>
      <ol>
      <?php
      $chapters_query = new WP_Query(array(
         'post_type'=>'page',
         'post_parent'=>get_the_ID(),
         'orderby'=>'menu_order',
         'order'=>'ASC'
      ));
      if($chapters_query->have_posts()) {
       while($chapters_query->have_posts()) {
         $chapters_query->the_post();
         ?>
         <li class="chapter">
           <h3 class="chapter-title">
             <a href="<?php the_permalink(); ?>">
                <?php the_title(); ?>
             </a>
           </h3>
           <?php the_excerpt(); ?>
         </li>
         <?php
```

```
        }
      }
    ?>
    </ol>
    <?php
  }
}
?>
</div>
</div>
<?php get_sidebar(); ?>
<?php get_footer(); ?>
```

When this page template is used, the book's title will be displayed as the main heading and will be followed by an ordered list of chapter titles and excerpts. If you've added your content correctly, and selected the Table of Contents page template for your main book page, you should be seeing something similar to the example shown in the following screenshot:

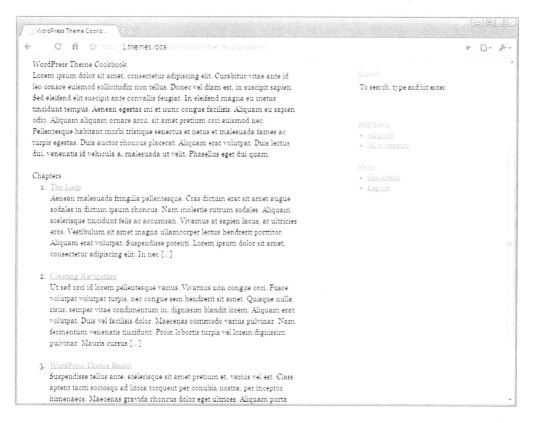

You'll see here that you have your book title at the very top of the page, followed by the full content of your book's description. After that, you have a link to each chapter, along with the chapter title and an excerpt.

How it works...

By this point you should have a pretty good idea of the way that custom page templates work. If you need a refresher, see the *How it works...* section of the *Creating a simple page template* recipe. In addition, you'll notice that we've used a custom Loop in this page template. For more on custom and multiple Loop constructs, see the recipe *Creating multiple loops on a single page* in *Chapter 3, The Loop*.

There aren't too many new and novel things in this recipe, but there is one particular item to note. Check out the `get_the_ID` function usage in the recipe code. Rather than hard-coding a parent ID to fetch the book's chapters, you're dynamically applying the ID from the currently-viewed page. This means that you can reuse the Table of Contents page template for multiple books on a single site.

There's more...

You've created a page template that links to each of the chapters in a book and this should prove quite useful to your site's visitors. However, wouldn't it be great if your chapters showed your visitor's progress through the book that they're reading? It's easy with another custom page template. Create a new file called `chapter-page-template.php`, insert and then save the following code, and then assign to each chapter the `Chapter` page template:

```php
<?php get_header(); ?>
<div id="container">
  <div id="content">
  <?php
  global $post;
  if(have_posts()) {
   while(have_posts()) {
     the_post();
     $current_chapter = $post;
     ?>
      <h2 class="chapter-title"><?php the_title(); ?></h2>
      <ol class="table-of-contents">
      <?php
      $chapters_query = new WP_Query(array(
        'post_type'=>'page',
        'post_parent'=>$current_chapter->post_parent,
        'orderby'=>'menu_order',
        'order'=>'ASC'
```

```php
));
if($chapters_query->have_posts()) {
  while($chapters_query->have_posts()) {
    $chapters_query->the_post();
    $viewing = $current_chapter->ID == get_the_ID();
    ?>
    <li class="chapter">
     <?php if($viewing) { ?>
     <strong>
     <?php } ?>
      <a href="<?php the_permalink(); ?>">
         <?php the_title(); ?>
      </a>
      <?php if($viewing) { ?>
     </strong>
     <?php } ?>
    </li>
     <?php
  }
}
setup_postdata($current_chapter);
?>
</ol>
<div class="chapter-contents">
<?php the_content(); ?>
</div>
<?php
  }
  }
?>
  </div>
</div>
<?php get_sidebar(); ?>
<?php get_footer(); ?>
```

With this template, you're generating a list of all chapters that are using the currently-viewed chapter's `post_parent` property. You're also highlighting the current chapter by checking the currently-viewed chapter's `ID` against the `ID` of each chapter in the list generation Loop. If you've done everything correctly, you'll be greeted with a short Table of Contents at the top of every chapter page, with the current chapter in bold. It should look like the example shown in the following screenshot:

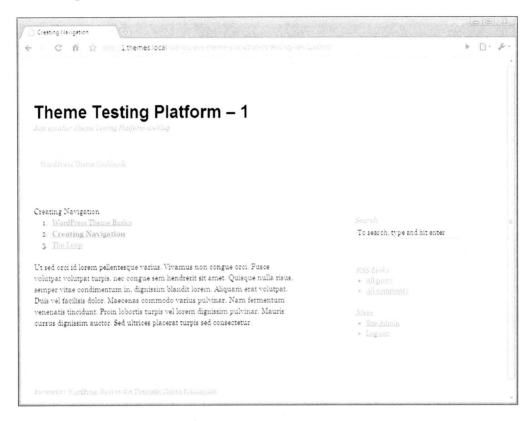

See also

▶ *Creating a simple page template*

▶ *Creating multiple loops on a single page*

Showing your pictures from Flickr

Flickr is a very popular photo upload and sharing site. Flickr has an excellent tagging, storage, and viewing system, and a lot of bloggers use Flickr for sharing pictures with friends and colleagues. In this chapter, you'll create a page template that pulls in a WordPress user's photos from their Flickr account, and displays these photos in a simple list.

Getting ready

To properly use the techniques in this recipe, you'll need to be working with a theme that you previously acquired or developed. If you haven't started developing a custom theme yet, I recommend using the Thematic theme. It can be freely downloaded from the WordPress.org Theme Repository, at `http://wordpress.org/extend/themes/thematic/`.

How to do it...

First, follow the steps in the recipe *Creating a simple page template* until you reach the point at which you start adding custom content. While following that recipe, modify the filename from `hello-world-page-template.php` to `flickr-page-template.php`, and change the value of the `Template Name:` header from `Hello World` to `Flickr`.

Next, you need to find your Flickr feed URL. You can do this by navigating to your Flickr photos page, scrolling to the bottom, and clicking on the Feed icon, as shown in the following screenshot:

Copy the resulting URL from your browser's address bar. It should be in the following format:

```
http://api.flickr.com/services/feeds/photos_public.
gne?id=44124424984@N01&lang=en-us&format=rss_200
```

Next, change the format parameter from `rss_200` to `json`, resulting in a URL like the following:

```
http://api.flickr.com/services/feeds/photos_public.
gne?id=44124424984@N01&lang=en-us&format=json
```

Now that you have your Flickr URL, you're ready to start adding the appropriate content. After the page template comment header, add the following markup to your page template, and then save the file:

```php
.<?php get_header(); ?>
<div id="container">
  <div id="content">
  <?php
  $flickr_username = 'nickohrn';
  ?>
    <h2>Latest Photos</h2>
    <?php
    $url = 'http://api.flickr.com/services/feeds/photos_public.
              gne?id=44124424984@N01&lang=en-us&format=rss_200';
```

```php
        $feed = fetch_feed($url);
        if(is_wp_error($items)) {
            ?>
            <h2>Error</h2>
            <p>Could not retrieve photos from Flickr.</p>
            <?php
        } else {
            ?>
            <ul>
            <?php
            foreach($feed->get_items() as $item) {
                ?>
                <li>
                <a href="<?php echo $item->get_link(); ?>">
                <?php
                echo esc_html($item->get_title());
                ?>
                </a><br />
                <a href="<?php echo esc_attr(
                                $item->get_enclosure()->get_link()); ?>">
                <img
                  src="<?php echo $item->get_enclosure()->get_link(); ?>"
                  />
                  </a>
                </li>
                <?php
                }
                ?>
            </ul>
            <?php
        }
        ?>
    </div>
  </div>
<?php get_sidebar(); ?>
<?php get_footer(); ?>
```

Make sure that you replace the value of the $url variable with your own feed URL. That way your photos are seen instead of Matt Mullenweg's photos. You can now use your Flickr page template. Go create a new page in the WordPress administrative area, and make sure that you've selected **Flickr** from the Template drop-down. If you need more information on how to do this, see the recipe *Creating a simple page template*. Visit your newly-created page. You should see an output similar to the following screenshot, depending on the photos that you have in your Flickr account:

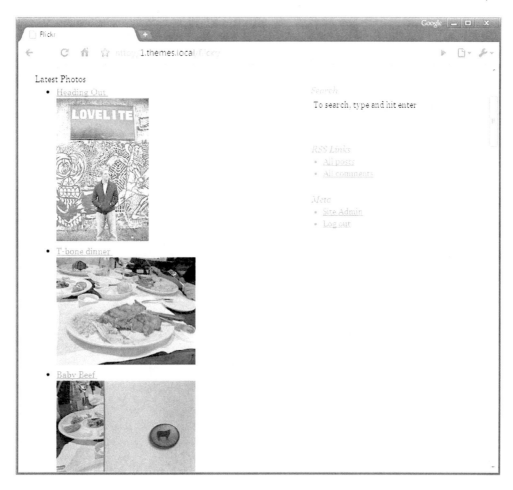

How it works...

By this point you should have a pretty good idea of the way in which custom page templates work. If you need a refresher, see the *How it works...* section of the *Creating a simple page template* recipe.

In this recipe, you used a few cool functions that you might want to use in other parts of your theme. The most obvious is `fetch_feed`: this is a utility function that WordPress provides, which gives access to the bundled `SimplePie` RSS library. The function returns a `SimplePie` object, which contains various methods and data.

The `SimplePie` library is very powerful, but in this recipe you're only using a few methods from the library. First, you use the `get_items` method on the main `SimplePie` feed returned from `fetch_feed`. This method returns an array of `SimplePie_Item` objects.

You then iterate over the array of items returned from `get_items`, and use a couple of different methods. You use `get_title` to retrieve the item title, `get_link` to retrieve the item link, and then you get access to the Flickr media enclosure (the image itself) by using `get_enclosure`. A deep dive into the `SimplePie` library is beyond the scope of this book, but you're encouraged to learn more by visiting the official API reference at `http://simplepie.org/wiki/reference/start`.

See also

▶ *Creating a simple page template*

Displaying a special template for a specific category

If you're running a professional or business blog, you may have specific categories that are required to fit in with the rest of your blog in general, but that need to stand out in some special way. For example, if you are using WordPress to power a design company's website, you'll probably have a portfolio category that needs to be displayed differently to the other blog categories (perhaps by showing images from each particular design).

Getting ready

To properly use the techniques in this recipe, you'll need to be working with a theme that you have previously acquired or developed. If you haven't started developing a custom theme yet, I recommend using the Thematic theme. It can be freely downloaded from the WordPress.org Theme Repository, at `http://wordpress.org/extend/themes/thematic/`.

How to do it...

Before you can create the special category template, you need to have some information about the category that it is going to be displayed. Open the WordPress administrative area and go to the **Categories** interface. Find the category that you wish to display in your new template, and take a look at the slug column in the **Categories** table. I've highlighted it in the following screenshot:

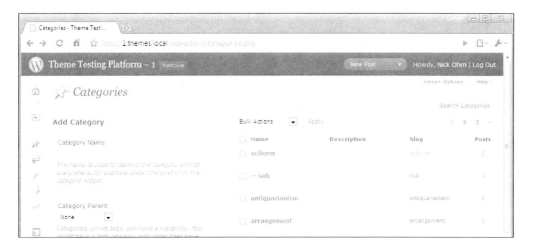

Remember the value of that slug. Now you need to create the special category template. The template should be named `category-CATEGORY_SLUG.php`, replacing `CATEGORY_SLUG` with the value from earlier. If you were using the category from the screenshot, you'd name your file `category-aciform.php`.

After creating your file, you have to populate it with content. In general, you'd probably copy the contents of `category.php` into your custom category template (alternatively using `archive.php` or `index.php` if `category.php` didn't exist) and work from there. To show the very basics of this technique, however, we're going to work with a small HTML skeleton for our custom category template. Open your new file and enter the following:

```
<!DOCTYPE HTML PUBLIC "-//W3C//DTD HTML 4.01//EN"
"http://www.w3.org/TR/html4/strict.dtd">
<html>
  <head>
    <title>
    Hello World!
    </title>
  </head>
  <body>
    <h1 style="text-align:center;"><?php
    global $wp_query;
    echo $wp_query->get_queried_object()->name;
    ?></h1>
  </body>
</html>
```

Now visit your blog and navigate to the URL for the category that you customized. When you visit that page, you should now see the category name and nothing else, as shown in the following screenshot:

How it works...

When WordPress is attempting to determine what template to display, it goes through a big long process that is encapsulated in the file located at `wp-includes/template-loader.php`. Once WordPress determines that a category listing is being shown, it calls the `get_category_template` function to retrieve the correct template filename.

Inside of `get_category_template`, WordPress calls the `locate_template` function with an array of strings, as follows:

- `category-slug.php`
- `category-id.php`
- `category.php`

`locate_template` scans the file system for each of these files in turn. If it finds one, then it returns that string immediately, and WordPress loads that template file.

8
Integrating Media

In this chapter, we will cover:

- ▶ Aligning images properly within a post
- ▶ Styling image galleries
- ▶ Styling image captions
- ▶ Creating a media template
- ▶ Creating a media template for a specific media type
- ▶ Displaying a related image for every post
- ▶ Creating video posts by using the Viper's Video Quicktags plug-in

Introduction

They say a picture is worth a thousand words. If that is the case, then audio must be worth a million, and video worth a billion. Luckily, WordPress provides users with great tools that allow you to quickly and easily attach different types of media directly to posts and, if desired, display that media in special ways directly in posts.

In this chapter, we're going to go over the different ways in which you can use media such as images, music, and video files in your theme. We'll look both at how to correctly display images for users based on WordPress conventions, and how to dig deeper and manipulate the display of media without user input.

You should know that if you are using the default *Kubrick* theme that it is not designed well for the display of videos or images within posts. We will be using the WordPress *Classic* theme, which is available with all new Wordpress downloads from `http://wordpress.org/download/`, for styling and displaying media in this chapter, but you can use any WordPress 2.8 or 2.9 compatible theme that you like, or apply these recipes to your own custom theme.

Aligning images properly within a post

One of the most important things for your theme to get right when it comes to displaying media is also one of the easiest. WordPress uses a certain set of markup to decorate images displayed in posts, and this markup includes instructions on how to align the images within a post. The class declarations shown below cover cases where images are inserted into a post by using the WordPress tools. This is very important to theme users, and forgetting to properly account for aligning images will give a very poor impression of your theme. Luckily, it is one of the easiest things to account for.

Getting started

For this recipe, you need to have a basic theme created already. It should have a template file that displays posts created by a user in their entirety.

How to do it...

First, we need to open up the theme's `style.css` file and place our cursor just after the introductory comment. Then, insert the following class declarations:

```css
img.centered {
  display: block;
  margin-left: auto;
  margin-right: auto;
  padding: 4px;
}

img.alignright {
  padding: 4px;
  margin: 0 0 5px 5px;
  display: inline;
}

img.alignleft {
  padding: 4px;
  margin: 0 5px 5px 0;
  display: inline;
}

.alignright {
  float: right;
}

.alignleft {
  float: left;
}
```

Be on the look-out for other similar tags. If you spot them, comment them out, beginning with /* and ending with */. As an example, see how similar code was commented out in the *Sandbox* style.css theme:

```
/* This is the standard layout Sandbox comes with
.alignright,img.alignright{
  float:right;
  border:none;
  margin:1em 0 0 1em;
} */
```

Save your changes, and then upload the `style.css` file to the current theme folder on your server. Upload three images into a post by using the media toolbar. Align each one to a different direction, and click on the **Insert into Post** button.

You can see an example of the image upload settings and button in the following screenshot:

In the previous example, **Center** alignment has been selected. Clicking on the **Insert into Post** button inserts generated markup, similar to the following, into the post editor text area:

```
<img src="rockcity1.jpg" alt="rocks" title="rock formations"
width="300" height="225" class="aligncenter size-medium wp-image-1" />
```

Copy this markup twice, and change `aligncenter` to `alignright` and `alignleft` respectively, to allow you to see each alignment in action. Your revised markup should look like the following:

```
<a href="03/05-06-07_12142.jpg"><img class="alignleft size-medium
wp-image-39" title="05-06-07_1214" src="05-06-07_12142-300x225.jpg"
alt="a tight squeeze" width="300" height="225" /></a>
<a href="05-06-07_1328.jpg"><img src="05-06-07_1328.jpg" alt="real
rock formations in a Rock City cave?" title="Rock City Cave #1"
width="160" height="120" class="aligncenter size-full wp-image-27"
/></a>
<a href=" 05-06-07_1228.jpg "><img src=" 05-06-07_1228.jpg" alt="view
from the top of rock city" title="View from the top of Rock City"
width="160" height="120" class="alignright size-full wp-image-28" />
</a>
```

After publishing the post, view it in your theme and you should see something similar to the following screenshot:

How it works...

When you click on the **Insert into Post** button, the WordPress system runs a JavaScript function that sends an HTML snippet to the post editor. This HTML snippet is formed in the function get_image_tag, before being sent to the post editor.

In the get_image_tag, the alignment is combined with the word **align** in order to produce one of four possible classes: alignnone, alignright, alignleft, and aligncenter. In the previous CSS that we wrote for our theme, the alignright, alignleft, and aligncenter classes are all accounted for, using the CSS float property and appropriate margin and padding values to ensure that the images align themselves properly within post containers.

Styling image galleries

Styling individual images is great when a user is uploading one or two images and manually inserting them. However, WordPress' real image-displaying prowess comes in the form of its gallery capabilities.

A WordPress gallery is output by using the `gallery` shortcode within a post. It collects all of the images attached to a post via the media uploader, and then outputs them using standard markup. Because the markup is consistent, styling it is easy.

Getting started

For this recipe, you need to have a basic theme created already. It should include a `page.php` or `single.php` file that displays full post content. If you don't have one, use the *Default* WordPress theme as a guide, or visit `http://codex.wordpress.com/Theme_Development` to learn more.

How to do it...

First, we need to open up the theme's `style.css` file and place our cursor just after the introductory comment. Then insert the following class declarations:

```
.gallery {
  border: 1px solid #f88;
}

.gallery-item {
  background: #000;
}

.gallery-icon {
  border: 1px solid #fff;
}

.gallery-caption {
  border: 1px solid #00f;
}
```

These style declarations will allow you to see where the different parts of the gallery markup start and end, so you can further style them as you wish. To see the gallery styles in action, you'll need to create a gallery. Go to the administrative interface, and create a new post. Click on the **Add an Image** button in the media toolbar, and upload multiple images. Then click on the **Save all changes** button.

After clicking on the **Save changes** button, you'll be presented with the gallery settings, as shown in the following screenshot:

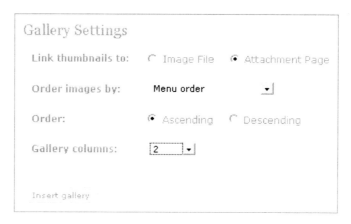

Select your desired gallery settings, and then click on the **Insert gallery** button. Something similar to the following markup will be sent to your post editor:

```
[gallery columns="2"]
```

After this has been inserted into the post editor, publish the post, and then view it in your theme. You should see something similar to the following screenshot:

How it works...

To understand how to style a gallery appropriately, we first have to understand how the gallery markup is output in the first place, and what exactly that markup looks like. Let's start with how it is generated and output.

When WordPress sees the shortcode [gallery] inside of a post's content, it auto-expands this, based on the images attached to that post. This expansion happens inside the gallery_shortcode function found in wp-includes/media.php.

The gallery_shortcode function does a few things when it is invoked. First, it determines if the post that the gallery is being called for has any image attachments. If it does, then the function starts to generate output. The output starts with a style tag that declares some basic layout information about the gallery. These styles include margin, width, and border declarations for the main elements of the gallery, and were defined in the style.css file earlier in the example.

Then, the function iterates over each of the image attachments, and outputs an HTML tag for it. The tag can be changed through the use of shortcode parameters, but the class attributes used in the tags will always be the same. The pertinent classes to pay attention to are:

- gallery
- gallery-item
- gallery-icon
- gallery-caption

So, at the very least, you should style these elements. After all of the image attachments have been iterated over, the gallery_shortcode function returns the HTML that has been produced, and this HTML is inserted wherever the gallery_shortcode is present in the post content.

For a simple four image, two-column gallery, the output would look something like this:

```
<style type='text/css'>
  #gallery-1 {
    margin: auto;
  }
  #gallery-1 .gallery-item {
    float: left;
    margin-top: 10px;
    text-align: center;
    width: 50%;
  }
  #gallery-1 img {
    border: 2px solid #cfcfcf;
  }
```

```
    #gallery-1 .gallery-caption {
      margin-left: 0;
    }
  </style>
  <!-- see gallery_shortcode() in wp-includes/media.php -->
  <div id='gallery-1' class='gallery galleryid-97'>
    <dl class='gallery-item'>
      <dt class='gallery-icon'>
        <a href='' title='Hydrangeas'><img width="150" height="150"
src="" class="attachment-thumbnail" alt="" title="Hydrangeas" /></a>
      </dt>
    </dl>
    <dl class='gallery-item'>
      <dt class='gallery-icon'>
        <a href='' title='Jellyfish'><img width="150" height="150"
src="" class="attachment-thumbnail" alt="" title="Jellyfish" /></a>
      </dt>
    </dl>
    <br style="clear: both"/>
    <dl class='gallery-item'>
      <dt class='gallery-icon'>
        <a href='' title='Koala'><img width="150" height="150" src=""
class="attachment-thumbnail" alt="" title="Koala" /></a>
      </dt>
    </dl>
    <dl class='gallery-item'>
      <dt class='gallery-icon'>
        <a href='' title='Lighthouse'><img width="150" height="150"
src="" class="attachment-thumbnail" alt="" title="Lighthouse" /></a>
      </dt>
    </dl>
    <br style="clear: both"/>
  </div>
```

Please keep in mind that the previous sample uses the default tags for gallery items, captions, and icons. These tags can be changed by changing the shortcode attributes. To learn more about this and all the parameters that a user can change in their gallery shortcode, see http://codex.wordpress.org/Gallery_Shortcode.

Styling image captions

Although some images are self-explanatory, many require a note about their contents in order to be relevant to the surrounding article. Luckily, this functionality is baked into WordPress, allowing users to enter a short caption when uploading an image.

These captions are marked up with a special format, and can be styled appropriately quite easily.

Getting started

For this recipe, you need to have a basic theme created already. This should include a `page.php` or `single.php` file that displays full post content.

How to do it...

First, we need to open the theme's `style.css` file and place our cursor just after the introductory comment.

Then, insert the following class declarations:

```
.wp-caption {
  border: 1px solid #ddd;
  text-align: center;
  background-color: #f3f3f3;
  padding-top: 4px;
  margin: 10px;
  border-radius: 3px;
}

.wp-caption img {
  margin: 0;
  padding: 0;
  border: 0 none;
}

.wp-caption p.wp-caption-text {
  font-size: 11px;
  line-height: 17px;
  padding: 0 4px 5px;
  margin: 0;
}
```

To see the captioning styles in action, you'll need to create a captioned image. Go to the administrative interface, and create a new post. Click on the **Add an Image** button in the media toolbar, and upload a single image.

Enter a short caption in the **Caption** field, as shown in the following screenshot:

Then, click on the **Insert into Post** button, and publish your post.

Viewing the post on the front-end, you should see something similar to the example shown in the following screenshot:

How it works...

The style declarations that were added to the `style.css` file will surround the image with a light gray box and a gentle border that gives the image and caption a sense of unity. The caption and image are centered in the caption container.

To understand how to appropriately style an image caption, it helps to understand how the caption markup is output, and what exactly that markup looks like.

When WordPress sees the shortcode [caption] inside of a post's content, it auto-expands this based on the parameters passed to the shortcode, and the image tag contained within it. This expansion happens inside the `img_caption_shortcode` function found in `wp-includes/media.php`.

The `img_caption_shortcode` function is really simple. It examines the parameters passed to the shortcode, and uses those parameters to build a surrounding `div` for the image and the caption, and appends a caption paragraph to the content within the shortcode. The surrounding `div` includes a couple of classes and an inline style declaration. The caption paragraph has the class `wp-caption-text`.

As such, the following shortcode:

```
[caption width="300" caption="Test Caption"]
<img src="http://wp.local/wp-content/uploads/2009/10/Tulips2-300x225.
jpg" alt="Test Caption" title="Tulips" width="300" height="225"
class="size-medium wp-image-105" />
[/caption]
```

results in the following HTML:

```
<div class="wp-caption alignnone" style="width: 310px"><img
src="http://wp.local/wp-content/uploads/2009/10/Tulips2-300x225.
jpg" alt="Test Caption" title="Tulips" width="300" height="225"
class="size-medium wp-image-105" />
<p class="wp-caption-text">Test Caption</p>
</div>
```

Here, the pertinent classes to style are:

► `wp-caption`
► `wp-caption-text`

Both of them are styled in this recipe's instructions.

See also

► *Aligning images properly within a post*

Creating a media template

Although in-line images and other media can be great in some circumstances, sometimes you really want to be able to highlight the importance of an attachment by placing the item on its own page and linking to it. Luckily, WordPress has support for attachment templates, allowing you to emphasize attachments appropriately.

Getting started

The only requirement for this recipe is that you are working on a modern WordPress theme that works with WordPress 2.8 or 2.9.

How to do it...

First, we need to create the attachment template. The basic attachment template that we are going to create must be called `attachment.php`. This template will be used to serve all attachment links.

Open `attachment.php`, and insert the following template code:

```
<html>
  <head>
    <title><?php the_title(); ?></title>
  </head>
  <body>
```

```
<?php
$meta = wp_get_attachment_metadata($post->ID);
$size = 'medium';
?>
<div
  style="margin: 0 auto;
    width: <?php echo $meta['sizes'][$size]['width'] + 20; ?>;
    text-align: left;
    padding: 10px;
    border: 5px solid #000;">
  <?php echo wp_get_attachment_link($post->ID,$size); ?>
</div>
</body>
</html>
```

Save the file, and upload it to your current theme folder.

You can see what the uploaded image would look like, by viewing the screenshot below:

Creating a basic media template

March 25, 2010 – 3:11 am

If you are creating a media template from scratch, you need an attachment file for users.

This is an example of a post using the media file to upload and post an image.

Vancouver Dawn

By Lee | Posted in Tutorials | Edit | Comments (0)

How it works...

The above example effectively highlights the attachment image by surrounding it with a simple bordered `div`, and aligning it to the left within the browser window. Here, the medium version of the image is used, and the full version is linked to directly, so that users can download it easily if they wish.

When WordPress is attempting to determine what template to display, it goes through a long process that is encapsulated in the file located at `wp-includes/template-loader.php`. Once WordPress determines that an attachment listing is being shown, it calls the `get_attachment_template` function, in order to retrieve the correct template filename.

Inside of `get_attachment_template`, WordPress defaults to looking for the `attachment.php` file that we have provided. The attachment information is provided in the global `$post` object. We can use that, and WordPress' template functions such as `wp_get_attachment_metadata` and `wp_get_attachment_link`, to display the attachment appropriately. This attachment template will work most effectively for images, but can handle other attachment types as well.

 You can easily replace the value of the `$size` parameter with one of `thumbnail`, `small`, `medium`, or `full`.

For more information on the attachment functions, see `http://codex.wordpress.org/Function_Reference#Attachments`.

See also

▶   *Creating a media template for a specific media type*

Creating a media template for a specific media type

Not all attachments are images, and so we shouldn't display them in the same way as we would display images. Perhaps you wish to link directly to a video or audio file, or you have a special Flash player that can read these files from the web and play them. Whatever your desired usage, it is easy to make sure that WordPress loads a specific template for certain media types.

Getting started

The only requirement for this recipe is that you are working on a modern WordPress theme (2.8 or 2.9). You will need to decide how granular you want your media type templates to be. For example, do you just want to display a certain attachment for all images, or do you want to display a specific template for JPEGs, GIFs, or PNGs? For now, we're going to assume that you want a different template for audio, video, and image files.

How to do it...

Back up any `attachment.php` file that you may have already created. Create `image.php`, `audio.php`, and `video.php` in your theme's folder. Copy and paste any media-specific attachment information, such as those used in the last recipe, into the appropriate file.

Add content to each of the specific media templates, starting with `image.php`:

```
<p>Image:</p>
<?php echo wp_get_attachment_link($post->ID); ?>
```

Add the content in the code below to the `audio.php` file:

```
<p>Audio:</p>
<?php echo wp_get_attachment_link($post->ID); ?>
```

Finally, add the following content to the `video.php` file:

```
<p>Video: </p>
<?php echo wp_get_attachment_link($post->ID); ?>
```

To test that the proper templates are being displayed, go to the administrative interface, and then click on **Add New** under the **Media** heading. Click on the **Select Files** button, and select an image, an audio file, and a video file. Then, click on **Save all changes**.

On the next screen, hover over each of the attachments that you just uploaded, and open their page by clicking on the **View** link that appears. You will see each template in action. The audio page will look like the following screenshot:

And the image template will appear as follows:

How it works...

After WordPress determines that it is displaying an attachment, it queries the file system to see if a template file exists for that attachment's specified mime type. If you're not familiar with mime types, you can find a good reference at `http://www.w3schools.com/media/media_mimeref.asp`.

Checking for a template is a three-step process, going from very broad to very narrow. Given a mime type of image/jpg, WordPress looks for the following files, in this order:

1. `image.php`
2. `jpg.php`
3. `image_jpg.php`

For a mime type of text/plain, the template file search would be for:

1. `text.php`
2. `plain.php`
3. `text_plain.php`

As you can see, you can get very specific with what you do for certain content types. Perhaps you have a player that can handle the mp3 audio format, but can't handle any other audio formats. Given this, you could create an mp3 template that handles that specific type of audio file, and a general attachment template that simply links to the attachment. In this way, you let WordPress handle what template code to display, and you focus simply on getting your implementation and presentation correct.

There's more...

It's worth taking the time to learn more about attachments and how they are handled in WordPress.

Using file and image attachments in WordPress

The main purpose of the `attachment.php` file, from a WordPress perspective, is to tie the media file (whether it is an image, audio file, document, or video) to its respective comments when the **link to page** option is chosen on file upload, or when creating or editing a post. You can learn more about it on the WordPress codex, at: `http://codex.wordpress.org/Using_Image_and_File_Attachments`.

See also

 ▶ *Creating a media template*

Displaying a related image for every post

As blogs become more and more like news magazines, it has become common to ensure that each post has an image associated with it, giving a clue to its contents. Before WordPress 2.9, retrieving this image for each post required a custom plug-in or some custom theme code. Now, it is built-in, and is easier than ever (refer to `http://markjaquith.wordpress.com/2009/12/23/new-in-wordpress-2-9-post-thumbnail-images/`).

Getting started

You need to have a basic theme created for this recipe, including `index.php`, `function.php`, and `single.php` template files.

How to do it...

First, open up your theme's `functions.php` file, and type the following code just below the comments section:

```
Add_theme_support('post-thumbnails');
```

Now the size of the thumbnails in the post and the corresponding image in a single page need to be set. Just below the code entered above, paste the following code:

```
set_post_thumbnail_size( 50, 50, true );
// Normal post thumbnails (cropped)
add_image_size( 'single-post-thumbnail', 400, 9999 );
// Permalink thumbnail size
```

Next, open up the `index.php` file, and look for the beginning of the WordPress *Loop*. Paste the following code just below `<?php while ( have_posts() ) : the_post() ?>` and any opening entry content div tag, such as `<div class="entry-content">`:

```
<!-- the image for each post or page function call -->
  <?php
if ( has_post_thumbnail() ) {
  // the current post has a thumbnail
} else {
  // the current post lacks a thumbnail
  } ?>
```

Finally, insert a tag to call the image on the single post page by opening up the `single.php` file (or `page.php`) and inserting the following tag below `<?php the_post(); ?>`:

```
<?php the_post_thumbnail( 'single-post-thumbnail' ); ?>
```

Save the changes, and then upload the files to the current theme folder on your server.

Create a new post, and then upload an image, to see the post thumbnail code in action. On the upload form in the **Size** section, you now have the option to **Use as thumbnail**. Click on the link to use the Post Thumbnail feature. An example of the form is shown in the screenshot below:

Save the post, and then view it in your browser.

Your post should look similar to the example shown in the next screenshot:

Creating Post Thumbnail Images for Every Post

March 25, 2010 – 4:46 pm

With WordPress 2.9 it is possible to create a thumbnail image for each post, and display a larger image on the single post page.

Nasa Photo - Blue view from space

How it works...

Adding the function call `add_theme_support('post-thumbnails');` to `functions.php` enables the post thumbnail UI on the image upload form for all post and page content. The `post_thumbnail()` function outputs the post thumbnail if it exists (in the loop). Next, the dimensions of the post thumbnails need to be specified by using `set_post_thumbnail_size`, which shrinks the image to a specific width and height. In this example, the height and width are both set to `50` pixels in the tag. Directly after that, the image size on a single post page is set by using `add_image_size`, which is set to a default width of `400` and an overstated maximum height of `9999`, which will allow for an image of any almost height needed in the post.

When an image is uploaded to a post and **Use thumbnail** is selected from the upload form, the thumbnail resize code automatically generates two sizes for the image: one for the index area on the site and one for the single post page. It does not matter what image size you choose if **Use thumbnail** link is selected. The code that we entered earlier will override all other size settings on the form. You will now have consistently-sized images on the index and post pages.

There's more...

Currently in the 2.9 version of WordPress, it is not possible to resize or use the above example for images that have already been uploaded to the media gallery.

Using Viper's Regenerate Thumbnails plug-in

Viper007Bond has created a thumbnail regeneration plug-in that can be downloaded from `http://wordpress.org/extend/plugins/regenerate-thumbnails/`.

Creating video posts by using the Viper's Video QuickTags plug-in

Getting started

You will need to have a modern WordPress theme installed that uses `<?php get_wphead ?>` on one of the theme pages, preferably in the header or index files.

How to do it...

Download the plugin files from `http://wordpress.org/extend/plugins/vipers-video-quicktags/`. Unzip the folder, and then upload it to the `plugins` folder under `/wp-content/`. Activate the plug-in, by navigating to the **Plugins** section of your WordPress administration panel and clicking on the **Activate** link.

After activating the plugin, visit the **Settings** link to configure default aspect ratios, remove or add video sites such as YouTube and Google Video, and even set alternate text for feeds. For example, click on the **Google Video** link. Under **Dimensions**, change the width to **300**. This will automatically update the aspect ratio.

Click on the **Save Changes** button, and leave the settings as they are, to test the plugin with a new post. You can see an example of these settings in the following screenshot:

Gather the link to the video you that want to use, and create a new post. Click on the **Google Video** button in the post editor. The form to insert the video link will appear. Paste your own video link, or use the default video URL for testing.

Click on **Dimensions** to verify that they are correct, and then click on the **Okay** button to finish inserting the video. You can see the form in the next screenshot:

Finish the post, and then publish it. View the site to see how the video post appears to visitors.

An example of a completed video post is shown in the next screenshot:

How it works...

The Viper's Video Quicktags plug-in eliminates the need to use embedded code in every video post, and gives you greater control on the layout and dimensions of videos. Viper contains highly-customized blocks of code that integrate with the WordPress post editor and provide a highly-customizable control panel area to manage video settings.

There's more...

Many people now use smart phones or other mobile devices to browse the web. To make your media content shine in those situations, you may want to consider using a specialized theme to control how your site will display on one of those devices.

Adapting your site for mobile content viewing by using the WPtouch theme

Visitors who reach your site from an iPhone, iPod touch, Android, or Blackberry device with touch screen capabilities will have an interactive experience, including AJAX loading articles and effects. The theme includes a theme switcher so that mobile visitors can view your site in the WPtouch theme or your standard site theme. The theme can be downloaded from `http://wordpress.org/extend/plugins/wptouch/`.

9
Showing Author Information

In this chapter, we will cover:

- ▶ Getting author data via an author's ID
- ▶ Dynamically displaying the author's name and linked e-mail address
- ▶ Listing all of the published authors on a site
- ▶ Listing the authors who most recently published a post
- ▶ Listing authors by the total number of comments that their posts have received
- ▶ Adding a custom user field to display an author's Twitter link

Introduction

The authors and editors of any reputable news source are almost as important as the content that they write. Often, readers try to identify with the authors whose material they like, and will gravitate towards their future works.

As such, it is very important that any serious, multi-author site run on WordPress should try to incorporate the display of author data (such as their name, biographical background information, posts or other blogs they participate in, and so on) in an interesting and useful way for the user. In this chapter, we are going to examine how you get at that data, and the different ways in which you might use it.

Getting author data via an author's ID

An author ID is the unique numeric identifier for any user on a WordPress site. The first user created on a new WordPress site generally has an ID with a value of 1.

Although it is rare that you'll have a numeric user ID without direct programmatic input, you can use this technique when defining custom template tags. We're going to create a custom function that prints a user's username and their e-mail address.

Getting started

You will need a theme that already has an `author.php` file created, such as Sandbox from `plaintxt.org`, or you can create your own basic `author.php` theme file by adding the code provided in this recipe.

How to do it...

First, open or create your theme's `author.php` file.

Place your cursor at the beginning of the `author.php` file, and then insert the following code:

```
<p>
<b>Our guest author this week</b>
<?php $user_info = get_userdata(2);
echo($user_info->user_nicename . ' has this email address:' .
$user_info->user_email . "\n"); ?>
</p>
```

Save the file and upload it to the current `theme` folder on your server.

When visitors go to the author page now, they should see a message about the **guest author**, as shown in the screenshot below:

> ## Author Archives: Lee
>
> **Author Email:** Contact Author
> Designer, artist, and author of two other books with Packt Publishing.
>
> **Our guest author this week:** leej has this email address: mamaphoenix@gmail.com

How it works...

When someone visits the author page, the `$user_info` variable calls the `get_userdata` function, passing the `user_id` with a value of 2 for the second user/author listed in the WordPress backend. It tries to retrieve user data by using the user ID, and will then display the "nice name" of the user and their e-mail address on the screen.

Dynamically displaying the author's name and linked e-mail address

It is useful to know how to dynamically display a post author's name and e-mail address (and potentially, other user data such as their author bio/description) on the author page.

Getting started

You will need a modern WordPress theme, such as Sandbox from `http://plaintxt.org`, and an `author.php` page.

How to do it...

First, open or create your theme's `author.php` file

Place your cursor at the beginning of the `author.php` file, immediately below the `comments` block, and insert the following code:

```
<h2 class="page-title author">
<?php printf( __( 'Author Archives: <span class="vcard">%s</span>',
'sandbox' ), "<a class='url fn n' href='$authordata->user_url'
title='$authordata->display_name' rel='me'>$authordata->display_name
</a>" ) ?>
</h2>
<div id="authorinfo">
<strong>Author Email:</strong> <a href="mailto:<?php echo
antispambot($curauth->user_email); ?>">Contact Author</a>
</div>
```

Save the `author.php` file, and upload it to the current theme on your server.

You can see an example of how the changes we just made will look to blog visitors, in the screenshot below:

How it works...

When visitors click on the nickname of the author in a post, the $authordata WordPress variable is called. The code that was placed in the author.php file will attempt to display the text **Author Archives**, along with the friendly author nickname, the text **Author Email:**, and their e-mail address, using the ID of the author whose nickname was clicked on in the post. This information is retrieved by WordPress via the get_userdata function. If the author ID is found, and their nickname and e-mail address are stored in the WordPress database, then an object is returned containing all of the information about the author, and the information requested in the code block is displayed on the screen. Information that can be used about users (and authors) on author pages includes their WordPress "nice name", nickname, e-mail address, website URL, display name, and their user ID. You can display or manipulate the user's name, description, level, and more.

There's more...

You can use $authordata and get_userdata to customize your theme in many ways.

Dive deeper into data

To learn more about ways to manipulate the display of information by using get_userdata, visit the WordPress codex: http://codex.wordpress.org/Function_Reference/get_userdata.

 Find your author ID by hovering your mouse over the nickname link below any post.

Listing all of the published authors on a site

The most common place to see author data is adjacent to content written by that author. However, it can be beneficial for both your site visitors and your site metrics to display a list of all authors somewhere on your site. The information displayed can range from a simple list of names with links to their posts, to their name, biography, and the last few posts that they made.

Getting started

For this recipe, you need to have a basic theme created already with a `sidebar.php` file. Also, you need to know where you want to put your list of authors. This could be within a page template or a sidebar. For this recipe, we'll assume that you want to display the listing inside of a sidebar.

How to do it...

Open up a `sidebar` file, and enter the following code into it:

```
<ul>
  <li>
    <ul>
    <?php
    $all_users = get_users_of_blog();
    foreach($all_users as $user ) {
      $num_authors_posts = get_usernumposts($user->ID);
      if( 0 < $num_authors_posts ) {
        $url = get_author_posts_url($user->ID);
        ?>
        <li>
          <a href="<?php echo $url; ?>">
            <?php echo get_the_author_meta('display_name',
              $user->ID); ?>
          </a>
          has published <?php printf(_n('%d post.', '%d posts.',
            $num_authors_posts),$num_authors_posts); ?>
        </li>
        <?php
      }
    }
    ?>
    </ul>
  </li>
</ul>
```

Save the `sidebar` file and upload it to the `theme` folder on your server. You should see something similar to the following:

As you can see, the code listing above creates a list of all of the authors who have published at least one post. The author's name links to their posts page (which lists all of their posts) and there is some descriptive text about how many posts they've published.

How it works...

There are a number of different functions in use in this example. First, we start by calling `get_users_of_blog`. This function returns an array of objects of user data. Each object contains a user's unique numeric identifier, login name, display name, user e-mail, and metadata. A listing of the objects' contents is as follows:

```
stdClass Object
(
     [user_id] => 1
     [ID] => 1
     [user_login] => admin
     [display_name] => Nick Ohrn
     [user_email] => example@example.com
     [meta_value] => a:1:{s:13:"administrator";b:1;}
)
```

After this, we call `get_usernumposts` to determine how many posts the user has published. `get_usernumposts` only includes posts that have actually been published, and does not include pages or media uploads.

If the user has published at least one post, we need to print their display name and a short message about how many posts they've published. To retrieve the user's display name, we use the `get_the_author_meta` function. This function accepts two arguments. The first argument is the name of the user meta to retrieve. The second argument is the user's ID whose information we are attempting to retrieve. The `get_the_author_meta` function accepts a variety of values for the first argument, including the following:

- user_login
- user_pass
- user_nicename
- user_email
- user_url
- user_registered
- user_activation_key
- user_status
- display_name
- nickname
- first_name
- last_name
- description
- jabber
- aim
- yim
- user_level
- user_firstname
- user_lastname
- user_description
- rich_editing
- comment_shortcuts
- admin_color
- plugins_per_page
- plugins_last_view
- ID

For more information on the use of this function, see `http://codex.wordpress.org/ Function_Reference/get_the_author_meta`.

The final function in use in this example is _n. This is a localization function that we will cover in a later recipe.

Listing the authors who most recently published a post

Although listing all authors is certainly nice, you don't want to give undue attention to authors who haven't been active in a while. In this recipe, we're going to develop a function that returns information about the users who most recently published a post on the site.

Getting started

The only requirement for this recipe is that you are working on a valid theme and that you have some place to put your author listing, ideally a sidebar file such as sidebar.php.

How to do it...

First, we need to create a couple of custom template tags. We'll call the first template tag get_recently_published_author_ids, and have it accept a single parameter that determines the number of author IDs to return. The second template tag is called get_last_post_id_published_for_author, and it accepts a single parameter that defines the author we are looking at.

Open or create your theme's functions.php file, and define the following functions in it:

```
function get_recently_published_author_ids($limit = 3) {
  global $wpdb;
  return $wpdb->get_col( $wpdb->prepare(
    "SELECT DISTINCT {$wpdb->posts}.post_author
    FROM {$wpdb->posts}
    WHERE {$wpdb->posts}.post_type = 'post'
    AND {$wpdb->posts}.post_status = 'publish'
    ORDER BY {$wpdb->posts}.post_date_gmt DESC
    LIMIT %d", $limit ));
}
function get_last_post_id_published_for_author($user_ID) {
  global $wpdb;
  return $wpdb->get_var( $wpdb->prepare(
    "SELECT {$wpdb->posts}.ID
    FROM {$wpdb->posts}
    WHERE {$wpdb->posts}.post_type = 'post'
    AND {$wpdb->posts}.post_status = 'publish'
    AND {$wpdb->posts}.post_author = %d
```

```
      ORDER BY {$wpdb->posts}.post_date_gmt DESC
      LIMIT 1", $user_ID ));
}
```

Now we need to use these functions somewhere. Borrowing from the recipe *Listing all published authors on a site*, we put the following code in one of our sidebars:

```
<ul>
  <li>Recent Authors
    <ul>
    <?php
    $recent = get_recently_published_author_ids();
    foreach($recent as $user_ID) {
      $num_authors_posts = get_usernumposts($user_ID);
      if( 0 < $num_authors_posts ) {
        $url = get_author_posts_url($user_ID);
        $pid = get_last_post_id_published_for_author($user_ID);
        $time = get_post_time('G', true, $pid);
        ?>
        <li>
          <a href="<?php echo $url; ?>">
            <?php echo
              get_the_author_meta('display_name',$user_ID); ?>
            <?php echo human_time_diff($time); ?>
          </a>
        </li>
        <?php
      }
    }
    ?>
    </ul>
  </li>
</ul>
```

If you've done everything correctly, you should have an output that looks something like the following:

Recent Authors
- Nick Ohrn - 9 days
- Test User 10 - 2 hours
- Test User 3 - 2 hours

How it works...

At the heart of this recipe are our two custom functions. They both invoke some raw SQL calls by using the `wpdb` class that WordPress provides. Our first function, `get_recently_published_author_ids`, queries the posts table for distinct author IDs, ordering them by the date on which the post was published. That function invokes the `get_col` method on the `$wpdb` object. The `get_col` method returns an array of values from a database column. In this case, that column is `post_author`.

The second custom function, `get_last_post_id_published_for_author`, simply returns the unique identifier for the last post published by a particular author. The function calls `get_var` on the `$wpdb` object. The `get_var` method returns a single value from a database query.

We combine these two functions to get the data that we use to generate the listing. First, we use a `foreach` loop to iterate over each of the user IDs returned from the call to `get_recently_published_author_ids`. Inside our `foreach` loop, we pass to the `get_last_post_id_published_for_author` function the user ID that we are currently working with to retrieve the post ID for that author's last published post. We use this post ID to retrieve the post's published time by using the `get_post_time` function. Then we pass the published time to WordPress's built-in `human_time_diff` function. `human_time_diff` returns a human readable time string, such as 9 days or 2 hours, detailing the difference between the lone timestamp argument and the current system time.

In this example, we use the `get_the_author_meta` function. For more information on this function and its use, please see *Listing all published authors on a site*.

See also

▶ *Listing all published authors on a site.*

Listing authors by the total number of comments that their posts have received

For most subject matters, one of the best ways to judge how interesting an author's posts are is to look at the level of discussion surrounding them. In the context of a blog, the discussion of a post happens in the comments designated for that post. In this recipe, we'll create a custom function that lets us find the authors who have generated the most discussion on their posts. Then we'll display some data about that author, along with the number of comments.

Getting started

You need to have a basic theme containing a `functions.php` file, and a sidebar file such as `sidebar.php` created for this recipe. You also need to know where you would like to place the listing of the most discussed authors. In this example, we will be displaying the data in a sidebar.

How to do it...

First, we need to create a custom template tag. We'll call the template tag `get_most_discussed_authors`, and have it accept a single parameter that determines the number of results to return. Open or create your theme's `functions.php` file, and define the function as follows:

```
function get_most_discussed_authors($limit = 3) {
  global $wpdb;
  return $wpdb->get_results( $wpdb->prepare(
    "SELECT COUNT({$wpdb->comments}.comment_ID) as
      number_comments,
    {$wpdb->users}.ID as user_ID
    FROM {$wpdb->comments}, {$wpdb->users}, {$wpdb->posts}
    WHERE {$wpdb->users}.ID = {$wpdb->posts}.post_author
    AND {$wpdb->posts}.ID = {$wpdb->comments}.comment_post_ID
    GROUP BY {$wpdb->users}.ID
    ORDER BY number_comments DESC
    LIMIT %d", $limit));
}
```

Now we need to use this function to display information to visitors. Borrowing from the recipe *Listing all published authors on a site*, we put the following code in one of our sidebars:

```
<ul>
  <li>Most Discussed Authors
    <ul>
    <?php
    $discussed = get_most_discussed_authors();
    foreach($discussed as $item) {
      $user_ID = $item->user_ID;
      $num_comments = $item->number_comments;
      $url = get_author_posts_url($user_ID);
    ?>
      <li>
        <a href="<?php echo $url; ?>">
          <?php echo get_the_author_meta
            ('display_name',$user_ID); ?>
```

```
        <?php printf( _n
          ( '%d comment', '%d comments', $num_comments ),
          $num_comments ); ?>
      </a>
    </li>
    <?php
  }
  ?>
  </ul>
  </li>
</ul>
```

Save the file, and then upload it to the current theme folder on your server.

If you've done everything correctly, you should have an output that looks something like the following screenshot of the sidebar:

Most Discussed Authors
- Test User 5 - 3 comments
- Test User 7 - 2 comments
- Test User 9 - 1 comment

How it works...

As with the previous two recipes, we've created a template tag that basically acts as a delegate for a raw SQL call, by using the `$wpdb` object that WordPress provides. In this recipe, the `get_most_discussed_authors` function calls the `wpdb` class's `get_results` method. This method returns an array of objects, including the authors, their related posts, and the comments attached to those posts, formed from the rows returned from a database call.

In our custom function, each item returned in the array has two properties: `user_ID` and `number_comments`. When iterating over the results from our call to `get_most_discussed_authors`, we use these two properties when displaying the nice list of author names and the amount of comments that their posts have received.

See also

▶ *Listing all published authors on a site.*

Adding a custom user field to display an author's Twitter link

We can use the data that describes the author, their "metadata", to display a variety of information, in most cases, the same as that retrieved by using $authordata or user_ data, as seen in previous examples in this chapter. However, sometimes a plugin gathers additional custom metadata such as an IM username or a Twitter name. In that situation, applying a special template tag called the_author_metadata to an author page is very useful.

In this example, we will create a custom user field for the user profile page in the WordPress control panel, and then use the Twitter metadata that it provides to display the author's Twitter username on the author page.

Getting started

You will need an author.php file in a modern 2.9 compatible WordPress theme, and a Twitter account (www.twitter.com).

How to do it...

Open up your functions.php file and insert the following code, in order to create the custom field:

```php
add_action( 'show_user_profile', 'my_show_extra_profile_fields' );
add_action( 'edit_user_profile', 'my_show_extra_profile_fields' );
function my_show_extra_profile_fields( $user ) { ?>
<h3>Extra profile information</h3>
    <table class="form-table">
    <tr><th><label for="twitter">Twitter</label></th>
    <td>
    <input type="text" name="twitter" id="twitter" value=
      "<?php echo esc_attr( get_the_author_meta
      ( 'twitter', $user->ID ) ); ?>" class="regular-text" />
      <br />
    <span class="description">Twitter username</span>
    </td>
    </tr>
    </table>
<?php }
```

Now we need to insert code into `functions.php` so that the data entered into the custom field will be saved. Enter the following code directly below the code in step 1:

```
//save the custom field
add_action( 'personal_options_update', 'my_save_extra_profile_fields'
);
add_action( 'edit_user_profile_update', 'my_save_extra_profile_fields'
);
function my_save_extra_profile_fields( $user_id ) {
if ( !current_user_can( 'edit_user', $user_id ) )
return false;
update_usermeta( $user_id, 'twitter', $_POST['twitter'] );}
```

Save the `functions.php` file, and then upload it to your server. You can now see the custom field area within your author profile, and can use it. It should look like the example shown in the screenshot below:

Next, a function to get the Twitter ID from the user profile needs to be created. Insert the following code into `functions.php`:

```
//author box function
  function my_author_box() { ?>
  <div class="author-profile vcard">
    <?php if ( get_the_author_meta( 'twitter' ) ) { ?>
    <p class="twitter clear">
    <a href="http://twitter.com/<?php the_author_meta
      ( 'twitter' ); ?>"
      title="Follow <?php the_author_meta
      ( 'display_name' ); ?> on Twitter">
      Follow <?php the_author_meta
      ( 'display_name' ); ?> on Twitter
    </a>
    </p>
<?php } // End check for twitter ?></div><?php
  }
```

Finally, we need to place a tag in `author.php` to call the `my_author_box()` function and display the **Follow on Twitter** link:

```
<div id="authorinfo">
  <strong>Author Email:</strong>
  <a href="mailto:<?php echo antispambot($curauth->user_email);
    ?>">Contact Author</a>
  <?php my_author_box(); ?>
</div>
```

Save the `functions.php` file and the `author.php` file, and then upload them to your server.

View the author page in your browser, and you should see a **Follow** link similar to the one shown in the screenshot below:

Author Archives: Lee

Author Email: Contact Author

Follow Lee on Twitter

Designer, artist, and author of two other books with Packt Publishing.

How it works...

First, the `add_action( 'show_user_profile', 'my_show_extra_profile_fields' );` and `add_action( 'edit_user_profile', 'my_show_extra_profile_fields' );` code was added to `functions.php` to allow a new custom user field to be created and edited as a part of the user profile form. Next, the form field and labels were created within the function `my_show_extra_profile_fields( $user )`. This added an input box label and description to the WordPress control panel's user profile screen. We then added code to `functions.php` file, in order to save any data entered into the custom field. We then created a function called `my_author_box()` that used the metadata function `get_author_meta()` to retrieve data stored in the WordPress database. The metadata function `the_author_meta()` displayed the display name and Twitter username meta information retrieved from the user profile. Finally, we added a tag to `author.php`, in order to call the `my_author_box` function and print the **Follow on Twitter** link on the screen.

You can use the previous example to create custom fields to display other information, including linking to podcasts, bookseller sites, and more.

Displaying an image next to the 'Follow' link

If you want to create a custom image, or use the default Twitter follow icon, you can add it to the above code by adding a link to the image in the author box function:

```php
function my_author_box() { ?>
<div class="author-profile vcard">
  <?php if ( get_the_author_meta( 'twitter' ) ) { ?>
  <p class="twitter clear">
  <img src="/images/twitter-link-logo.png"alt="twitter logo"/>
  <a href="http://twitter.com/<?php the_author_meta
    ( 'twitter' ); ?>" title="Follow
    <?php the_author_meta( 'display_name' ); ?>
    on Twitter">Follow <?php the_author_meta
    ( 'display_name' ); ?> on Twitter</a>
  </p><?php } // End check for twitter ?>
</div><?php
}
```

10
Adding JavaScript Effects

In this chapter, we will cover:

- ▶ Linking to your theme's JavaScript files directly
- ▶ Adding JavaScript files to your theme programmatically
- ▶ Adding a bundled library to your theme programmatically
- ▶ Creating a featured post slider
- ▶ Making sidebar widgets toggle-able
- ▶ Adding a font-size toggle

Introduction

In the last couple of years, web users have become quite a bit more sophisticated. As this happened, many came to expect a certain level of dynamic interaction with a web page. The dynamic element can be many things, the most popular being animating elements and dynamic content loads.

Luckily for developers, this rise in interest in dynamic elements coincided with the maturation of JavaScript libraries and techniques. This makes creating fun and useful interactions on your site simpler.

To make things even easier for a WordPress developer, the WordPress package comes bundled with many popular JavaScript libraries built-in and ready-to-use. In this chapter, we'll look at how to use those libraries, where they live, and some interesting things that you can do with them in the context of your theme.

Linking to your theme's JavaScript files directly

The easiest way to include JavaScript functionality in your theme is to link directly to the file from the `<head>` element of your theme. In this recipe, we'll examine how you determine the URL to link to and where to, put the linking element.

Getting started

You need to have created a WordPress theme that contains at least a `style.css` file and an `index.php` file.

How to do it...

First, you're going to create a JavaScript file to link to. Open the folder that your theme lives in, and create a new folder called `js`. This folder exists for the purposes of organization of your JavaScript files.

Inside of the `js` folder, create a new file called `my-theme.js`. Open this file for editing, and insert the following test script:

```
/*
 * Created for test purposes.
 */
alert('This is a test.');
```

Now you need to link to the JavaScript file from your theme, to ensure that the script is loaded and run. To do so, open up the theme file where your `<head>` element is located. This will most likely be `header.php`.

Between the `<head>` and `</head>` tags, insert a new line with the following content:

```
<script type="text/javascript" src="<?php bloginfo('stylesheet_
directory'); ?>/js/my-theme.js"></script>
```

After doing this, load your WordPress site with your theme active, and you'll be greeted by a dialog box similar to the one pictured in the screenshot below:

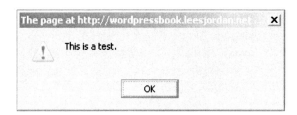

How it works...

There are two possible uses of an HTML script tag. The first is to add JavaScript directly to a page. This would look something like the following:

```
<script type="text/javascript">
alert('This is a test.');
</script>
```

In this example, the visitor's browser of choice interprets the script as it parses the page, taking whatever action is called for. If you followed along in the example, you noticed that the alert appeared before the rest of the page loaded in the browser, and once the visitor clicked on **OK**, the alert box disappeared and the page resumed loading.

However, in most instances, it is desirable to put JavaScript that is used throughout a site in a separate file that can be used again and again. There are many reasons for this, including smaller overall page size, and the fact that most browsers can—and wil —cache the external file so that it doesn't have to be fetched multiple times for a single site.

To specify an external file, we use a `<script>` tag without any content, and add the `src` attribute to tell the browser where to find the file. The browser reads the `src` attribute and attempts to fetch and parse the file located at the specified URL.

In this particular case, the `src` attribute is dynamically-generated by using the `bloginfo` function. As reviewed in the recipe *Displaying the blog name* from Chapter 1, the `bloginfo` function has a variety of different parameter values that you can use to get different information. Passing `stylesheet_directory` returns a URL that points to the directory containing your theme's `style.css` file. The URL will often be something in the form `mysite.com/wp-content/themes/my-theme`. Please note that no trailing slash is included, so you need to include it yourself if necessary.

See also

▶ *Displaying the blog name*

Adding JavaScript files to your theme programmatically

Although you can certainly link to your JavaScript files directly (and in some cases, you may need to, for one reason or another), the preferred method of generating script tags for your theme is to add references programmatically. This allows for the reuse of popular scripts, and ensures that a script is not linked to twice within the same page.

Getting started

You need to have created a WordPress theme that contains at least a `style.css` file and an `index.php` file. Inside the template file containing your theme's `<head>` tag, you need to call the `wp_head` function. If you have also completed the previous example, open up the `header.php` file (or whichever file you placed the `<script>` tag code in) and remove the code added in the last recipe.

How to do it...

First, you must create a JavaScript file to link to. This file will reside within your theme. Open your theme's folder and create a `js` folder. Inside the `js` folder, create a file called `my-theme.js`.

Open the `my-theme.js` file, and insert the following JavaScript, which will produce an alert dialog box on page load:

```
/*
 * Created for test purposes.
 */
alert('This is an enqueue script test.');
```

Now, open or create your theme's `functions.php` file. In `functions.php`, add the following code inside a PHP block:

```
if( !is_admin() ) {
wp_enqueue_script(
  'my-theme',
  get_bloginfo('stylesheet_directory') . '/js/my-theme.js'
);
}
```

Upload the updated `my-theme.js` file and `functions.php` file. Go to your WordPress site with your theme enabled, and you'll be greeted with something like the following screenshot, in your browser:

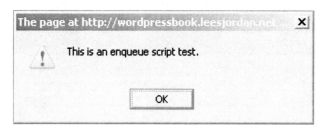

How it works...

When you call `wp_enqueue_script`, you're taking advantage of one of several JavaScript-specific functions included with WordPress. Some of the others include `wp_register_script`, `wp_is_script`, and `wp_print_scripts`.

The `wp_enqueue_script` function accepts the following parameters: `$handle`, `$src`, `$deps`, `$ver`, and `$in_footer`. Let's talk about which ones are required, and which ones are optional. Earlier in our example we used the following function to call a simple JavaScript file:

```
wp_enqueue_script( 'my-theme', get_bloginfo('stylesheet_
directory') . '/js/my-theme.js' );
```

This contained a handle (the name of the script, a lowercase string) and the URL (also a string) where the script could be found. When you call `wp_enqueue_script`, you must pass in a string value for `$handle` as the first parameter, and the URL (`$src`) at which the script can be found as the second parameter. These are the required parameters. Optionally, you can pass in an array of script handles as a third parameter (the `$dep` parameter), a version string as the fourth parameter (the `$ver` parameter), and a flag (`$in_footer`, a Boolean value), indicating that the script should be printed in the footer, as the fifth and final parameter.

After a script has been enqueued, WordPress knows that a link to it should be printed whenever `wp_print_scripts` is called. Normally, this is called within the `wp_head` function inside of the `<head>` tag.

When you are creating a theme using multiple JavaScript functions or feature-rich libraries such as JQuery, it is a best practice to place the `wp_enqueue_script` function in `functions.php` and use the `$in_footer` parameter to automatically call the script in the footer. We will cover that in the next section.

If you go back and check the source for your blog homepage after adding the code specified previously, you'll see something like the following:

```
<script
type='text/javascript'
src='http://wp.local/wp-content/themes/my-theme/js/my-theme.
js?ver=2.8.5'></script>
```

You can see that WordPress parsed the relative path information provided in the `$src` parameter of our example (`get_bloginfo('stylesheet_directory') . '/js/my-theme.js'`), and printed an absolute path to the script when the page was called by the browser.

This may lead you to ask why you should use wp_enqueue_script instead of linking to the file directly. There are several reasons, including the fact that wp_enqueue_script lets you set up dependencies on other scripts, allows you to enqueue scripts bundled with WordPress, and allows you to separate your determination of when a script should be referenced from the actual reference point.

There's more...

There is much more that can be done with scripts in WordPress. Read on for two more ways to improve your site by using the default WordPress JavaScript functions.

Placing wp_enqueue_script in the footer for better site performance

WordPress recommends that script tags be called in the footer area of themes. The reason for this is improved site performance, due to the way in which browsers load site files. Let's look at an example:

Open up your my-theme.js file, and update the code so that it looks like the following example:

```
/*
 * Created for test purposes.
 */
alert('An example of wp_enqueue_script and $in_footer! Click on Ok to
continue.');
```

Now we need to check for the WordPress footer function call, to make sure that it exists so that the Boolean value for $in_footer will evaluate to true. Open the footer.php file. You should have a WordPress footer function call that looks like <? php wp_footer() ?>. If it is not located there, it is probably in the index file just above the closing </body> tag. The tag needs to be present in your theme.

Paste the following code within the functions.php file, just below the comment area at the beginning of the file:

```
if( !is_admin() ) {
wp_enqueue_script( 'my-theme', get_bloginfo('stylesheet_directory') .
'/js/my-theme.js', $in_footer);
}
```

Save the my_theme.js file and the functions.php file, and upload them to your current theme.

You should see an alert box appear, similar to the one shown below, when you visit your site:

The code that we just placed within the `functions.php` file will not load first in the head of the theme when the page is first requested. Instead, it will load in the footer, after all of the other scripts and images are ready. The alert box will then appear just before all other page information has been displayed. You can learn more about the `wp_enqueue_script` function in the WordPress codex, at: `http://codex.wordpress.org/Function_Reference/wp_enqueue_script`.

Taking advantage of wp_register_script

As mentioned previously, WordPress includes a function called `wp_register_script`. This function stores a script handle, URL, and options for use in the future.

This is useful in cases where you want to tell WordPress that a script is available for use, without immediately requesting it. It also simplifies the `wp_enqueue_script` declaration, making it easier to maintain multiple declarations, and reducing typos. The following code is usually placed within `functions.php`:

```php
<?php
/**
 * @package WordPress
 * @subpackage Classic_Theme
 */

automatic_feed_links();

if ( function_exists('register_sidebar') )
    register_sidebar(array(
        'before_widget' => '<li id="%1$s" class="widget %2$s">',
        'after_widget' => '</li>',
        'before_title' => '',
        'after_title' => '',
    ));
/* register script example */
```

```
wp_register_script('my-alerts', get_bloginfo('stylesheet_directory') .
'/js/my-alerts.js');
wp_register_script('my-colors', get_bloginfo('stylesheet_directory') .
'/js/my-colors.js');
wp_register_script('my-switch', get_bloginfo('stylesheet_directory') .
'/js/my-switch.js');

if( !is_admin() ) {
  wp_enqueue_script( 'my-alerts' );
}
?>
```

Here, we register three different script files that our theme can reference. Later on in the code sample, we'll check to determine that we are not on an admin page. The statement if (!is_admin()) must evaluate true for the my-alerts.js script to be called, meaning we must be on a front-end page of the site

Adding a bundled library to your theme programmatically

As mentioned in the introduction to this chapter, WordPress comes bundled with a bevy of useful scripts and libraries. Because of WordPress' JavaScript functions (covered in the recipe *Adding JavaScript files to your theme programmatically*), you can use these bundled scripts with very little effort.

Getting started

You need to have created a WordPress theme that contains at least a style.css file and on index.php file. Inside the template file containing your theme's <head> tag, you need to call the wp_head function. For this recipe, we'll assume that you want to use the jQuery library in your theme. jQuery is quite powerful, and is bundled with WordPress.

How to do it...

Open or create your theme's functions.php file, and add the following code inside a PHP block:

```
If( !is_admin() ) {
  wp_enqueue_script( 'jquery');
}
```

Now load your WordPress site with your theme activated. Go to **View | Page Source**, and you should see a script reference similar to the following:

```
<script type='text/javascript' src='http://wp.local/wp-includes/js/
jquery/jquery.js?ver=1.3.2'></script>
```

How it works...

When WordPress loads, it automatically registers a wide range of JavaScript files that it uses internally. By default, none of these scripts are enqueued on the front-end of the site. However, as the theme author, you can make the decision to enqueue any one of them.

Here, you enqueued the jQuery framework for your theme. Because the jQuery framework had been previously registered when WordPress loaded, all you had to do was pass the handle name that WordPress had used when registering it. You did not have to specify the location of the framework, or any other information about the script file, or how it should be loaded.

There's more...

There are many more tools and JavaScript libraries that are available for use in WordPress. Taking advantage of these tools can increase the appeal and functionality of your theme.

List of bundled scripts

As stated previously, WordPress comes bundled with a bevy of utility scripts and JavaScript frameworks that you can use in your theme. At the time of writing, the following script handles are registered when WordPress loads. You can use any one of them by simply calling `wp_enqueue_script( $handle )` in your `functions.php` file.

- utils
- common
- sack
- quicktags
- colorpicker
- editor
- prototype
- wp-ajax-response
- autosave
- wp-lists
- scriptaculous-root
- scriptaculous-builder

- scriptaculous-dragdrop
- scriptaculous-effects
- scriptaculous-slider
- scriptaculous-sound
- scriptaculous-controls
- scriptaculous
- cropper
- jquery
- jquery-ui-core
- jquery-ui-tabs
- jquery-ui-sortable
- jquery-ui-draggable
- jquery-ui-droppable
- jquery-ui-selectable
- jquery-ui-resizable
- jquery-ui-dialog
- jquery-form
- jquery-color
- interface
- suggest
- schedule
- jquery-hotkeys
- jquery-table-hotkeys
- thickbox
- jcrop
- swfobject
- swfupload
- swfupload-swfobject
- swfupload-queue
- swfupload-speed
- comment-reply

If you want further information on the file that any particular handle refers to, you can examine the source of the file located at `wp-includes/script-loader.php`.

▶ *Adding JavaScript files to your theme programmatically*

Creating a featured post slider

One of the most popular uses of JavaScript on a WordPress site is to create a content slider that shows particular types of posts or media. Some of the most popular sites use this effect, including eBay, Amazon, and ESPN.

Getting started

For this recipe, you need to have already created a theme, and decided where you'd like to put your featured content slider. In addition, you should have a special category that you assign to posts that you want to be featured.

How to do it...

First, you need to identify which set of posts will be part of your featured content slider. For the purposes of this recipe, we're going to assume that you assign all featured posts a category of `Featured`, which has a category `ID` of 3. Next, you need to create a file to hold the code. Create a file, and name it `featured-slider-markup.php`.

Now, to define the markup for the featured content slider, open the `featured-slider-markup.php` file, and insert the following code:

```php
<?php
$featured_query = new WP_Query(array('cat'=>3,'posts_per_page'=>4));
if( $featured_query->have_posts() ) { ?>
<div id="featured-posts-container">
  <ul id="featured-posts-tabs">
    <?php while( $featured_query->have_posts() ) {
                              $featured_query->the_post(); ?>
    <li><a href="#featured-post-<?php the_ID(); ?>" id="featured-post-
        selector-<?php the_ID(); ?>"><?php the_title(); ?></a></li>
    <?php } ?>
  </ul>
  <?php $featured_query->rewind_posts(); ?>
  <?php while( $featured_query->have_posts() ) {
                              $featured_query->the_post(); ?>
    <div id="featured-post-<?php the_ID(); ?>">
      <h3><a href="<?php the_permalink(); ?>"><?php the_title(); ?>
                                                  </a></h3>
      <div>
```

```
            <?php the_excerpt(); ?>
        </div>
    </div>
    <?php } ?>
</div><?php } ?>
```

Save the file and upload it to the server.

The featured content slider code now needs to be called on a theme page. Most sliders are either on the index page or in the sidebar. We will place it on the index page in this example, just above the WordPress post loop and below the opening `<body>` tag and any `<div id="content">` opening tags. To do this, we need to call the `featured-slider-markup.php` file that we created earlier. Insert the code shown next:

```
<!-- /featured content slider is called here/-->
<div id="featuredwrapper">
<?php if(is_home()){include('featured-slider-markup.php'); }?>
</div>
<!--/ featured content slider ends/ -->
```

Save the `index.php` file.

To enable the slider, you need to create a JavaScript file and then reference it. First, open your theme's containing folder, and create a new directory called `js`. Inside of the `js` folder, create a file named `featured-slider.js`. Open `featured-slider.js`, and insert the following code:

```
jQuery(document).ready(function() {
  jQuery('#featured-posts-container').tabs(
    {
      fx: {
        opacity: 'toggle',
        duration: 'normal'
      }
    }
  ).tabs('rotate', 5000);
});
```

Now that the JavaScript file has been created, you need to reference it. You'll do this the WordPress way, by using `wp_enqueue_script`. Insert the following code into your `functions.php` file, inside a PHP block:

```
wp_enqueue_script( 'featured-slider', get_bloginfo('stylesheet_
directory') . '/js/featured-slider.js', array( 'jquery', 'jquery-ui-
core', 'jquery-ui-tabs' ) );
```

Finally, you need to add the appropriate styles to get the content item looking good. Open your theme's `style.css` file, and add the following style declarations:

```
#featuredpwrapper{
width: 30em;
border: 0.1em solid #2b2b2b;
margin-bottom: 2em;
}
.ui-tabs-hide {
  display: none;
}

#featured-posts-tabs {
  width: 20%;
  float: right;
  padding:5px;
  font-size:10px;}
```

Now load the page in your browser. If you've done everything correctly, you should see something similar to the following screenshot:

In this example, the `title` and `excerpt` from each of the four featured posts fades in and out in turn.

How it works...

There are a lot of moving parts in this recipe, so let's go through them one at a time.

First, you created the necessary markup in your template file. Generally, you'll want to separate this markup into a new file, such as `featured-slider-markup.php`, and then use the PHP include construct `<?php if(is_home()){include('featured-slider-markup.php'); }?>` to check if the current page is the home page, by using `is_home()`, and then include the `featured-slider-markup.php` file into the main template page. This helps considerably with organization.

In the `featured-slider-markup.php` code, you created a new `WP_Query` object that loads up to four posts from a category with the `ID` of `3` (in our recipe, we assumed this was the `Featured` category; hover your mouse over the name of your preferred category in the admin panel to verify your category ID). Then, you used the standard loop functions `while(` `$featured_query->have_posts())` to iterate over the posts in this query, creating a list of items for the posts. Then, you called `rewind_posts` on the query object so that you can iterate over the posts again. This time, you displayed the `title` and `excerpt` from each post inside a `<div>` tag.

After the markup was complete, you created the JavaScript necessary for the operation of the featured content slider, saving it in a separate folder within the theme. When the theme file is rendered, the previous code outputs the appropriate markup that you need for the slider. If a visitor does not have JavaScript enabled, then the links will show up as a nice set of post titles.

You took advantage of the `jQuery` and `jQuery UI` libraries bundled with WordPress, and utilized the `jQuery UI Tabs` functionality. `jQuery UI Tabs` has a bundle of available options. In this instance, you used the `fx` parameter to specify a custom animation, and the `rotate` option to specify that the tabs should be rotated every `5000 milliseconds`. For more on using `jQuery UI Tabs`, please see `http://docs.jquery.com/UI/Tabs`.

Next, you needed to reference the JavaScript file that you created. You did this using the `wp_enqueue_script` function. For more information on this function, please see the recipe *Adding JavaScript files to your theme programmatically*.

Finally, you added a few styles to the `style.css` file in order to control the layout and appearance of the content slider. The `#featuredwrapper` div positioned the content slider and gave it a defined border. The `.ui-tabs-hide` class hid tabs that shouldn't be showing at a particular time. The `#featured-posts-tabs` div floated the tab selector to the right for a nice appearance, as well as adding padding to the tabs and decreasing the font size of the text within the tabs. After all of these steps, you ended up with a functionally-complete content-featured content rotator.

Building on this, you can style the content rotator however you want: add images and display any post information that your heart desires. For inspiration, try searching on Google for **beautiful content sliders**. The examples that you can find can help you to create a stunning way to feature your best content.

There's more...

There is much more that can be done with this basic content slider. The `jQuery UI Tabs` does come with its own styles, to create nice looking tabs, but you will probably want to create your own look.

Theming your slider with Themeroller

You can quickly generate great-looking designs for your content slider and other jQuery-based objects, by using Themeroller.

Go to `http://jqueryui.com/themeroller/` and begin clicking on the color pickers and other tools on the left-hand side of the page to customize the widgets (including a tabbed box) that appear on the right. You can also click on the **Gallery** link to choose from an already-designed theme. After playing with several of the options, your screen should look similar to the one shown next:

Now click on the **Download theme** button. It will take you to the **Build Your Download** screen on which you can finalize your choices. Just stick to the default settings, and click on **Download** on the right-hand side of the screen.

A window will appear to verify where you want to save the zipped theme file. Save it locally on your computer. Open the zipped folder and you will find a complete bundle of sample scripts, CSS theme files, and jQuery JavaScript files.

Try out the different examples in your favourite HTML editor and browser. All of the examples have an index page that will instantly load them so that you can test their behaviour locally. Be sure to examine the CSS files contained within the `/themes/base/` folder, particularly `jquery.ui.theme.css`. This is where you can experiment by changing colors and other style declarations.

Enjoy the many options that jQuery gives you to control the look and behaviour of your interactive page elements.

See also

▶ *Adding JavaScript files to your theme programmatically*

Making sidebar widgets toggle-able

The extensible nature of widgets and sidebars in WordPress opens those items up to a whole range of possibilities when it comes to making them dynamic. One of the easiest and most noticeable things that you can do is to modify your widgets so that users are able to interact with them. Even the rudimentary interaction provided in this recipe can go a long way to increasing user participation with the site that your theme is deployed on.

Getting started

You need to have a theme created with at least one sidebar registered.

How to do it...

First, you need to change the parameters that you are passing to your sidebar registration function. Find the declaration for your sidebar (usually contained within the `functions.php` file) and change the code to the following:

```
register_sidebar(array(
    'before_widget' => '<li id="%1$s" class="widget %2$s">',
    'after_widget' => '</div></li>',
    'before_title' => '<h2 class="widgettitle">',
    'after_title' => '</h2><div>',
));
```

You'll see that this differs from the default WordPress sidebar arguments in that a `<div>` start tag has been appended to the `after_title` argument, and a `</div>` end tag has been prepended to the `after_widget` argument. Doing this causes all widget contents to be enclosed by a `div` tag that we can use for manipulation.

Now, you need to create the JavaScript code that controls slide toggling. First, create a new folder in the directory containing your theme, called `js`. In the `js` directory, create and open a new file called `widget-slide-toggle.js`. Inside the `widget-slide-toggle.js` file, put the following code:

```
jQuery(document).ready(function() {
jQuery('.widget h2.widgettitle').click(function(event) {
  event.preventDefault();
  jQuery(this).siblings('div:first').toggle();
});
});
```

Now, to make sure this JavaScript gets run, we need to reference it. Ensure that your `<head>` tag has a call to `wp_head` within it, and then open or create your theme's `functions.php` file. Inside the `functions.php` file, place the following code:

```
<?php wp_enqueue_script( 'widget-slide-toggle', get_
bloginfo('stylesheet_directory') . '/js/widget-slide-toggle.js',
array( 'jquery' ) ); ?>
```

Now, load your WordPress admin panel and put some widgets in the sidebar for your theme. Load any page that displays your sidebar, and click on the widget title for any widget. You'll see the content of the widget slide up or slide down, based on how many times you've clicked on the title.

You can see the before and after results in the following screenshot:

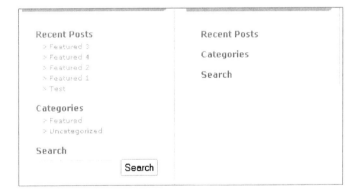

How it works...

This is a perfect example of how a little bit of markup and a little bit of JavaScript can make a big difference. First, you added a little bit of extra markup to your theme's sidebar. This markup encloses each widget's content inside an extra `<div>` position, as a sibling to the widget's title.

After this, you added a reference to a script that contained a small bit of jQuery. The jQuery contains a statement binding an event handler to the click event on each widget's title. When a user clicks on the title of a widget, the specified event handler fires, causing the browser to toggle the state of the first `div` adjacent to the title. Because of the extra markup that we registered with the sidebar in the `functions.php` file, this `div` is always guaranteed to surround the content of the widget.

There's more...

The sidebar widgets expand again each time the page is reloaded. This is not ideal if you want users to have the satisfaction of seeing their changes persist on the page.

Remembering the widget's state

As it is currently implemented, the slide toggle only persists during a single page load. If you want to remember the widget's state between page loads, you can take advantage of a great jQuery plugin called jQuery Cookie. Download the jQuery plugin from `http://plugins.jquery.com/project/cookie`, and put the JavaScript file into your theme's `js` directory. Then place the jQuery Cookie enqueue script below the widget slide toggle enqueue script:

```
wp_enqueue_script( 'jquery-cookie', get_bloginfo('stylesheet_
directory') . '/js/jquery.cookie.js', array( 'jquery' ) );
```

After enqueuing the Cookie plugin, change the contents of your `widget-slide-toggle.js` file to the following code:

```
jQuery(document).ready(function() {
  jQuery('.widget').each(function() {
    var widgetId = jQuery(this).attr('id');
    var slideStatus = jQuery.cookie('slide-status-'+widgetId);
    if( slideStatus == 'hidden' ) {
jQuery(this).find('h2.widgettitle').siblings('div:first').hide();
    }
  });
  jQuery('.widget h2.widgettitle').click(function(event) {
    event.preventDefault();
    jQuery(this).siblings('div:first').slideToggle('normal',
    function() {
      var widgetId = jQuery(this).parents('.widget').attr('id');
      if(jQuery(this).is(':visible')) {
        jQuery.cookie('slide-status-'+widgetId,'visible',{
                                        path: '/', expires: 10 });
      } else {
        jQuery.cookie('slide-status-'+widgetId,'hidden',{
                                        path: '/', expires: 10 });
      }
    });
  });
});
```

Now, when a user toggles a widget's state and returns to the page later, the state will be restored. That is, if the user hid the widget, it will be hidden on page load. Otherwise, the widget will be shown.

Adding a font size toggle

Using JavaScript to create fancy animations and add unnecessary but interesting interaction is great. However, the real boon comes when you use it to provide users with something that helps them to use your site, and that emphasizes your content.

How to do it...

First, you need to decide what text you want to be able to resize. For every element that you want resizable text in, add the `text-resizable` class. In this example, let's set the post content to be resizable, within the WordPress loop in the `index.php` file, placing the `font-resizable` opening `div` tag just above the `entry-content` opening `div` tag, then closing both tags, as shown in the following code:

```
<!-- make the content entry text resizable --> <div class="font-
resizable">
        <div class="entry-content">

<?php the_content( __( 'Read More <span class="meta-nav">&raquo;</
span>', 'sandbox' ) ) ?>

        <?php wp_link_pages('before=<div class="page-link">'
                . __( 'Pages:', 'sandbox' ) . '&after=</div>') ?>
        </div><!-- end post content entry -->
                                        </div><!-- #text resize-->
```

In addition, you need to create two links with the IDs `increase-font-size` and `decrease-font-size`. You can put these links anywhere on your page. We will place ours just below the opening `content` div tag, within the `index.php` file. Do not place this within the WordPress loop.

```
<p>Font Size:
   <a id="increase-font-size" href="#">[+]</a>/<a id="decrease-font-
size" href="#">[-]</a> </p>
```

Let's have a quick preview of what the font resize links will look like once they are live on the site:

Font Size: [+]/[-]

Now you need to create the JavaScript code that controls text resizing. First, create a new folder in the directory containing your theme, and call it `js`. Inside the `js` directory, create and open a new file called `text-resize.js`. In the `text-resize.js` file, put the following code:

```javascript
jQuery(document).ready(function() {
  jQuery('#increase-font-size').click(function(event) {
    event.preventDefault();
    jQuery('.font-resizable').each(function() {
                                    changeFontSize(this, change); });
  });
  jQuery('#decrease-font-size').click(function(event) {
    event.preventDefault();
    jQuery('.font-resizable').each(function() {
                                    changeFontSize(this, -change); });
  });
});

var min = 8, max = 32, change = 2;

function changeFontSize(element, value) {
  var currentSize = parseFloat(jQuery(element).css('font-size'));
  var newSize = currentSize + value;

  if (newSize <= max && newSize >= min) {
    jQuery(element).css('font-size', newSize + 'px');
  }
}
```

Now, to make sure that this JavaScript gets run, we need to reference it. Ensure that your `<head>` tag has a call to `wp_head` within it, and then open or create your theme's `functions.php` file. Inside the `functions.php` file, place the following code:

```php
wp_enqueue_script( 'text-resize', get_bloginfo('stylesheet_directory')
. '/js/text-resize.js', array( 'jquery' ) );
```

Then load your WordPress site and click on the [+] or [-] links. You'll see the text resize appropriately for every element with the appropriate class, as seen in the following screenshot:

Twitter Tools for WordPress

March 26, 2010 – 4:25 pm

Twitter tools is a multipurpose plugin that gives blog authors the ability to send blog posts as tweets by category, set hash tags, and display Twitter information in other areas of a site.

By Lee | Posted in Featured, Tutorials | Tagged Tutorials | Edit
| Comments (0)

Twitter Tools for WordPress

March 26, 2010 – 4:25 pm

Twitter tools is a multipurpose plugin that gives blog authors the ability to send blog posts as tweets by category, set hash tags, and display Twitter information in other areas of a site.

By Lee | Posted in Featured, Tutorials | Tagged Tutorials | Edit
| Comments (0)

How it works...

In this example, we used jQuery to resize the text within posts on the home page. Whenever the [-] or [+] font size links were clicked, the text resized from 8 to 32 pixels in increments of 2 pixels. First, we identified an area that we wanted to be resizable—in this case, any post content text on the home page—and created a div tag called text-resizable to wrap around the entry-content tags. This created a container that jQuery could then affect.

Next, we added our font resize links to index.php, just below the main opening content div, outside of the WordPress post loop. This placed the links near the top of the page, a location where people are used to seeing resizable text links.

Then we created a JavaScript file named text-resize.js to contain the functions for the resize actions. The (document).ready(function() verified that the page was loaded, and then allowed the text size to be decreased or increased. Next, the variable var min was created and defined, to control the range of font size values. The function changeFontSize(element, value) accepted two parameters: element and value. This allowed the function to determine what to resize and what size the element should become.

Finally, we referenced the text-resize.js script within functions.php, by using wp_enqueue_script. This contained the parameter array('jquery') that also indicated to WordPress that the text-resize script had a dependency on the jQuery library in order for it to function properly, and allowed us to make sure that the jQuery library was loaded to handle any hard labor. Once the files were all uploaded, clicking on the text resize links clearly caused all of the text within post entries on the home page to resize.

11
Advanced WordPress Themes

In this chapter, we will cover:

- ▶ Adding a theme options page
- ▶ Allowing for multiple theme color schemes
- ▶ Changing the default Gravatar icon for your theme
- ▶ Registering shortcodes for your theme
- ▶ Localizing your theme
- ▶ Displaying information based on the logged-in user's role
- ▶ Packaging your theme for distribution
- ▶ Uploading your theme to the WordPress.org theme repository

Introduction

Creating a basic WordPress theme is great. You learn about *The Loop*, find the appropriate template tags to display the information that you want, and then you write some HTML and CSS to tie it all together. However, there comes a time when you're ready to take your themes to the next level. That is what this chapter is all about.

In this chapter, you'll learn how to provide your theme's users with options about what is displayed and how is displayed. You'll also learn about localizing your theme for an international audience and showing users information based on their current role.

Finally, this chapter covers the essentials for packaging and distributing your theme via the WordPress.org theme repository. You'll need to follow a few simple steps to make sure that your theme is accepted and that it provides users with the best possible experience.

Adding a theme options page

As a theme developer, you have to make a lot of choices when you create a theme. What text should be displayed in certain locations? Will that text always be appropriate? How many posts should you display in a featured item carousel? How many levels should the nested navigation menu have?

Part of being a good developer is knowing when to make these decisions for your theme's users, and when to give the users a choice. Many WordPress users are not comfortable with editing PHP files, so you need to provide some other way for users to make these choices. The best way, in the context of a WordPress theme, is to provide the users with a theme options panel.

Getting started

You need to have created a WordPress theme containing at least a `style.css` file and an `index.php` file.

How to do it...

First, you need to decide what choice you want to give your users. In this recipe, we're going to assume that you want users to be able to change the color of the name of their site, which is located in the site header.

Next, you have to create the `options` page that lets users make their choice and save it. Open your theme's directory and create a new directory inside it called `admin`. Inside the `admin` directory, create a file called `options.php`.

Open the `options.php` file, and insert the following code:

```php
<?php
$settings = $this->get_settings();
?>
<div class="wrap">
  <h2><?php _e('My Theme Options' ); ?></h2>
  <?php if('1'==$_GET['updated']) { ?>
  <div id="my-theme-options-updated" class="updated fade"><p><?php _e(
'Settings saved!' ); ?></p></div>
  <?php } ?>
  <form method="post">
```

```
<table class="form-table">
  <tbody>
    <tr>
      <th scope="row"><label for="custom-theme-header-color">
                         <?php _e('Header Color'); ?></label></th>
      <td>
        #<input type="text" class="regular-text"
             name="custom-theme-header-color"
             id="custom-theme-header-color"
             value="<?php echo esc_attr( $settings[
                                   'header-color' ] ); ?>" />
      </td>
    </tr>
  </tbody>
</table>
<p class="submit">
  <?php wp_nonce_field( 'custom-theme-save-options' ); ?>
  <input type="submit" class="button-primary"
       name="custom-theme-save-options"
       id="custom-theme-save-options"
       value="<?php _e( 'Save' ); ?>" />
</p>
  </form>
</div>
```

This file contains all of the code necessary for the theme options page.

The next thing that you need to do is to hook the admin page into the WordPress administrative menu. Open or create your theme's `functions.php` file and insert the following code:

```
if (!class_exists('My_Theme')) {
    class My_Theme {

        var $settings = null;

        function My_Theme() {
            add_action('admin_init', array(&$this, 'save_settings'));
            add_action('admin_menu', array(&$this, 'add_admin_stuff'));
        }

        function add_admin_stuff() {
            add_theme_page( __('My Theme'), __('My Theme'),
            'switch_themes', 'my-theme', array(&$this,
            'display_theme_admin_page'));
        }

        function display_theme_admin_page() {
            include (TEMPLATEPATH.'/admin/options.php');
        }
```

```
        function save_settings() {
            if (isset($_POST['custom-theme-save-options']) &&
check_admin_referer('custom-theme-save-options') && current_user_
can('switch_themes')) {
                $settings = $this->get_settings();
                $settings['header-color'] = stripslashes($_
POST['custom-theme-header-color']);
                $this->set_settings($settings);
                wp_redirect(admin_url('themes.php?page=my-
theme&updated=1'));
            }
        }


        function get_settings() {
            if (null === $this->settings) {
                $this->settings = get_option('My Theme Custom
Settings', array());
            }
            return $this->settings;
        }


        function set_settings($settings) {
            if (is_array($settings)) {
                $this->settings = $settings;
                update_option('My Theme Custom Settings', $this-
>settings);
            }
        }

    }

    $my_theme = new My_Theme();
    function get_custom_theme_header_color() {
        global $my_theme;
        $settings = $my_theme->get_settings();
        $color = $settings['header-color'];
        if(empty($color)) {
            $color = '000000';
        }
        return $color;
    }
    function the_custom_theme_header_color() {
        echo get_custom_theme_header_color();
    }
}
```

This file hooks into two different WordPress administrative hooks. First, you add the administrative menu page by hooking into `admin_menu`. Then, you hook to `admin_init` to process and save the custom options present on the custom admin page.

After you save these files, go to your administrative menu and look at the sidebar on the left-hand side under the **Appearance** heading. You should see a **My Theme** link, as shown in the following screenshot:

Now, click on the **My Theme** link under the **Appearance** menu heading. If you've done everything correctly, you should see a page that looks like the following screenshot:

Enter a value such as `99000` and click on the **Save** button, and you'll see a **Settings saved!** success message, as seen in the following screenshot:

Now, you need to use your custom value somewhere in your theme. Open up your theme header (usually `header.php` or `index.php`) and insert the following code between the opening and closing `<head>` tags:

```
<h1 style="color:#<?php the_custom_theme_header_color(); ?>;"><?php
bloginfo(); ?></h1>
```

View your site in a browser to see the change in color of the site title (this is usually the only text that uses the `<h1>` tag) with the custom option set to hexadecimal color value `990000`:

Test WordPress

Now, whatever value you set for the custom option that we created will be used as the color for the site title.

How it works...

There are quite a few moving parts here, so let's go through them one by one. First, you created the administrative page. This was saved to `/yourthemefolder/admin/options.php`. This file contains all of the items contained on a typical WordPress admin page:

- A containing `<div>` with the `wrap` class
- A `<h2>` tag with the custom theme options title
- A form that posts back to itself
- Form elements arranged inside a `<table>` with the `form-table` class

With all of these elements in place, you get a slick looking administrative page that blends in with the rest of the WordPress admin control panel.

Next, you created a small script within the `functions.php` file that hooks the administrative menu into place and saves the options when the page is posted. You hooked to `admin_menu` to add the administrative page and `admin_init` to save the options using the WordPress `add_action()` function that accepts a key value pair of the named action as a descriptive string and the actual action to take place. Your custom options are saved when three conditions are met:

1. The form posts back to itself.
2. The system verifies the security nonce from the form.
3. The currently logged-in user has the ability to switch themes (usually just the blog administrator).

The options are saved as an array to the WordPress options table by using the `update_option` function. When you need to retrieve the options, you call `get_option` and pass the appropriate key.

In addition to the hooks that provide the core functionality of this script, you created two template tags. The tag `the_custom_theme_header_color()` allowed you to access, and `get_custom_theme_header_color()` allowed you to print the values you stored on the custom options page.

Finally, you used the template tags that you created to take advantage of your custom option on the front-end by adding `<?php _the_custom_theme_header_color(); ?>;` to the style of the `<h1>` tag that controls the color and size of the blog title. In this particular instance, you're allowing your theme's users to modify the color of the theme's header. However, endless possibilities exist as you become more familiar with WordPress, and by expanding the options, you allow your users to modify your themes.

There's more...

You can add additional theme option settings to customize how users can edit your theme.

Diving into administrative settings for themes

Visit the WordPress codex at `http://codex.wordpress.org/Function_Reference` to learn more about the functions available to you for creating custom theme edit forms in the administrative area of WordPress.

Allowing for multiple theme color schemes

In the previous recipe, we covered the general way in which you provide your theme's users with an options page. In this recipe, you'll implement one of the most straightforward features that many premium themes possess: a theme color scheme chooser.

Getting started

You need to have created a WordPress theme containing at least a `style.css` file and an `index.php` file. Inside the template file containing your theme's `<head>` tag, you need to call the `wp_head` function.

How to do it...

You're going to be controlling the color schemes that users can select, by putting each one in a different CSS file. As such, the first thing that you have to do is to create these files. Open your theme's directory and create a new directory named `schemes`. Inside the `schemes` directory, create the files `blue.css`, `red.css`, and `green.css`. They should contain the following styles:

```
@charset "utf-8";
/* Blue.CSS Color Schemes Document Chapter 11 Example 2 */
body{
  color:#00f; /* very bright medium blue*/
  background-color:#99ccff; /* light blue*/}
/* theme links*/
a., a:link, a:hover, a:visited {}
```

```css
a., a:link{color:#000099;} /* medium dark blue*/
a:hover{color: #0066FF;} /* bright medium blue*/
a:visited{color:#000099;}
/* blog title styles*/
h1.blog-title, h1.blog-title a{
  color:#000033; /* dark blue*/
  text-decoration:none;}

#header a {
  color: #000033;
  text-decoration: none;
}

#header a:hover {
  color: #0066FF;
  text-decoration: underline;}

#header a:visited{color:#000099;}

h2{
  color:#003399; /* medium  blue*/
  text-decoration:none;}
  #header{
    background:none;
    font-family:arial, verdana, sans-serif;
  }

h2 a {
  color:#003399;/* medium blue */
  text-decoration:none;}
h3.storytitle, h3.storytitle a{
  color:#003399; /* medium blue*/
  text-decoration:none;}


@charset "utf-8";
/* Red.CSS Color Schemes Document Chapter 11 Example 2 */
body{
  color:#660000; /* dark red */
  background-color:#ffffcc; /* light orange-pink*/}
/* theme links*/
a., a:link, a:hover, a:visited {}
a., a:link{color:#ff0000;} /* bright red */
a:hover{color: #ff0033} /* bright pink */
a:visited{color:#ff0000;}
```

```
/* blog title styles*/
h1.blog-title, h1.blog-title a{
  color:#ff3333; /* medium pink-red*/
  text-decoration:none;}
#header a {
  color: #ff3333;
  text-decoration: none;
}

#header a:hover {
  color: #ff0033;
  text-decoration: underline;}

#header a:visited{color:#ff3333;}
h2{
  color:#660000; /* medium  medium dull red*/
  text-decoration:none;}
h2 a {
  color:#660000; /* medium  medium dull red*/
  text-decoration:none;}

h3.storytitle, h3.storytitle a{
  color:#ff3333; /* medium pink-red*/
  text-decoration:none;}


@charset "utf-8";
/* Green.CSS Color Schemes Document Chapter 11 Example 2 */
body{
  color:#009933; /* dull medium green*/
  background-color:#005826; /* dull dark green */}
/* theme links*/
a., a:link, a:hover, a:visited {}
a., a:link{color:#00ff00;} /* bright light neon green*/
a:hover{color: #33ff00;} /* bright green*/
a:visited{color:#00ff00;}
/* blog title styles*/
h1.blog-title, h1.blog-title a{
  color:#99cc99; /* light pale green */
  text-decoration:none;}
h2{
  color:#33cc66; /* medium  green */
  text-decoration:none;}

h2 a {
```

```
    color:#33cc66; /* medium  green*/
    text-decoration:none; }

  h3.storytitle, h3.storytitle a{
    color:#33cc66; /* medium green*/
    text-decoration:none; }
```

Next, you have to create the options page that lets users make their choice and save it. Open your theme's directory and create a new directory inside it called `admin`. Inside the `admin` directory, create a file called `options.php`.

Open the `options.php` file, and insert the following code:

```php
<?php
$settings = $this->get_settings();
$custom_schemes = $this->get_custom_themes();
?>
<div class="wrap">
  <h2><?php _e('My Theme Options' ); ?></h2>
  <?php if('1'==$_GET['updated']) { ?>
  <div id="my-theme-options-updated" class="updated fade">
                    <p><?php _e( 'Settings saved!' ); ?></p></div>
  <?php } ?>
  <form method="post">
    <table class="form-table">
      <tbody>
        <tr>
          <th scope="row"><label for="custom-theme-header-color">
                    <?php _e('Custom Color Scheme'); ?></label></th>
          <td>
            <select name="custom-theme-color">
              <option <?php selected( $settings[ 'color' ], '' ); ?>
                          value=""><?php _e('None'); ?></option>
              <?php foreach( (array)$custom_schemes as $key =>
                                                     $name ) { ?>
              <option <?php selected( $settings[ 'color' ], $key );
                      ?> value="<?php echo esc_attr($key);
                      ?>"><?php echo esc_html($name); ?></option>
              <?php } ?>
            </select>
          </td>
        </tr>
      </tbody>
    </table>
    <p class="submit">
      <?php wp_nonce_field( 'custom-theme-save-options' ); ?>
```

```
        <input type="submit" class="button-primary" name="custom-theme-
save-options" id="custom-theme-save-options" value="<?php _e( 'Save'
); ?>" />
    </p>
  </form>
</div>
```

This file contains all of the code necessary for the theme options page. This particular options page contains a `<select>` drop-down menu that displays the available color schemes to the theme's user.

The next thing that you need to do is to hook the admin page into the WordPress administrative menu. Open or create your themes `functions.php` file, and insert the following code:

```php
<?php
if (!class_exists('My_Theme')) {
    class My_Theme {

        var $settings = null;

        function My_Theme() {
            add_action('admin_init', array(&$this, 'save_settings'));
            add_action('admin_menu', array(&$this, 'add_admin_stuff'));
    add_action('init', array(&$this, 'enqueue_color_css'));
        }

        function add_admin_stuff() {
            add_theme_page(__('My Theme'), __('My Theme'),
            'switch_themes', 'my-theme', array(&$this,
            'display_theme_admin_page'));
        }

        function display_theme_admin_page() {
            include (TEMPLATEPATH.'/admin/options.php');
        }

    function enqueue_color_css() {
      $settings = $this->get_settings();
      if( !empty( $settings['color'] ) && !is_admin() ) {
        wp_enqueue_style( 'custom-theme-color',
        get_bloginfo( 'stylesheet_directory' ) . '/schemes/' .
        $settings[ 'color' ] );
      }
    }
  }

    function get_custom_themes() {
      $schemes_dir = TEMPLATEPATH . '/schemes/';
```

```
        $schemes = array();
        if( is_dir($schemes_dir) && is_readable( $schemes_dir ) ) {
          $dir = opendir($schemes_dir);
          while(false !== ($file = readdir($dir))) {
            if('.' != $file && '..' != $file) {
              $scheme_name = ucwords(str_replace(
                      array('-','_','.css'), array(' ',' ',''), $file));
              $schemes[$file] = $scheme_name;
            }
          }
        }
        return $schemes;
    }


    function save_settings() {
        if (isset($_POST['custom-theme-save-options'])
            && check_admin_referer('custom-theme-save-options')
            && current_user_can('switch_themes')) {
            $settings = $this->get_settings();
            $settings['color'] = stripslashes(
                            $_POST['custom-theme-color']);
            $this->set_settings($settings);
            wp_redirect(admin_url(
                    'themes.php?page=my-theme&updated=1'));
        }
    }


    function get_settings() {
        if (null === $this->settings) {
            $this->settings = get_option(
                        'My Theme Custom Settings', array());
        }
        return $this->settings;
    }


    function set_settings($settings) {
        if (is_array($settings)) {
            $this->settings = $settings;
            update_option('My Theme Custom Settings',
                                    $this->settings);
        }
    }

}

$my_theme = new My_Theme();
}
```

This file hooks into two different WordPress administrative hooks. First, you add the administrative menu page by hooking to `admin_menu`. Then, you hook to `admin_init` to process and save the custom options present on the custom admin page. Finally, you hook to the `init` hook to enqueue the custom CSS stylesheet the user has selected.

After you save these files, go to your administrative menu and look at the sidebar on the left-hand side, under the **Appearance** heading. You should see a **My Theme** link, as shown in the following screenshot:

Now, click on the **My Theme** link under the **Appearance** menu heading. If you've done everything correctly, you should see an administrative page that looks like the one shown in the following screenshot:

Select a value, such as `Red`, from the drop-down selection menu, and then click on the `Save` button. You'll see the **Settings saved!** message, as well as the chosen color scheme selected in the **Custom Color Scheme** drop-down menu.

Finally, you can view the results of the color scheme change by opening up your site in a browser window. In the following screenshot, you can see what the page header of each of the three color schemes will look like:

How it works...

You've done quite a few things in providing your theme's users with the ability to switch color schemes. First, you hooked a custom admin menu into the WordPress administrative interface, in order to provide a place for users to select their desired color scheme. You did this by taking advantage of the WordPress plugin API and the hooks `admin_menu` and `admin_init`.

You used the `admin_menu` hook to register your custom administrative page with a title of **My Theme**. After getting your administrative page to display, you allowed the user to save the values by using the `admin_init` hook to record the values in the WordPress database.

The most interesting part of the administrative menu that you created was the dynamic nature of the possible values in the `<select>` element. The `get_custom_themes` method opens the `schemes` directory located inside your theme. It then reads through all of the files in the schemes directory, sanitizes the filename, and provides these custom CSS files as options for the user to select. You can add or remove schemes in the future. Perhaps you want to give your users the option of using an ochre or monochrome color scheme. This is as easy as creating the files `ochre.css` and `monochrome.css` in your `schemes` directory. The system will automatically detect and offer these files as options to your theme's users.

The final WordPress hook that you took advantage of in this recipe is `init`. The `init` hook is fired after WordPress has initialized itself. Here, your hook callback checks to make sure that the user has chosen a color scheme and that a front-end page is being displayed. If both of these conditions are met, then the `wp_enqueue_style` function is used to enqueue the custom CSS file that your theme's user has chosen for their color scheme.

See also

▶ *Adding a theme options page*

Changing the default Gravatar icon for your theme

A great way to build a community around a blog is to allow the users to personally identify themselves, either as authors or when commenting. Luckily, WordPress has built-in support for user avatars, by using the Gravatar service. Unfortunately, not all users have registered their e-mail address with Gravatar.com and they get stuck with a boring mystery man outline.

Luckily, WordPress allows administrators to change the default Gravatar for users who don't have them, and allows theme authors to provide custom defaults when their theme is active.

Getting started

You need to have created a WordPress theme containing at least a `style.css` file and an `index.php` file. Also, you should be using the `get_avatar` function somewhere within your theme. The `wp_list_comments` function uses the `get_avatar` function, so most themes satisfy this requirement.

How to do it...

First, you have to decide what your custom avatar for unknown users is going to be. The following smiley avatar will be used for the purposes of this recipe:

After you've selected the avatar that you'd like to use for unknown users, open your theme's directory and create a subdirectory named `images`. Inside the `images` directory, place the image file that you're going to use as your avatar, naming it something like `avatar.jpg`.

Next, open your administrative menu and go to **Settings | Discussion**. Scroll to the bottom of the page and look at the current list of possible default avatars. This should look like the example shown in the following screenshot:

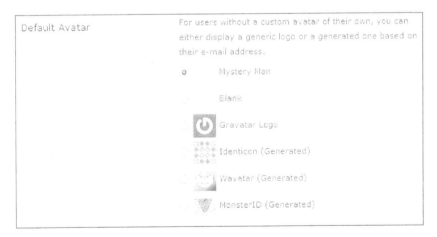

Now, open or create your theme's `functions.php` file. Inside this file, insert the following code:

```
add_filter( 'avatar_defaults', 'add_my_theme_default_avatar' );

function add_my_theme_default_avatar($avatars) {
  $avatars[get_bloginfo('stylesheet_directory') . '/images/avatar.
jpg'] = __( 'My Theme Avatar' );
  return $avatars;
}
```

Save the `functions.php` file and reload the **Settings | Discussion** page. You should see something similar to the following screenshot:

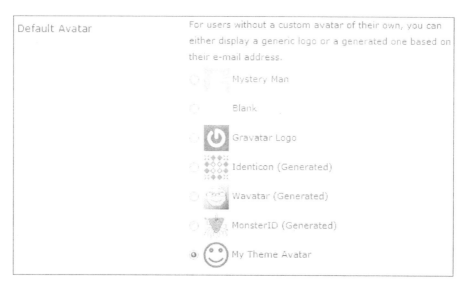

The previous screenshot shows that your custom avatar has been added to the avatar options.

Select your theme avatar and save the discussion options. Then, when an unknown user has their avatar displayed on the frontend of the site, it will look something like the following screenshot:

How it works...

Providing a custom avatar is a simple matter of hooking to the correct filter and returning the correct values. Here, you hook to the `avatar_defaults` filter. Your callback function receives an array of avatars that WordPress and other plugins provide. You add an `array` item by using your image location as the `key` and your avatar description string `My Theme Avatar` as the array value.

In this instance, the key is a `URL` to an image located in the theme's `images` directory, and the description is the string `My Theme Avatar`. Of course, after you provide the default avatar, the theme's user still has to select it for it to become active.

There's more...

Sometimes, either for design purposes or as part of other project requirements, you may want to have more control over when and how your avatar is used.

Forcing your theme to use your default avatar

Although it is great to give the user a choice, sometimes you just want to make sure that the theme uses your custom default avatar. This is appropriate in cases where your end user doesn't have a lot of technical expertise, or you are setting up a site for someone and don't want to let them change the default avatar while your theme is active.

Open or create a `functions.php` file, and insert the following code:

```
add_filter('avatar_defaults', 'add_my_theme_default_avatar');
add_filter('pre_option_avatar_default', 'force_my_theme_default_
avatar');
function add_my_theme_default_avatar($avatars) {
  return array();
}
function force_my_theme_default_avatar($value) {
  return get_bloginfo('stylesheet_directory') . '/images/avatar.jpg';
}
```

Save and upload the `functions.php` file to your server.

Within the `functions.php` file, you're doing a few things. First, with the preceding code, you remove all the options from the default avatar options selection on the **Settings | Discussion** menu.

This results in the screen displaying no avatar choices to the user as shown in the following screenshot:

Next, you're overriding the `get_option` return value when the option being fetched is `default_avatar`. In this case, you're overriding the return value by providing the URL to your own custom avatar.

Registering shortcodes for your theme

If you've ever used forum bbcode, then WordPress shortcodes should look very familiar to you. In an earlier chapter recipe, we used the `[gallery]` shortcode to specify the number of columns for a post photo gallery. You can add your own custom shortcodes to the `functions.php` file of your theme in order to add easy functionality for theme users.

In this recipe, we will create a permalink shortcode so that the theme users can quickly add permalinks to posts that will automatically update if those links change.

How to do it...

First, open up or create a `functions.php` file. This is where we will add the permalink shortcode function and register our permalink shortcode.

Next, enter the following code to create the permalink shortcode:

```
/* Chapter 11 permalink shortcode starts here */
function do_permalink($atts) {
  extract(shortcode_atts(array(
    'id' => 1,
    'text' => ""  // default value if none supplied
  ), $atts));

  if ($text) {
    $url = get_permalink($id);
    return "<a href='$url'>$text</a>";
  } else {
    return get_permalink($id);
  }
```

```
    }
    add_shortcode('permalink', 'do_permalink');

/* closing shortcode example */
```

Now, register the shortcode within the `functions.php` file, so that it can be added to posts, by placing the `add_shortcode()` tag below the preceding code. It will accept two parameters: the value of the shortcode itself (`permalink`) and `do_permalink`, which is the name of the function creating the shortcode. The following example shows how they should look:

```
add_shortcode('permalink','do_permalink');
```

The custom shortcode permalink is now ready to be added to posts. To test it, create a new post and enter a link by using the `permalink id` of another post:

```
<a href="[permalink id=57]">Creating Post Thumbnail Images for Every
Post</a>
```

View the post in your browser. The custom permalink shortcode will now cause the permalink to appear in the post as shown in the next screenshot:

Testing a custom shortcode

April 4, 2010 – 2:53 am

I've created a custom shortcode that allows me to quickl

Creating Post Thumbnail Images for Every Post

By Lee | Posted in Tutorials | Edit | Comments (0)

There's more...

You can examine the `shortcodes.php` file provided by WordPress in the `wp-includes` folder. There is a lot more to learn about shortcodes, and a great place to dig deeper is the shortcode API in the WordPress codex, at: `http://codex.wordpress.org/Shortcode_API`.

Displaying Twitter trends by using shortcodes in posts

Aaron Jorbin has created a series of shortcodes that you can use to add quick Twitter functionality to the post pages of your theme.

First, open up your `functions.php` file, and create the custom shortcode function by adding the following code to the file:

```php
<?php
/*
Name: Jorbin Twitter Trends Shortcodes  URI: http://aaron.jorb.in/
Description: Shortcodes I use - Twitter Trends
Author: Aaron Jorbin Version: 0.0
Author URI: http://aaron.jorb.in/       License: GPL2
*/
function jorbin_twitter_trends(){

  $transient='twitter-trends';
  $url = 'http://search.twitter.com/trends.json';

  if ( $tweet_display = get_transient($transient) ){

  }
  else{
    $search = wp_remote_get( $url );

    $results = json_decode($search['body']);
    $trends = $results->trends;
    ob_start();
      echo "<ul class='twitter-trends'>";
      foreach ($trends as $trend){
        echo '<li><a href="' . esc_url($trend->url) .
                        '"> '. esc_html($trend->name) . '</a></li>';
      }
      echo "</ul>";
    $tweet_display = ob_get_clean();
    set_transient($transient, $tweet_display, 120);
  }
  return $tweet_display;
}
?>
```

Now register the shortcode by placing the `add_shortcode()` function in the `functions.php` file. It accepts two parameters: the shortcode value as a string, and the name of the shortcode function as a string.

```php
add_shortcode(__('twitter-trends'),'jorbin_twitter_trends');
```

Save the file, and upload it to your server. You can now include the shortcode [twitter-trends] in a post. It should result in a post that looks similar to the following screenshot:

Check out these Twitter Trends!

April 6, 2010 – 2:33 am

I'm using Jorbin's Twitter trends shortcode to display some trends on Twitter:

- #ZodiacFacts
- #NowPlaying
- #iwishicould
- #whatsThePoint
- #stoplying
- Justin Bieber
- Easter
- #pisces
- NCAA
- Adam Lambert

By Lee | Posted in Featured, Tutorials | Edit | Comments (0)

Visit http://aaron.jorb.in to learn more about using shortcodes with WordPress themes.

Localizing your theme

WordPress themes are used by people all over the world. Luckily, it is relatively easy to localize your theme by modifying code. We will be adding localization functions to text strings, then creating a .po file, adding a tag within our theme so that WordPress knows the theme is localized, then optionally converting any translated .po files to .mo files, and changing the language setting of our theme. The GNU gettext localization system (also referred to as GetText) is used by WordPress to allow strings of text to be tagged as translatable and then looked up in a dictionary. GetText is available by default on all web servers.

How to do it...

Back up your theme files. In this recipe, we will be updating text seen on the administration side of WordPress and the front-end side, by using the localization functions __() and _e().

Go through all customized files and look for any existing text strings that are already contained within <php ?> tags. Add two underscores (__), and surround any output text string with parentheses. As an example, we will use the localization function __($text) to flag the Edit link in the WordPress posts loop as translatable text. Open up your index.php file, and find the Edit link within the posts loop: edit_post_link('Edit'); and add the __() function so that it looks like the following example:

```
edit_post_link (__('Edit'));
```

Next, check your template files for any text strings that print to the front-end screen view of your WordPress site and that are not currently contained within PHP tags. These will need to be flagged as translatable, by using the `_e()` function.

Open up your `index.php` file, or any other file such as `author.php` or `single.php`, and find a block of display text. As an example, we will use the localization function `_e($text)` to flag the `<strong>Author Email:</strong>` text from an `author.php` page example created in Chapter 9 as translatable text. Add the `_e()` function, along with any needed PHP tags, so that it now looks like the following example:

```
<?php <strong> _e('Author Email:')</strong> ?>
```

Create a folder named `translation`, and save it in your theme folder. This is where any translation files should be kept for users and translators.

Now a localization tool must be run over the code in order to compile all of the marked text into a specialized file called a PO (Portable Object) file. The PO file is a text file that is organized so that each instance of translatable text is identified by using comments. The easiest way to create the file is to use the `.po` file generator at `http://www.icanlocalize.com/tools/php_scanner`. Navigate to the site, and you will be able to upload one of your PHP files, or a `.po` file if you already have one:

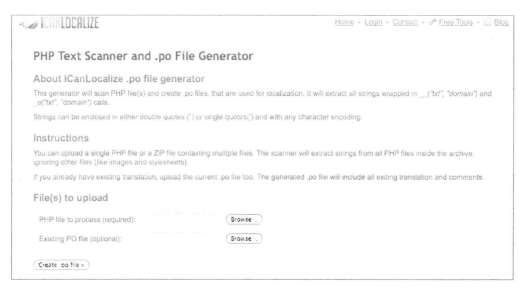

Save the `.po` file, and upload any more PHP files and the `.po` file, until all of the translatable text is processed. Save the final `.po` file to your `translation` folder so that it is available to translators.

Check your PO file. It should have each text string block formatted like the following example, which shows the text string Dashboard from the administration panel, along with a comment block directly above it that describes where the text string is located within the template:

```
#: wp-admin/menu.php: 10
msgid "Dashboard"
msgstr ""
```

Add a comment to the readme file of your theme about the availability of the PO file, and specifying that your theme is prepared for translation and localization. You may also want to add an additional readme file in your translation folder that describes the purpose of the PO file.

Now that the template has been localized, you will need to add a tag to either your functions.php file or header.php file, so that any translated text will be loaded, if desired by the user. Open up or create a functions.php file, and add the following code, contained within PHP tags, where themename is the name of your theme folder on your server:

```
// Translate, if applicable
load_theme_textdomain('themename');
```

As an extra step, you can also create your own localization files. Open your PO file and augment the msgstr for each item so that it now contains the translated text. Following is an example of the text string Dashboard translated to Spanish:

```
#: wp-admin/menu.php: 10
msgid "Dashboard"
msgstr "Tablero de instrumentos"
```

Save the file with the extension .po within your translation folder, using the language abbreviation as the file name. For example, if your .po file is in Spanish, it would usually be called es_ES.po, where the lowercase text represents the dialect or regional language and the uppercase text represents the core language abbreviation.

The .po file now needs to be formatted as an .mo (Machine Object) file in order for the text to be properly read by the server side GetText translation utility used by WordPress. You can download the free editor POEdit from http://www.poedit.net, so that you can make any additional translation changes and then save the file in .mo format.

Next, you will need to upload a copy of the .mo file to your languages folder within wp-content, if you would like to test your previous localization edits. Otherwise, you can place the file within your main theme folder. If your theme does not already have a languages folder within the wp-content folder, you will need to create one so that the path to the .mo file is /wordpress installation root folder/wp-content/languages/.

Next you need to edit the `WPLANG` setting in the `wp-config.php` file, in order to add a language parameter. By default, if your WordPress installation is currently English, it will look like: `define ('WPLANG','');`. Notice that `WPLANG` accepts an additional string parameter, which by default is empty. To specify a language, add the name of the `.mo` file as a string to `WPLANG`. In the following example, the `it_IT.mo` file is being referenced to set the language of the WordPress site to Italian:

```
define ('WPLANG', 'it_IT');
```

Save the `wp-config.php` file, and upload it to your server. When you view your WordPress site, you should now see any text strings that were identified as translatable in your theme, and translated within the `.mo` file, displayed in Italian (or other language that you specified). You can see an example of translated theme text in the following screenshot, where the `author`, `category identification`, `edit`, and `comments` link text have been translated:

Testing a custom shortcode

April 4, 2010 – 2:53 am

I've created a custom shortcode that allows me to quickly add a permalink to this post:

Creating Post Thumbnail Images for Every Post

Di Lee | Archiviato in Tutorials | Modifica | Nessun Commento

How it works...

`__($text)` is a WordPress function that takes a text string as a parameter, and looks for a translated version of `$text` within a provided dictionary file and returns the result, if any. It is used for controlling the display of text already contained within PHP tags. If no localization files other than English exist, then the text will remain the same.

There is a second localization function used to print text to the screen so that it is visible to site visitors. The `_e($text)` WordPress function looks for a translated version of `$text` and echoes the result to the screen. This should be used for titles and headings that will display on the screen and are not already contained within PHP tags (pay special attention to text in plugins, and the `index.php`, `functions.php`, `header.php`, and `sidebar.php` files).

Once all text within a theme is localized, it can then be processed into a `.po` file or POT (Portable Object Template) file for translation. The structure of these types of files makes it easy for translators to quickly translate text strings into another language by listing only the text strings and brief comments explaining the location of the text in the theme. After a `.po` file is created, it can then be made available to translators in the theme package, or the theme creator can work with someone to translate the strings (or translate the file themselves). The translated `.po` file should be saved in a `translation` folder so that other users can use it as a reference, or edit it later as they make changes to the template.

The WordPress back-end now needs to know that the theme has been localized. This is done by using the WordPress tag `load_theme_textdomain($text)`, which accepts a text string that is the short name (the name of your theme's folder on the server) of your theme. Any translatable text will now be looked up and processed into a specified language, as necessary.

If no other steps are taken, the theme will be localized, but will not be able to display the theme text in another language, as it still needs a special object file for GetText to read, in `wp-content/languages/`. As a theme author, you can stop at this point and let other volunteers take over, or you can provide any `.po` files that have already been translated as `.mo` files.

Converting a file to Machine Object (`.mo`) format so that it can be read by the server-side translation utility GetText, which is provided by default on all web servers and leveraged by WordPress to process translation files, creates a library that can be referenced by the utility to replace text strings in the old language with text strings in the new language. GetText will automatically look in the `/wp-content/languages/` folder for any `.mo` files.

There's more...

Translating themes for other WordPress users is a great way to give back to the WordPress community. Who knows, your participation may encourage others to help provide translations for your theme as well!

Becoming a WordPress theme translator

If you are fluent in multiple languages, you may want to consider giving back to the WordPress community as a translation volunteer. You can learn more about active translation projects at `http://codex.wordpress.org/Translating_WordPress`.

Displaying information based on the logged-in user's role

Sometimes you want to be able to display messages to new users or users with specific roles, such as authors or contributors. This recipe will display a message to users of the site based on their user role.

How to do it...

Open the `index.php` file of your theme. We are going to create a message area on the home page. Paste the following code below the content `div` tag and above the WordPress loop:

```php
<?php
/*
* Chapter 11 Example 6
* Creates a user message area on the home page.  Paste above the
WordPress loop.
*/
function get_my_user_message() {

    if (is_user_logged_in() && current_user_can('level_1')){
    echo "Remember we publish posts on Tuesdays, Wednesdays, and
        Thursdays!";
    } /* closing contributer role or higher text bracket */
    else if (is_user_logged_in() && current_user_can('level_0')){
    echo "Let us know if you see any grammatical errors in any
        posts!";
    } /* closing else if subscriber text */
    else { /*here is a paragraph that is shown to anyone not
        logged in*/
    echo "Howdy! Thanks for visiting. Please leave a comment.";
    }  /* closing  else visitor text bracket */

} /* closing bracket for function my_user_message */
?>
```

Next, we need to create an area on the home page for the message to be displayed and call the `get_my_user_message` function. Enter the following code before the WordPress loop:

```html
<!-- display the message on the home page -->
<div class="mymessagearea">

<?php if (function_exists ('get_my_user_message'))
    echo get_my_user_message();  ?> </div>
```

Save the file, and upload it to your server. Next, the `style.css` file should be edited so that the message will be noticed by visitors. Open your `style.css` file, and create a new class called `div.mymessagearea{}`.

Now specify the `background-color`, `padding`, `border`, `color`, and positioning of the class. Insert the following code between the opening and closing brackets of the class:

```
display:block;
background-color:#ffffff;
padding-left:10px;
color:#990000;
font-weight:bold;
font-size:small;
border-left:#FF3300 5px solid;
border-right:#FF3300 5px solid;
height: 50px;
width:400px;
```

Save the CSS file, and upload it to your server. Now, the next time that a person visits your site, they will see different messages if they are logged in and have user-level privileges than if they are site visitors and are not logged in.

To view the message yourself, view the home page in your browser. It should look similar to the next screenshot:

How it works...

First, a div class called `mymessagearea` is created to contain the user message. Then a function call, `current_user_can('level_1')`, is made that accepts the WordPress user level as a string parameter. If a user is logged-in and has a WordPress user role of contributor or higher (levels 1-10), they will be able to see the message text that begins with `Remember...` on the home page. The next `else if` statement checks to see if a user is logged in and has a user level of `level_0`. If both of these statements are true, then the user is a subscriber and can read, but not edit posts. An additional `else` statement then provides the option to display a different message if the visitor is not logged-in. This is the simplest way to determine the user role. Even though the use of user levels is not the preferred method to determine user roles, the process to grab a user's role is very clunky. In fact, if you go to the WordPress codex via the link provided in the following section, you will notice that there is no direct user data for a user's role.

Finally, the display of the message text is styled by using the `div` class `mymessagearea` created earlier. The positioning and size of the `div` are controlled using the `display`, `padding-left`, `width`, and `height` declarations, while the `border-left`, `border-right`, `color`, and `background-color` declarations control the look of the message box.

There's more...

There is much more that can be done to create custom messages within your theme, for users of different roles. Visit `http://codex.wordpress.org/Function_Reference/get_currentuserinfo` to learn more about user roles and levels.

Easier ways to use user roles in WordPress 3.0

Currently, users of WordPress 2.9 or earlier have no easy way to leverage user roles in the way they do other user data. That will be changing somewhat in WordPress 3.0, when roles are supposed to act as containers of permissions. Check out the WordPress forums (`http://wordpress.org/support/`) to learn more.

Packaging your theme for distribution

In this recipe, we will go over the steps necessary to package your theme for distribution. Even if you never share your theme with the public, following these steps can help you organize your theme better, and test for any potential compatibility issues with plugins or other code.

How to do it...

First, you need to prepare any plug-ins or custom functions that you have created, so that any tags or callbacks that were inserted into template files will not "break" or corrupt the theme. To do this, the function `function_exists()` can be used to check for a plug-in or function, and detect if it exists or is active. If `function_exists()` returns a value of `false` or not found, the plugin tag or function callback will be ignored and the page will continue loading. For example, earlier in this chapter we used the function check for a user message function. The code used was:

```php
<?php if (function_exists ('get_my_user_message'))
    echo get_my_user_message();  ?>
```

The previous example function uses `get_my_user_message()` to print out information to the screen. Check all of your core template files, along with any other custom template files that you have created; otherwise don't be surprised if things break!

Make sure that you include all of the core WordPress template files, like `index.php`, `sidebar.php`, `single.php`, `comments.php`, `header.php`, and `footer.php`. Your template folder should also contain a `style.css` file. Using a `functions.php` file to contain loose functions (that is, those that are not plug-ins) is also preferred.

Test your template files, including the comments functionality, for any weird layout issues. You may want to visit the WordPress Forums, or review the basics of HTML, PHP, and CSS at `http://www.w3schools.com`, for most issues.

Organize your theme structure to match the way that other themes are set up. This means keeping your `style.css` file in the main theme folder, and adding any additional styles for `schemes` and others to a special subfolder, for neatness. If you will have multiple files of the same type, such as `.po` files, then you should put them in a `translations` subfolder. Other files, such as `.mo` files, should be left in the main theme folder, where WordPress expects to find them.

Don't rename default WordPress style definitions just to be different. Keep any main structural styles such as `#header` and `#content` named the same. Be aware that many people use `.primary` and `.secondary` to denote the main sidebar and secondary sidebar, if you are styling more than one. It is a best practice to add any new classes that you create below the standard WordPress classes in your `style.css` sheet, and use `/**/` to comment liberally about the purpose of your styles.

Comment, comment, and comment some more. Remember: your more adventurous users will be reading your code. They may be looking to do something similar, or may just want to understand what you were thinking.

Test, test, test, and then test your theme some more, using various test blogs, different plug-ins, when the theme is active and inactive, and in other instances. You cannot test your theme enough.

Double-check that you have documented any custom tweaks, tips, plug-ins, or other things that the user must know, in a readme file.

Put all of your theme files, including a readme text file with information and description, in a ZIP file for easy downloading. If possible, provide two or more file compression types, such as RAR, ZIP, GZIP, and so on, in order to maximize user choices.

There's more...

Releasing a theme for public use is not for the faint of heart. Read on for more information about letting your theme go public.

Is your theme really ready for public release?

Packaging your theme is one thing, but exposing your efforts to public view and criticism is another. Are you ready for the requests for support, e-mails about grammatical errors, and complaints about things you never even considered before? If so, then you may have the courage to release your theme to the public. Visit `http://codex.wordpress.org/Designing_Themes_for_Public_Release` for more ways to prepare your little theme for the great big WordPress community.

Uploading your theme to the WordPress.org theme repository

This recipe covers uploading your theme to WordPress.org, and promoting your theme on the codex and the WordPress.org forum.

Getting started

You will need to have tested, validated, and packaged your theme for distribution. Learn more about packaging your theme in the recipe *Packaging your theme for distribution*.

How to do it...

Create a page on your site by logging in to your WordPress control panel and selecting **Pages** and then **Add New** on the control panel menu. Using the screenshot shown below, follow along with the next step in order to create a page for your theme:

Name your page descriptively, such as **Download Awesome Theme** in the page title field. Use the main content area field to describe your theme, and include the following: demo or screenshot of various page views (capture screenshots using *Ctrl + F5* on the PC or *Cmd + Shift + 4* on a Mac), and link to a downloadable ZIP file. (Don't forget—the easiest way to show off multiple screenshots is to use the **Gallery** feature of the WordPress **Media Library** to insert a gallery into your page). The new page should now look like the example shown in the following screenshot:

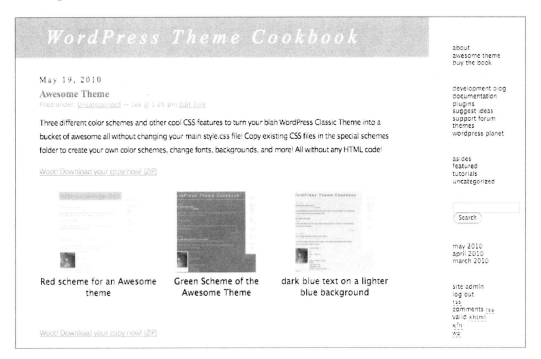

Go to the Free Themes Directory (http://wordpress.org/extend/themes/upload/) and log in (register if you haven't done so; it is quick and easy). Under **Add Your Theme To The Directory**, click the **Browse** button to select the ZIP file of your packaged theme from your computer. Click on the **Upload** button to upload your theme. It will be reviewed and then posted on the Free Themes Directory if the review team is satisfied with the quality of the theme.

Post a note about your new theme on the WordPress Forum, under **Themes and Templates** (http://wordpress.org/support/forum/5), describing the theme. The more descriptive keywords you use, the more likely people's search for themes will turn up your theme. Include links to your theme and the downloadable ZIP file.

Visit the WordPress theme repository at http://www.wordpress.org/extend/themes to view other themes, and then log in to upload your own.

How it works...

Previously, everyone uploaded their WordPress themes to a central repository on WordPress. org. Times have changed, and as themes have grown more complex, so has sharing your theme. Even though you can still go to `http://www.wordpress.org/extend/themes` to find themes, your theme may not make it to that list until after it has been through a gauntlet of testing and commentary by other WordPress users. Test, test, and test your theme, and then share it with others on the WordPress forums, making edits when you receive constructive criticism and suggestions. In the end, you will benefit by having a more stable theme to offer.

12
Layout

In this chapter, we will cover:

- Adding a skip navigation link for usability
- Centering your site's layout in the browser window
- Setting up a randomly-rotating header image
- Making theme components drag-and-drop
- Creating a global toolbar for your theme
- Creating tabbed navigation for your theme

Introduction

The basis of any good WordPress theme is a solid layout. The layout that you choose will be used throughout the site. So picking one suitable for your particular purposes is important.

It is also important to recognize the standard conventions of a blog layout. You want to make sure that visitors know how to navigate your site and can recognize where different elements, such as search forms and main content, should be. Following long-standing conventions regarding blog design makes this a snap.

Adding a skip navigation link for usability

In general, most blog themes have four main sections:

- Header with site title and logo
- Navigation links and other navigation aids, such as search forms
- Main content; the main focus of the page
- Site footer, containing extra site information

If a sighted user navigates to a page, they'll often be able to immediately locate and start consuming the content. They can click on links, scroll though articles, and find the information that they want, quickly and easily.

However, for non-sighted users, or other users who make use of browsing aids (such as screen readers), a large navigation section with scores of links can have a highly detrimental effect. These users can't get to your content and read about your services, products, or opinions. To solve this problem, you'll rely on a simple technique that has been around for quite a while—the skip navigation link.

Getting started

You should have created the basic structure of your WordPress theme before starting this recipe. You need to have the basic skeleton of your site implemented in HTML, so that you know where your main content lives and can effectively link to it.

How to do it...

There are two parts to the skip navigation link technique. The first part is the link itself. This link should be the first link within the <body> tag of your theme. It should go after your page's main heading or company name, but before anything else. To implement this, open up the file containing your theme's header (this should be the header.php file), and add something similar to the following code:

```
<div id="header">
  <h1><?php bloginfo('name'); ?></h1>
  <a id="skip" href="#content">Skip Navigation</a>
</div>
```

Styling Skip Navigation

You'll probably want to style your skip navigation links very discreetly. Try to incorporate the link into your design and use the :focus and :active CSS modifiers to style it for tabbed navigation. Examples of styling skip navigation links for usability and accessibility can be found at http://www.section508.gov/SSA_BestPractices/lessons/css/skipnav.htm.

The second part of this technique is the target for the skip link. When a user selects the skip link, the target receives the browser's focus, and the user should be able to immediately read and peruse your content. To create the appropriate target for your skip navigation link, find the HTML element in your theme files that contains the majority of your article content. Most designers like to name their content containers with an ID of `content`, so you might want to start looking for something like that. If you can't find an element with an appropriate ID, you'll have to add one. You are looking to have something like this:

```
<div id="content">
    <!--content goes here --></div> <!--end content  -->
```

Save your changes, and update the files on your server. As soon as you have implemented the two parts of this technique, you should have a functional skip navigation link. If you styled the skip navigation link such that it is visible, you'll probably have something that looks like the example shown in the following screenshot:

When users who rely on screen readers or prefer to use their keyboard for navigation visit your page, they'll be able to instantly skip your navigation links and reach your content.

Try it out by visiting your page and clicking on the link. You'll be able to scroll down to your content immediately. The following screenshot shows our example theme after clicking on the **Skip Navigation** link:

How it works...

When a hyperlink (<a>) tag contains a string consisting of a hash sign (#) and then some other characters, the browser looks within the page for a series of things, in order. First, it looks for any element in the page that has its id attribute equal to the characters after the hash sign. If an element is found, then the browser scrolls the viewable area so that the top of the viewable area coincides with the found element.

If no element with the id attribute equal to the characters after the hash sign is found, then the browser looks for an element with its name attribute equal to the characters after the hash sign. If it finds one, the browser scrolls to that element.

In this example, you're using a hyperlink tag to link to your main content so that non-sighted or other users relying on alternative navigation technologies can quickly and easily bypass your navigation menu and reach the element containing the majority of your content. You used a container with an `id` attribute equal to `content` that matches up with the `href` attribute equal to `#content` on your skip navigation link.

Centering your site's layout in the browser window

One of the most popular ways to classify designs on the web is to delineate them as either fixed-width or elastic. Designers who want maximum control over the layout of text, images, and other site elements generally created fixed-width designs. Current trends dictate that fixed-width designs belong in the center of the browser viewing window.

In this recipe, you'll learn how to center your design and make certain that your content is going where you want it to.

Getting started

You should have started writing the basic skeleton HTML of your theme. You need to make sure you have The Loop somewhere in your theme and an overall containing element that wraps all your content: header, main content, and footer.

How to do it...

First, you need to discern what the ID of the containing element for your content is. Take the following header code, which is usually contained within the `header.php` file, as a starting point, as it is fairly typical of a simple WordPress theme. The `<div id="wrap">` tag is the key to using CSS to center the theme. If your file does not contain a site layout wrapping div tag above the header tag, then you will need to add one to your theme. In this example, the div is named `wrap`, but you may also see the same type of div named `wrapper` or `rap` or `container`, depending on the theme:

```
<body <?php body_class(); ?>
  <div id="wrap">
    <?php /*note: the wrapper div may be called "rap",
    "wrapper","wrap", or "container" in your theme. The book example
    uses the standard "wrap". */ ?>
    <h1 id="header">
      <a href="<?php bloginfo('url'); ?>/">
        <?php bloginfo('name'); ?>
      </a>
    </h1>
```

Now, we take a look at the `footer.php` file and add a closing `</div>` tag for the `wrap` div:

```
<div id="footer">

  <p class="credit">
    <!--<?php echo get_num_queries(); ?> queries. <?php
    timer_stop(1); ?> seconds. -->
      <cite><?php echo sprintf(__("Powered by
      <a href='http://wordpress.org/' title='%s'>
        <strong>WordPress</strong></a>"), __("Powered by WordPress,
        state-of-the-art semantic personal publishing platform.")); 
      ?>
      </cite></p>

<?php wp_footer(); ?></div>
<!--- close footer --->
</div><!-- close wrap (wrapper div) -->
</body>
</html>
```

In this code sample, you can see that all of the content for the theme is wrapped in an element with an `id` attribute of `wrap`. Seeing this, we can start to correctly style the theme to center the theme in the browser.

Next we need to style the `wrap` div in the `style.css` file. We need to decide on a fixed `width`, and for simplicity's sake, you'll use `860` pixels for this example. Open up your theme's stylesheet (`style.css`), and enter the following styles:

```
/* note: WordPress Classic calls it "rap" but many themes refer to
it as "wrapper" or "wrap". It is ok to change it here as long as you
change it in your other files. */
#wrap{background-color:#ebe8b1;/* if you are not sure what is actually
wrapped, set the background color to something easy to see and
different from the rest of the theme colors */
  border:1px solid #666666;
  margin:0 auto;
  width:860px;
}
```

After you enter the styles in the stylesheet, you should upload your theme and display your site in a browser and you'll see a bordered fixed-width design similar to the following screenshot:

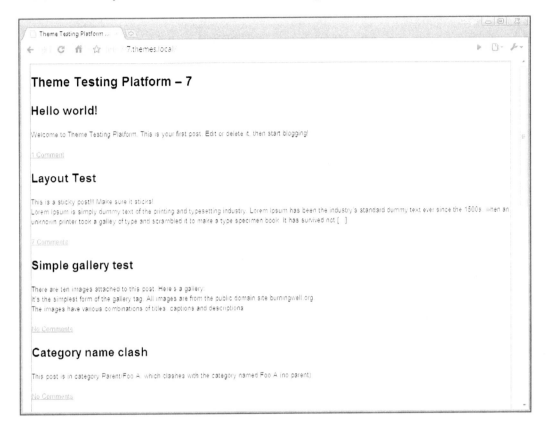

How it works...

In this example, you've created a `div` element with an `id` attribute of `wrap` and explicitly set the `width` to `860` pixels. Then, you've declared the `margin` property for the element and added some other styles so that you could see the centering in action.

The centering works because of the CSS box model that is defined by the W3C and followed by all major browsers. A discussion of the box model is beyond the scope of this book, but the basics of this technique are as follows:

- ▸ Set an explicit width so that the browser knows exactly how much space the element will occupy
- ▸ Set the top and bottom margins of the wrap element to 0
- ▸ Set the left and right margins of the wrap element to auto, and the browser calculates the correct margin to allow the element to remain centered

- ▸ The browser applies the margins it previously calculated
- ▸ The element is centered

Please note that this technique will work with all block-level elements that have a specified width. For example, you can center images or blockquotes in posts, or center widgets within your sidebar.

Setting up a randomly-rotating header image

To add some real design pizzazz to your WordPress theme, every time the page loads, you can randomly display different photos or other images in the header section of your theme. You can use this as a technique to generate interest for your visitors, or just as a fun personal experiment. With the method in this recipe, you'll be up and running in no time.

Getting started

You should have a basic theme skeleton created, in order to take advantage of this recipe. In addition, you should also have created a variety of possible header background images, preferably each of the same size.

How to do it...

For the purpose of this recipe, you'll be working under the assumption that you want to randomly rotate the image displayed in the header section of your theme each time the page reloads. The blog title will sit on top of the random image.

First, you need to place the images in the correct place so that the code we're going to write can get to them.

Open the directory that your theme lives in, and create a new subdirectory called `header-images`. Inside this directory, place all of the images you want to rotate through your header. The following are some examples of images you could use for an application like this:

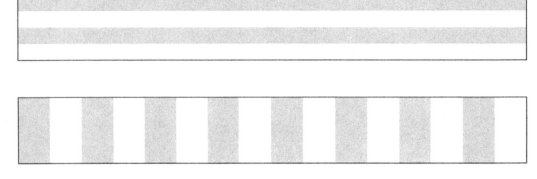

After gathering the images, you need to write the function that will return the appropriate image URL. Open or create your theme's `functions.php` file, and insert the following code into this file:

```
function wptc_get_header_image() {
  $headers_path = TEMPLATEPATH . '/header-images/';
  $headers = array();
  if(file_exists($headers_path)&&is_dir($headers_path)) {
  $dir = opendir($headers_path);
  $stylesheet_dir = get_bloginfo('stylesheet_directory');
    while(false !== ($file = readdir($dir))) {
      if('.' == $file || '..' == $file) {
        continue;
      }
      $image_info = getimagesize($headers_path.$file);
      if(false !== $image_info) {
        $headers[]="$stylesheet_dir/header-images/$file";
      }
    }
  }
  if(!empty($headers)) {
    $rand = array_rand($headers);
    return $headers[$rand];
  } else {
    return false;
  }
}
```

This function returns the URL to one of the images in the `header-images` directory that you created. Alternatively, if there are no images in the `header-images` directory, the function returns `false`.

Next, after creating this function, you're ready to write the appropriate HTML and CSS. You should know ahead of time what size your images are, so this part is pretty straightforward. First, write the header HTML (this may belong in either the `index.php` file or the `header.php` file):

```php
<?php
$header_image = wptc_get_header_image();
if( $header_image ) {
  $style = "background-image:url('{$header_image}');";
}
?>
<div id="wrap">
  <div id="header" style="<?php echo $style; ?>">
    <h1><?php bloginfo('name'); ?></h1>
  </div>
</div>
```

Then follow up with the appropriate CSS in the `style.css` file:

```css
.wrap {
  margin: 0 auto;
  width: 960px;
}

#header {
  background-repeat: no-repeat;
  color: #000000;
  text-align: center;
  height: 120px;
  line-height: 120px;
  width: 960px;
}
```

In this code sample, you can see that you first attempt to retrieve a random image from the `header-images` directory, using the new function that you wrote, you then assign a style declaration to the `$style` variable. When you create the header element, you assign an inline style with the random image as the background image. In addition to the inline style, the header element has some styles applied that color the text contained within and center it, both vertically and horizontally, to increase the aesthetic appeal.

After you do all of this, you get a nice random header. The following screenshots show a random header image:

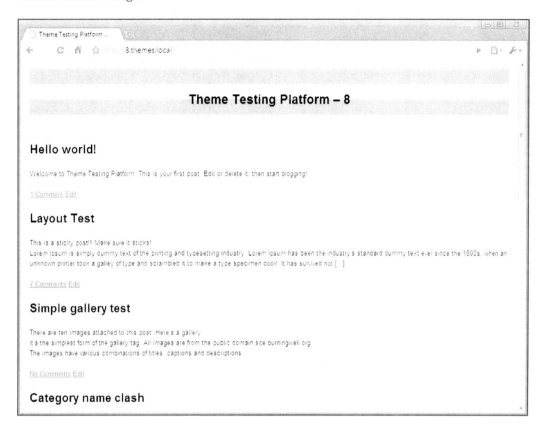

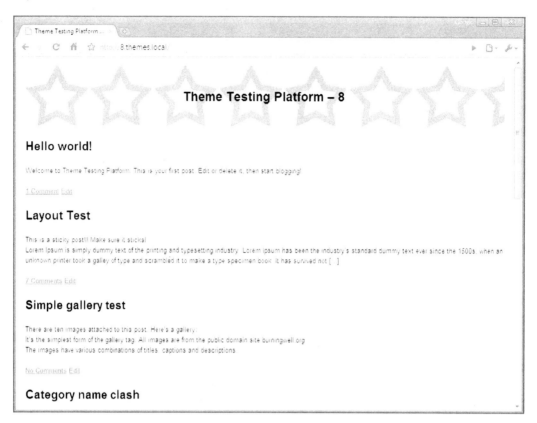

How it works...

The most important part of this recipe is the random image determination function. You make the function available throughout your theme by creating it in the `functions.php` file that WordPress loads as part of its startup process.

First, the `wptc_get_header_image` function checks to make sure that the appropriate directory exists in your theme and is available for reading. After these conditions are verified, PHP opens the `header-images` directory and iterates over each file in the directory. The filenames `.` and `..` are excluded because they have special meanings in the context of the file system and do not need to be considered in this case. Every other filename in the directory is verified to be an image, and if it is, it's added to an array of header image possibilities.

After the array of possible image URLs is complete, the function verifies that at least one item is present in the array. If the array is not empty, a random key is retrieved from the array using `array_rand`, and the array item for that key is returned. If the array does not have any items in it, then the `false` literal is returned.

On the front-end, directly above the markup for the header, you call `wptc_get_header_image` to get a random URL for an image. If an image URL is returned, you populate the value of the `$style` variable with the appropriate background-image declaration. Otherwise, the `$style` variable remains undeclared.

In the declaration for the header `div`, you add the contents of the `$style` variable as an inline style, in order to make the background image of the header change at render time. When the page is displayed, the image is fetched and placed in the background of the header div, and the header text (in this case the blog's name) renders on top of the image.

Making theme components drag-and-drop

The best websites provide means for their users to shape a custom experience, allowing them to interact with site content and components in the way that they want to. In this recipe, you'll learn how to create a drag-and-drop interface for site components. You'll let users order your content in the way that they want to experience it, letting each individual user decide what is most important.

Getting started

To start, you should have a basic theme skeleton created with at least a `style.css` file, and an `index.php` file. For this recipe, you'll create a custom page template to demonstrate the technique, so you should have some knowledge of page templates.

How to do it...

The first component of the drag-and-drop interface you're going to create is the custom page template. Create a new file in your theme's directory and name it `category-overview.php`. This template will display the six most used categories with up to five posts for each. It will let the visitor easily sort the categories they want to view by dragging the category name. Open the `category-overview.php` file, and insert the following code:

```php
<?php
/*
Template Name: Category Overview
*/
?>
    <?php get_header(); ?>

  <body <?php body_class('wptc-theme'); ?>>
  <div id="wrap">
    <div id="content">
      <?php
      $categories = get_categories(
```

```php
    array(
      'number'=>6,
      'hide_empty'=>false,
      'orderby'=>'count',
      'order'=>'DESC'
    )
);
foreach($categories as $category) {
  $category_posts = new WP_Query(
    array(
      'cat'=>$category->term_id,
      'posts_per_page'=>5
    )
  );
  if( $category_posts->have_posts() ) {
  ?>
  <div
  class="piece"
  id="user_cat_<?php echo $category->term_id; ?>"
  >
    <h2>
    <?php echo esc_html($category->name); ?>
    </h2>
    <ul>
    <?php
    while($category_posts->have_posts()) {
      $category_posts->the_post();
      ?>
        <li>
          <a
            href="<?php the_permalink(); ?>"
            title="<?php the_title(); ?>">
            <?php the_title(); ?>
          </a>
        </li>
      <?php
      }
    ?>
    </ul>
  </div>
  <?php
  }
}
?>
```

```
    </div>
   </div>
  </body>
 </html>
```

After you've inserted this code, save the file and go to your WordPress administrative panel. Create a new page, and change the `Template` to `Category Overview`. If you need more information on page templates and how to activate them, see the recipe *Creating a simple page template* in Chapter 7.

Next, you need to create the CSS to properly display each category and its posts. Currently, unstyled, your category items should look something like the example shown in the following screenshot:

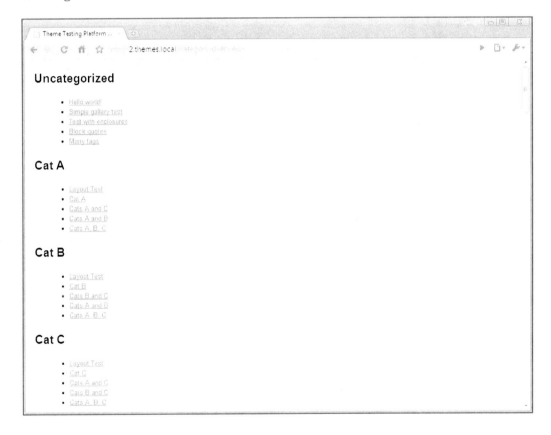

Open up your theme's stylesheet, `style.css`, and insert the following styles:

```
#wrap {
  margin: 0 auto;
  width: 960px;
}

#content {
  width: 100%;
}


#content .piece {
  border: 5px solid #666666;
  float: left;
  height: 290px;
  margin: 5px;
  overflow: hidden;
  padding: 5px;
  width: 290px;
}

#content .piece h2 {
  text-align: center;
  cursor: move;
}

#content .piece.ui-sortable-helper {
  border: 2px dashed #ff0000;
}

#content .piece.ui-sortable-placeholder {
  background: #dddddd;
  border-color: #aaaaaa;
}

#content .clear {
  clear: both;
  height: 0;
  width: 0;
}
```

Now, reload your category overview page, and view it in your browser. It should look something like the example shown in the following screenshot:

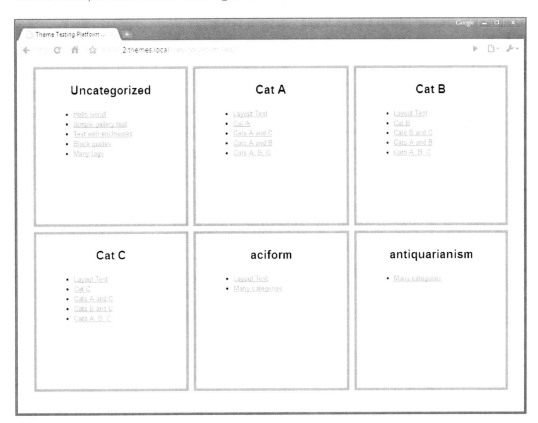

Now that you've got your basic styles set up, it is time to write the JavaScript that will enable the drag-and-drop functionality that you're looking for. Create a new sub-directory in your theme's directory and name it `js`. Inside this new directory, create a file named `scripts.js`, and insert the following JavaScript code:

```
jQuery(document).ready(function($) {
  $('#content').sortable({
  items:'div.piece',
  handle:'h2',
  placeholder:'piece ui-sortable-placeholder'
  });
});
```

This script is quite simple, but you should recognize a few things. First, this snippet uses the jQuery and jQuery UI libraries, so they are dependencies that we will have to take into account shortly. Second, you're targeting the element with id equal to `content` and telling the browser that you want to make the items inside sortable. Finally, you're passing a few options that make the sorting behave in a certain way:

- Only `div` elements with the `piece` class are sortable
- To drag an item, the user needs to grab the `h2` element and drag
- The placeholder that the library creates has the classes `piece` and `ui-sortable-placeholder`

Now that you have written the appropriate JavaScript, you just need to get WordPress to include the script in the page with the proper dependencies. First, ensure that your theme's head element has a `wp_head` function call within it. Then, open or create your theme's `functions.php` file, and insert the following code:

```
add_action('init','wptc_enqueue_site_scripts');
function wptc_enqueue_site_scripts() {
  if( !is_admin() ) {
    wp_enqueue_script(
    'wptc-scripts',
    get_bloginfo('stylesheet_directory').'/js/scripts.js',
    array('jquery','jquery-ui-sortable')
    );
  }
}
```

This snippet tells WordPress to print a link to your custom JavaScript file in the head of the theme, and to make sure that the jQuery and jQuery UI Sortable libraries are loaded first.

After saving the `functions.php` file, reload your category overview page, and then click and drag on a category title. You should see something like the following screenshot:

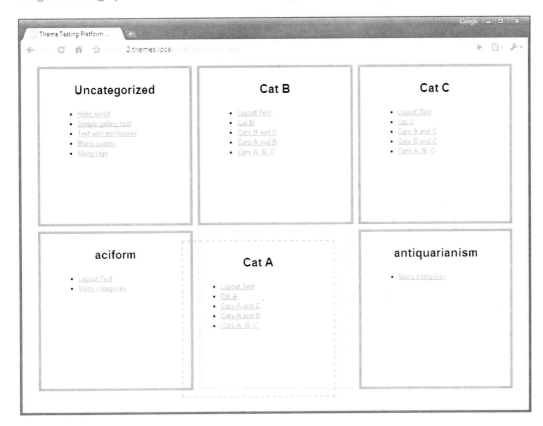

You can see in the preceding screenshot that the placeholder is styled as a simple gray box with a light gray border, and the element you're currently dragging has a red dashed border so that you can easily see where you are with the drag.

How it works...

There are a lot of elements at play in this recipe, so let's go through them one by one. First, you created the markup necessary to display your top categories in a page template. You called the `get_categories` function with specific parameters, in order to retrieve the six most used categories and then created a custom loop for each category to list the latest five posts from that category.

The markup for each category box is simple, consisting of a containing `div` with a class of `piece`, a second-level heading for the category name, and an unordered list of links to posts from that category.

After creating the markup, you opened up your main stylesheet, and made the category sections look nice. The styles that you entered created a simple grid of 290 by 290 pixel boxes, with a centered header for the category name and an unstyled list. You also created some styles, that were specific to the dragging capabilities that you will add later.

Then, after checking out the category grid that you styled, it was time to create the actual dragging functionality. You created a custom JavaScript file that takes advantage of the jQuery and jQuery UI libraries. Inside of the JavaScript file, you wrote a single statement specifying that the items with a class of `piece` inside the `div` with an `id` of `content` should be sortable. The sortable items' handle is the `h2` element contained within the item, which in this case, is the category name.

> **Learn more about jQuery UI**
>
> The jQuery UI library is very powerful and can help you to create some stunning effects. To learn more, consult the official jQuery UI documentation at `http://jqueryui.com/demos/`.

Finally, you enqueued the custom JavaScript file that you wrote, and specified that it depended on the jQuery and jQuery UI Sortable libraries. Loading up the category overview page, you can now grab any category name and drag the box around, observing the styles that you entered earlier coming into play.

There's more...

Putting some draggable items on your site is great, but so far it doesn't really benefit your users at all. Let's change that by giving them the ability to save the order of the boxes after they sort them.

Saving the category order

There are only a few things that you need to add to your current set-up to allow a user to save a custom order for their categories. First, open up your `functions.php` file and add the following code to it:

```
/* here is the code for the drag and drop of category boxes */
add_action('init','wptc_enqueue_site_scripts');
function wptc_enqueue_site_scripts() {
  if( !is_admin() ) {
    wp_enqueue_script(
      'wptc-scripts',
      get_bloginfo('stylesheet_directory').'/js/scripts.js',
      array('jquery','jquery-ui-sortable')
      );
  }
}
```

```
add_action('parse_request','wptc_save_user_cat_order');
function wptc_save_user_cat_order($wp) {
  if( isset( $_POST['save-user-cat-order'] ) ) ) {
    $args = wp_parse_args(stripslashes($_POST['user-cat-order']));
    $cats = (array)$args['user_cat'];
    setcookie('user-cat-
    order',maybe_serialize($cats),time()+3600*24*31);
    exit();
  }
}


global $user_cat_order;
$user_cat_order = unserialize(stripslashes($_COOKIE['user-cat-
order']));
$user_cat_order = is_array($user_cat_order) ? $user_cat_order : false;

function wptc_sort_categories($categories) {
  global $user_cat_order,$current_categories;
  if(!$user_cat_order) {
    $current_categories = array();
    foreach($categories as $category) {
      $current_categories[] = $category->term_id;
    }
    $user_cat_order = $current_categories;
  }
  usort($categories,'wptc_order_category_overview');
  return $categories;
}


function wptc_order_category_overview($catA, $catB) {
  global $user_cat_order,$current_categories;
  if($user_cat_order) {
    $posA = array_search($catA->term_id,$user_cat_order);
    if(false === $posA) {
      $posA = -1;
    }

    $posB = array_search($catB->term_id,$user_cat_order);
    if( false === $posB) {
      $posB = -1;
    }

    return $posA - $posB;
  } else {
    return -1;
  }
}
```

This code intercepts the save request that you'll make use of when a user finishes sorting the categories. Also, you've added a custom sorting function that makes sure that the categories are in the correct order before rendering them to the browser.

Next, open up your JavaScript file `scripts.js`, and change your code to the following. This code adds an event handler that fires when your user finishes sorting the categories on the front-end. The handler fires off a request when the user finishes sorting. The request contains the necessary variables to save the categories being sorted. Particular areas of interest have been marked in bold:

```
jQuery(document).ready(function($) {
    $('#content').sortable({
    stop:wptc_user_cat_order,
    items:'div.piece',
    handle:'h2',
    placeholder:'piece ui-sortable-placeholder'
    });

    function wptc_user_cat_order(event,ui) {
      jQuery.post(
        '/',
        {
        'save-user-cat-order':1,
        'user-cat-order':$(this).sortable('serialize')
        }
      );
    }
});
```

To test this functionality, refresh the category overview page that you've been working on. You'll notice that the categories are in the order that they were before. We took special care to ensure that if the user hasn't sorted the categories previously, they'll be rendered in the order determined by number of posts in a category. Next, sort the categories by dragging and dropping them into the position that you desire. Refresh the page, and the category boxes should remain in their custom-sorted positions.

See also

▸   *Creating a simple page template*

Creating a global toolbar for your theme

Having a great site is one thing, but building a community is quite another. To really push your site's community efforts, it can pay to put the most desirable actions right at the top of your site's theme. This is what WordPress.com does, and in this recipe, is what you'll do.

Getting started

You need to have a basic theme constructed and, for the best experience, you need to have separated your header elements out into `header.php`.

How to do it...

First, you need to decide what components you wish to put into your site's toolbar. For this recipe, we'll follow the lead of WordPress.com. The toolbar on that site allows users to perform the following actions:

- Access the currently logged-in user's profile
- Log in and log out
- Search the site
- Access a random post

The WordPress.com toolbar also allows for a variety of other actions, but these won't be discussed in this recipe.

Next, you need to create the HTML for the toolbar. To keep the toolbar markup as clear as possible, you'll create a new file and then include it where necessary. Inside your theme's directory, create a subdirectory called `components`. Inside this new subdirectory create a file called `toolbar.php`.

Insert the following markup into the new `toolbar.php` file:

```
<ul id="toolbar">
  <?php if ( is_user_logged_in() ) { ?>
  <li>
    <a href="<?php echo esc_url(admin_url('profile.php')); ?>">
      <?php _e('My Profile'); ?>
    </a>
  </li>
  <li>
    <a href="<?php echo esc_url(wp_logout_url(site_url('/'))); ?>">
      <?php _e('Log Out'); ?>
    </a>
```

```
</li>
<?php } else { ?>
<li>
  <form
  name="loginform"
  id="loginform"
  action="<?php echo site_url('wp-login.php', 'login_post'); ?>"
  method="post">
      <label><span class="hidden"><?php _e('Username'); ?></span>
      <input type="text" name="log"
          id="user_login" class="input" />

      </label>

      <label><span class="hidden"><?php _e('Password') ?></span>
      <input type="password" name="pwd"
          id="user_pass" class="input" />
      </label>


      <input type="submit" name="wp-submit"
          id="wp-submit" class="button-primary"
          value="<?php esc_attr_e('Log In'); ?>" />

      <label>
      <input name="rememberme" type="checkbox"
          id="rememberme" value="forever" />
      <?php esc_attr_e('Remember Me'); ?>
      </label>

      <input type="hidden" name="redirect_to"
        value="<?php echo esc_attr(site_url('/')); ?>" />
      <input type="hidden" name="testcookie" value="1" />
  </form>
</li>
<?php } ?>
```

```php
<?php
$random_posts = get_posts(array('orderby'=>'rand'));
if( !empty($posts) ) {
$random_post = array_shift($random_posts);
?>
<li>
  <a href="<?php echo esc_url(get_permalink($random_post->ID)); ?>">
  <?php _e('Random Post'); ?>
  </a>
</li>
<?php } ?>

<li class="right">
  <form method="get">
    <input type="text" name="s" id="s" />
    <input type="submit" name="search"
        id="search-submit" value="<?php _e( 'Search' ); ?>" />
  </form>
</li>
</ul>
```

The markup does a few things. First, it checks to see if a user is logged in. If they are, then a link to the logged-in user's account profile page, and a link for logging out, are rendered. Otherwise, a login form is output to the browser. Next, the toolbar retrieves a random post that has been published and links to it. Finally, a search form is placed in the toolbar, allowing the user to search the blog.

After you've constructed your toolbar, it is time to put it in the appropriate place. Open up `header.php` file (or the `index.php` file, depending on your template structure) and insert the following code directly after the opening body tag:

```php
<?php include( TEMPLATEPATH . '/components/toolbar.php' ); ?>
```

This line references the toolbar file, and makes PHP include it in line with the rest of your template's content.

Open your site in a browser window (making sure that you are not logged in) and take a look at the results. If you've done everything correctly up to this point, you're likely to have something that looks like the following, if you're logged out:

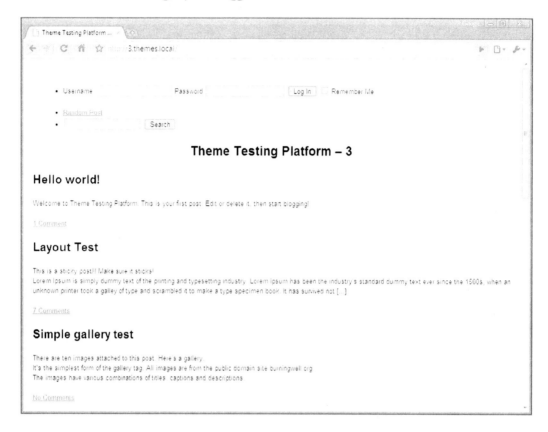

Now log in to your site to test the view when users are logged in. If you're logged in, your site should look like the following screenshot:

Now that the markup is complete, it's time to style the toolbar. Open up your theme's stylesheet, `style.css` file, and insert the following styles. These styles will fix the toolbar to the top of the browser window, and ensure that, as the user scrolls down, the toolbar always remains in place. In addition, the styles define text, background colors and appropriate margin and padding for all elements:

```css
/*note: you may have to increase the padding (top) of the header div
as shown below:*/

#header {
  background: #90a090;
  border-bottom: 3px double #aba;
  border-left: 1px solid #9a9;
  border-right: 1px solid #565;
  border-top: 1px solid #9a9;
```

```
    font: italic normal 230% 'Times New Roman', Times, serif;
    letter-spacing: 0.2em;
    margin: 0;
    padding: 50px 10px 15px 60px;
}
/* menu top changed from 0 to 120px;*/
#menu {
    background: #fff;
    border-left: 1px dotted #ccc;
    border-top: 3px solid #e0e6e0;
    padding: 20px 0 10px 30px;
    position: absolute;
    right: 2px;
    top: 120px;
    width: 11em;
}
/* note: you may have to adjust the placement of the top of your
sidebar /side menu since this toolbar runs across the top of the
theme. */
#toolbar a {
    color: #ffffff;
    display: block;
    text-decoration: none;
    padding: 4px 6px;
}

#toolbar a:hover {
    background: #666666;
}

#toolbar form {
    padding: 0 5px;
}

#toolbar li {
    display: block;
    float: left;

    margin: 0;
    padding: 0;
}

#toolbar .right {
    float: right;
```

```
}

#toolbar .hidden {
  display: none;
}
```

Refresh your browser, and you should see something similar to the following screenshot, assuming that you are logged out:

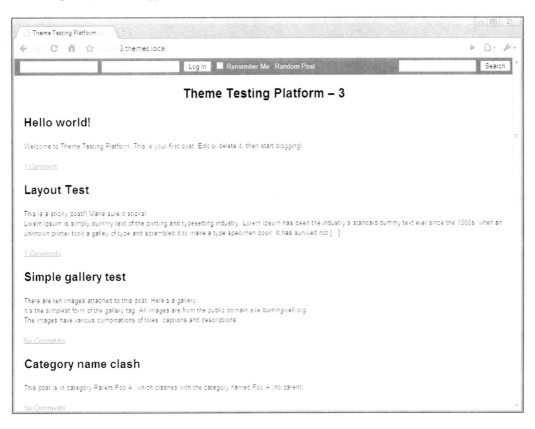

When you're logged in, your display should resemble the following screenshot:

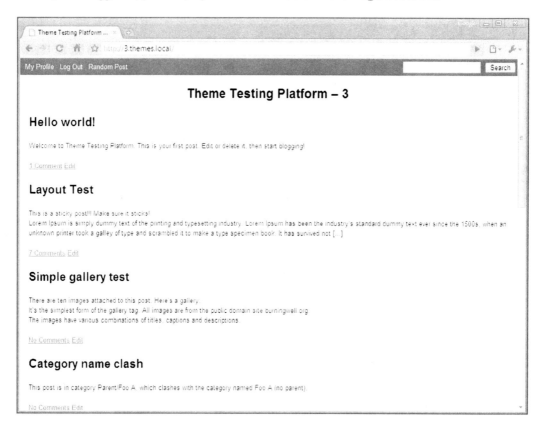

How it works...

The concepts here are simple, but we'll go through them one by one. First, you created a separate PHP file that contains the entire toolbar component. In this case, you made the toolbar relevant both to site functions (logging in and out) and to site content (random post and search toolbar).

To do so, you took advantage of a few WordPress functions to get the necessary conditions and content. First, you used `is_user_logged_in` to determine whether to show the log-in form, or to give the user the option to modify their profile, or log out. You used `wp_logout_url` to retrieve the appropriate log-out URL for the site in question, rather than manually constructing it.

You also created two forms. The first was a log-in form mimicking the one shown at your site's `wp-login.php` page. The second was a search form containing a single input, as required by WordPress.

Finally, you included this component into your `header.php` file so that it shows across every page of your site. Once it was included appropriately, you styled it by using some good looking colors and layout.

Creating tabbed navigation for your theme

One of the easiest visual clues that you can offer your users is that of active and inactive tabs. This lets them know exactly where they are on your site at any moment. In this recipe, you'll learn the markup and styles you need to bring an easy tabbed interface to life.

Getting started

You need to have a basic theme constructed, and need to have separated your main navigation items into their own pages in the WordPress back-end.

How to do it...

For this recipe, we're going to concern ourselves with a simple, one-column site with horizontal, tabbed navigation. While this technique can be applied to a variety of situations, the horizontal tabs are definitely the easiest. Your `index.php` file should look something like the following:

```php
<?php
get_header();
?>
<div id="content">
  <?php
  if( have_posts() ) {
  while( have_posts() ) { the_post(); ?>
  <div <?php post_class('post-container'); ?>>
    <h2 <?php post_class('post-title'); ?>>
      <?php the_title(); ?>
    </h2>
    <div <?php post_class('post-excerpt'); ?>>
      <?php the_excerpt(); ?>
    </div>
    <div <?php post_class('post-controls'); ?>>
      <a href="<?php comments_link(); ?>">
      <?php
      comments_number(
          __('No Comments'),
          __('1 Comment'),
          __('% Comments')
```

```
        );
        ?>
        </a>
        <?php if( is_user_logged_in() ) { ?>
          <?php edit_post_link('Edit'); ?>
        <?php } ?>
      </div>
    </div>
    <?php } } ?>
  </div>
  <?php
  get_footer();
  ?>
```

Next, make sure that your `header.php` file resembles the following:

```
<!DOCTYPE html PUBLIC "-//W3C//DTD XHTML 1.0 Transitional//EN"
"http://www.w3.org/TR/xhtml1/DTD/xhtml1-transitional.dtd">
<html xmlns="http://www.w3.org/1999/xhtml" <?php language_
attributes(); ?>>

<head profile="http://gmpg.org/xfn/11">
  <meta http-equiv="Content-Type" content="<?php
  bloginfo('html_type'); ?>; charset=<?php bloginfo('charset'); ?>"
  />

  <title> <?php bloginfo('name');
  wp_title('&mdash;', true, ''); ?></title>

  <style type="text/css" media="screen">
    @import url( <?php bloginfo('stylesheet_url'); ?> );
  </style>

  <?php wp_head(); ?>
</head>

<body <?php body_class('classic'); ?>>

<div id="wrap">
<div id="header">
<h1><?php bloginfo('name'); ?></h1>
<?php wp_page_menu(array('depth'=>1, 'show_home'=>true)); ?>
</div><!-- closing of the header div -->
<!-- end header -->
```

Open your browser to view the changes. Assuming that you haven't added any styles yet, your theme will resemble the following screenshot:

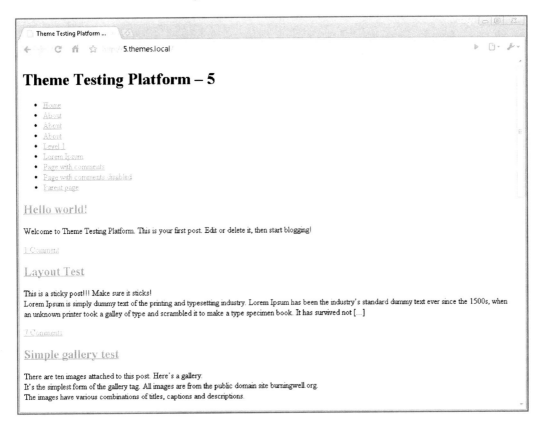

Now to make the magic happen, and get those tabs aiding your users, you need to add some styles. For now, you'll just get the basic tabs down. In the future, you can use variations on this technique to make your sites' navigation beautiful. First, let's establish a solid container that wraps all of the content. Luckily, you already have an element to style that wraps everything. Add the following code to your theme's stylesheet, `style.css`:

```css
.wrap {
  margin: 0 auto;
  width: 960px;
}
```

Now let's separate the content by setting up a `border` around it. Here, we'll use a simple black border that surrounds the entire `content div`. Insert the following code into your stylesheet:

```
#content {
  border: 1px solid #000000;
  padding: 10px;
  clear: left;
}
```

If you've got everything done correctly, you should have something that resembles the following screenshot, which shows a standard vertical list of links:

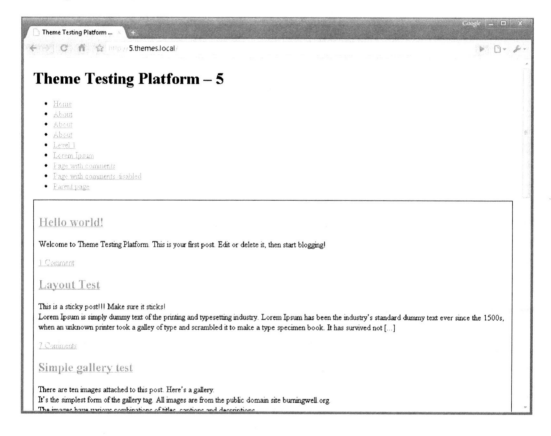

Now you can style the header navigation links to look like tabs. For the purposes of this recipe, the `active` tab will be shown by removing the `border` between the tab and the main content area. Inactive tabs will be gray, but will brighten to a slight off-white color on `hover`. For now, we just need to get the items in the correct positions, though. We'll start by styling the list and list elements. Insert the following code into your stylesheet:

```
#header {
  float: left;
}

#header .menu {
  border: 1px solid #000000;
  border-width: 1px 0 0 1px;
  float: left;
  margin-bottom: -1px;
}

#header .menu ul, #header .menu li {
  float: left;
  list-style: none;
  list-style-type: none;
  margin: 0;
  padding: 0;
}

#header .menu li {
  border: 1px solid #000000;
  border-width: 0 1px 1px 0;
  display: block;
  font-weight: bold;
  text-align: center;
}

#header .menu li a{
  display:block;
  padding:10px;
  text-decoration:none;
  background: #dedede;
}
```

This code floats the list items appropriately, and makes them display along the top edge of the content div.

Save your changes, and then open your browser to view the results. The result is something like the example shown in the following screenshot, which shows the list items now in a horizontal row, surrounded by rectangular shapes, and no list-style type (bullet or number):

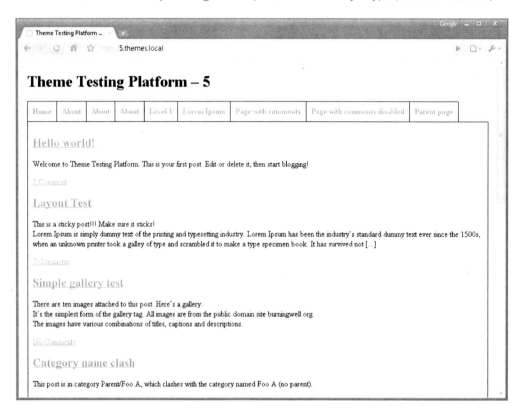

All that's left to do at this point is to handle the `colors` and the `active` tab. Insert the following code into your stylesheet:

```
#header .menu li a{
  background: #dedede;

#header .menu li a:hover{
  background: #efefef;
}
#header .menu li.current_page_item{
  border-bottom-color:#ffffff; /*note: you can use a different color
  here as needed */
}
#header .menu li.current_page_item a{
  background:#ffffff; /*note: you can use a different color here as
  needed */
}
```

At this point, you should have some fully-styled tabs. Try them out by hovering over and clicking on another tab. You'll see the active tab changes on page reload. The following screenshot shows the end result when you're visiting the **About** page and hovering over another tab:

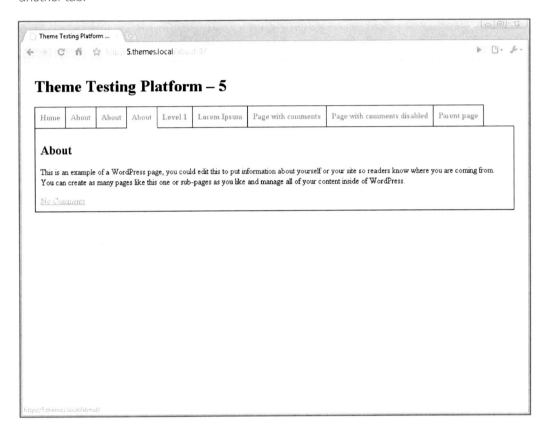

How it works...

The key to this recipe is the styles applied in your theme's stylesheet. Most of the techniques used are not worth a rehash. However, there is one important set of styles that deserves to be highlighted.

In the markup generated when WordPress renders this template, you end up with something that looks like the following code:

```
<div id="header">
    <h1>Theme Testing Platform &#8211; 5</h1>
    <div class="menu">
      <ul>
        <li>
```

```
        <a href="http://5.themes.local"
          title="Home">Home</a>
      </li>
      <li class="page_item page-item-2">
        <a href="http://5.themes.local/about/"
          title="About">About</a>
      </li>
      <li class="page_item page-item-119">
        <a href="http://5.themes.local/about-2/"
          title="About">About</a>
      </li>
    </ul>
  </div>
</div>
<div id="content">
<!-- Lots of stuff -->
</div>
```

Ordinarily, this markup would cause the menu div to sit directly on top of the content div. If you were to apply a border to the bottom of the items in the menu div and the top of the content div, you would get a doubled-up border.

However, you'll notice the following style declaration was created in your style.css file:

```
#header .menu {
  margin-bottom: -1px;
}
```

This declaration tells the browser to overlap the menu and content divs by moving the menu div down 1 pixel on top of the content div. Now, the items inside the menu div that have bottom borders don't double up with the content div; they overlap the border of the content div.

Later on in your stylesheet, you'll notice that the current page list item is styled differently to the rest:

```
#header .menu li.current_page_item {
  border-bottom-color: #ffffff;
}
```

This declaration tells the list item of the current page to style its bottom border with the same color as the background of the main content area. Because this bottom border overlaps the top border of the content div, this style effectively makes the border seem to disappear underneath the active item.

There's more...

Maybe you want to use images as backgrounds on your menu items, or learn about other ways to structure your navigation in order to make your theme more unique. There are many more resources on the web to help you out.

Many menus, many resources

Due to the flexibility of WordPress, you can use many different kinds of CSS and JavaScript driven menus, with a dash of PHP if you like. Visit the following resources to learn more about different types of menus and other navigation structures:

- http://www.alistapart.com/topics/code/css/
- http://www.w3schools.com/css/css_navbar.asp
- http://codex.wordpress.org/Dynamic_Menu_Highlighting

Index

D

E

F

G

Thank you for buying
WordPress 2.8 Themes Cookbook

About Packt Publishing

Packt, pronounced 'packed', published its first book "*Mastering phpMyAdmin for Effective MySQL Management*" in April 2004 and subsequently continued to specialize in publishing highly focused books on specific technologies and solutions.

Our books and publications share the experiences of your fellow IT professionals in adapting and customizing today's systems, applications, and frameworks. Our solution based books give you the knowledge and power to customize the software and technologies you're using to get the job done. Packt books are more specific and less general than the IT books you have seen in the past. Our unique business model allows us to bring you more focused information, giving you more of what you need to know, and less of what you don't.

Packt is a modern, yet unique publishing company, which focuses on producing quality, cutting-edge books for communities of developers, administrators, and newbies alike. For more information, please visit our website: www.packtpub.com.

About Packt Open Source

In 2010, Packt launched two new brands, Packt Open Source and Packt Enterprise, in order to continue its focus on specialization. This book is part of the Packt Open Source brand, home to books published on software built around Open Source licences, and offering information to anybody from advanced developers to budding web designers. The Open Source brand also runs Packt's Open Source Royalty Scheme, by which Packt gives a royalty to each Open Source project about whose software a book is sold.

Writing for Packt

We welcome all inquiries from people who are interested in authoring. Book proposals should be sent to author@packtpub.com. If your book idea is still at an early stage and you would like to discuss it first before writing a formal book proposal, contact us; one of our commissioning editors will get in touch with you.

We're not just looking for published authors; if you have strong technical skills but no writing experience, our experienced editors can help you develop a writing career, or simply get some additional reward for your expertise.

WordPress 2.8 Theme Design

ISBN: 978-1-849510-08-0   Paperback: 292 pages

Create flexible, powerful, and professional themes for your WordPress blogs and web sites

1. Take control of the look and feel of your WordPress site by creating fully functional unique themes that cover the latest WordPress features

2. Add interactivity to your themes using Flash and AJAX techniques

3. Expert guidance with practical step-by-step instructions for custom theme design

4. Includes design tips, tricks, and troubleshooting ideas

WordPress 2.7 Complete

ISBN: 978-1-847196-56-9   Paperback: 296 pages

Create your own complete blog or web site from scratch with WordPress

1. Everything you need to set up your own feature-rich WordPress blog or web site

2. Clear and practical explanations of all aspects of WordPress

3. In-depth coverage of installation, themes, syndication, and podcasting

4. Explore WordPress as a fully functioning content management system

5. Concise, clear, and easy to follow; rich with examples

Please check **www.PacktPub.com** for information on our titles

WordPress 2.9 E-Commerce

ISBN: 978-1-84719-850-1   Paperback: 284 pages

Build a proficient online store to sell products and services

1. Earn huge profits by transforming WordPress into an intuitive and capable platform for e-Commerce

2. Build and control a vast product catalog to sell physical items and digital downloads

3. Configure and integrate various payment gateways into your store for your customers' convenience

4. Promote and market your store online for increased profits

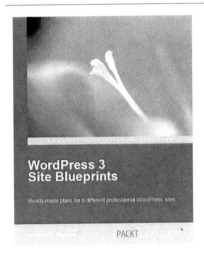

WordPress 3 Site Blueprints

ISBN: 978-1-847199-36-2   Paperback: 230 pages

Ready-made plans for 9 different professional WordPress sites

1. Everything you need to build a varied collection of feature-rich customized WordPress websites for yourself

2. Transform a static website into a dynamic WordPress blog

3. In-depth coverage of several WordPress themes and plugins

4. Packed with screenshots and step-by-step instructions to help you complete each site

Please check **www.PacktPub.com** for information on our titles

WordPress 2.7 Cookbook

ISBN: 978-1-847197-38-2   Paperback: 316 pages

100 simple but incredibly useful recipes to take control of your WordPress blog layout, themes, widgets, plug-ins, security, and SEO

1. Take your WordPress blog to the next level with solutions to common WordPress problems that make your blog better, smarter, faster, and more secure

2. Add interactivity to your themes using Flash and AJAX techniques

3. Expert guidance with practical step-by-step instructions for custom theme design

4. Includes design tips, tricks, and troubleshooting ideas

WordPress MU 2.8: Beginner's Guide

ISBN: 978-1-847196-54-5   Paperback: 268 pages

Build your own blog network with unlimited users and blogs, forums, photo galleries, and more!

1. Design, develop, secure, and optimize a blog network with a single installation of WordPress

2. Add unlimited users and blogs, and give different permissions on different blogs

3. Add social networking features to your blogs using BuddyPress

4. Create a bbPress forum for your users to communicate with each other

Please check **www.PacktPub.com** for information on our titles

Choosing an Open Source CMS: Beginner's Guide

ISBN: 978-1-847196-22-4   Paperback: 340 pages

Find the best CMS and start working with it to create web sites, blogs, communities, e-commerce sites, and intranets

1. Understand different types of CMSs and select the one that best fits your needs

2. Install and customize a CMS with themes and plug-ins

3. Learn key concepts of Content Management Systems and how to systematically assess your requirements

4. Introduction to the major CMSs including Joomla!, Drupal, WordPress, Plone, Magento, Alfresco, and more

WordPress and Flash 10x Cookbook

ISBN: 978-1-847198-82-2   Paperback: 268 pages

Over 50 simple but incredibly effective recipes to take control of dynamic Flash content in Wordpress

1. Learn how to make your WordPress blog or website stand out with Flash

2. Embed, encode, and distribute your video content in your Wordpress site or blog

3. Build your own .swf files using various plugins

4. Develop your own Flash audio player using audio and podcasting plugins

Breinigsville, PA USA
26 November 2010

249921BV00005B/24/P